BORN IN MALTA IN 1948, Aline P'nina Tayar grew up in Israel and Australia. She has lived in France, Tunisia, Italy, Belgium and Portugal. For the last twenty years her permanent home has been in the UK. From Bath, she commutes to Brussels and Strasbourg where she works as a freelance conference interpreter for the institutions of the European Union.

A Mediterranean Journey Through
a Jewish Family

\* \* \*

how shall we sing?

ALINE P'NINA TAYAR

PICADOR
Pan Macmillan Australia

I would like to thank all the people who have helped me put these stories together: Edith Benmussa, Phyllis Grant, Jeanne Halliday, Ninette and Giacomo Israel, Foued Jellalia, Liliana Tayar Levison, Ida Nahum, Jacques and Nicoletta Mawas, Susie Tayar Santarlasci, Maria Manuel Stocker, Enzo Tayar and George Tayar. My parents Douglas and Lina, my aunts Ondina and Margot Tayar, as well as my uncles Oscar Tayar and Daniel Lumbroso are the sources of many of the tales that I have hoarded over the years.

I am grateful to Sylvia Sher Wyner, Alexia Whiting, Susan North and Veronica Balfour for all those long discussions on identity and to Stefanie Woodbridge, Al Garotto and Alan Lindsay for their very useful initial editorial comments. Margaret Bouffler and Nikki Christer had faith. Vivian Gornick told me where I was going wrong and Jane Arms, my editor, set me right.

I would also like to thank Gayna Murphy for her design, and Marilyn Jackson for the illustrations.

Acknowledgements are due to the following authors and publishers for permission to quote from:

*The History of the Jews* of Italy by Cecil Roth, published by the Jewish Publication Society, 1946. Used by permission.

*Black Sea* by N. Ascherson, published by Jonathan Cape.

'Church Going', from *The Less Deceived* by Philip Larkin, published by The Marvell Press.

*Oleander, Jacaranda* by Penelope Lively, published by Viking, 1994.

*The Scent of Dried Roses* by Tim Lott, published by Viking, 1996.

*The Nature of Blood* by Caryl Phillips. © Caryl Phillips 1997. Reprinted with the permission of Gillon Aitken Associates Ltd.

*Histoire des Juifs de Tunisie* by Paul Sebag, published by Harmattan, 1991.

First published 2000 in Picador by Pan Macmillan Australia Pty Limited
St Martins Tower, 31 Market Street, Sydney

National Library of Australia
Cataloguing-in-publication data:

Tayar, Aline P'nina.
How shall we sing? : a Mediterranean journey through a Jewish family.

ISBN 0 330 36211 9.

1. P'nina Tayar family. 2. Jews – Malta – Biography. 3. Jews – Malta – Fiction.
4. Jews – Mediterreanean Region – Fiction. 5. Jews – Australia – Fiction.
6. Jewish diaspora – Fiction. I. Title.

Typeset in 12.5/15 pt Bembo by Post Pre-press Group, Brisbane, Queensland
Printed in Australia by McPherson's Printing Group

Designed by Gayna Murphy, Greendot Design

*This book is dedicated to the memory of
Bernard Radoff, without whom I would not
have embarked on this journey, and to my
late aunt Simone (Semcha) Lumbroso.*

*By the rivers of Babylon, there we sat down,*

*Yeah we wept, when we remembered Zion.*

*We hanged our harps upon the willows in the midst thereof.*

*For there they that carried us away captive required of us a song;*

*And they that wasted us, required of us mirth,*

*Saying sing us one of the songs of Zion.*

*How shall we sing the Lord's song in a strange land?*

*PSALM cxxxvii*

# contents

\* \* \*

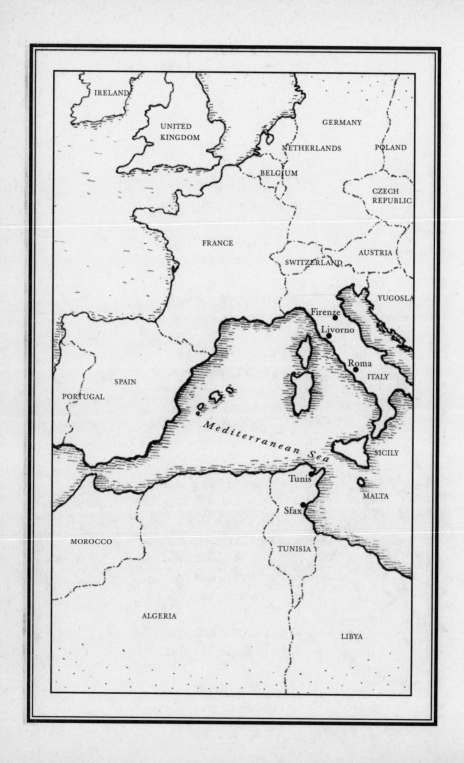

*I became obsessed by the idea of certainty, since it is clearly*
*what I crave. Yet, as I read about fascism and communism,*
*about the French Revolution and the Spanish Inquisition,*
*it seems to me that certainty, and the need for identity,*
*which it serves, is a sort of virulent and dangerous disease.*
*Yet it becomes clear that the need for it is the deepest*
*impulse there is.*

TIM LOTT, *The Scent of Dried Roses*

PROLOGUE

# what are you? who are you?

Although I have lived in many different places, I have been evicted only once – for stepping on the tail of a saluki. Salukis are an exotic breed of dusty-coloured dogs, which look impossibly more anorexic than whippets and are certainly more jittery. The offended dog was one of four hounds kept by my landlords, an Anglo-German woman and her stateless Hungarian lover. Their house was located in the heart of Tunis's souks, on a cul-de-sac in a maze of lanes which, by the early 1970s, had long ceased to be the quarter where female slaves were put up for auction. In the past it must have been a rich man's house.

I had not deliberately stepped on the saluki's tail. Without my lenses I see only a dandelion fuzz and, since the dog was the same colour as the stone-slab floor of my rented room, I only realised it was lying by my bed when it started to howl more pitifully than a professional ululator at a funeral. My landlord accused me of torturing his pet. He gave me no chance to defend myself and ordered me to vacate his property by the end of the week.

I wasn't sure where to go to next but was relieved to be leaving. I had grown weary of the landlord's habit of creeping up on me, his hair brilliantined into two devil's horns designed to make me yelp in fright. More than that, however, I was tired of his peremptory manner which, before my expulsion, I had taken to be a problem of translating his thoughts from his mother tongue into French, the only language we had in common. Or rather his version of French, because he stubbornly refused to learn how to conjugate verbs and used only infinitives. His theory, formulated with lucidity, was that if he accepted the grammatical strictures and ready-made expressions of a language other than his own, he would lose his identity. Beached in Tunisia, without a passport, he had no doubts who or what he was. When asked, he always answered with complete certainty, 'I be Hungarian.'

When faced with this question his girlfriend and I were much less sure. She had grown up in Britain, but always specified that her parents were from Dresden. I still chirruped that I was Australian. Yet, by this time, I was less confident of my label, uncomfortable when prodded to demonstrate allegiance to any group, national or religious.

I had just spent a year in Paris where my precarious Australian identity had come under attack in an unexpected way. Before my arrival, teachers at the school in which I was to give English conversation lessons had been discussing me. Knowing that I was arriving from Down Under, they laid bets on my having red hair, freckles, broad swimmer's shoulders and possibly a well-developed tennis arm. I don't know if one of the teachers had staked a lot on those physical traits, but I was astonished when later he introduced me to a stranger as '*notre petite juive*'(our little Jewess).

Just three months off the ship from Sydney, I wasn't comfortable about being labelled in this way. Through my mother's family in Paris, I had only recently got a taste of France's North African Jewish diaspora and felt that it had nothing to do with me.

Though I loved the food, growing briefly plump on deep-fried sweets and savouries, and was enchanted by the hospitality, I longed for privacy and a lowering of decibels. I found the men boorish and sat bewildered through religious celebrations. I felt foolish that, apart from the words for bellybutton, cucumber and tiger, I was unable to remember a single word of Hebrew, which had been my first language. When I tried to argue the case for the atheism I had been brought up with in the Antipodes, I could not shake off the impression that family members suspected I was ashamed of my origins. My immediate impulse was to shout that I was Australian and that if this was all I wished to include in my self-definition then my wish should be respected.

A year later, living in that house in Tunis's souks with two people who, like me, were the products of the displacements caused by the confusions of history, I began to see how difficult it is to reduce identity to a single component. When faced with the question of who we are, those of us living in places where neither we nor our parents were born will never be able to give a simple reply. Though I have had a home in England now for twenty-five years, I cannot get away with saying that I am English. When strangers hear my first name, which is French, and my second, which is Hebrew, and a surname, which is certainly Semitic, I catch the shadow of a frown. It says that by the look of me – thick dark hair, sallow skin, full mouth – this cannot be true. So I rush in to qualify that although I hold a British passport I was born in Malta. This needs further clarification, however, for the assumption most people make is that all Maltese are Catholics. I came into this world as one of those great rarities, a Maltese Jew.

When I was a baby my parents took me to Israel and we settled in a kibbutz. Disillusioned with Israel, after five years we returned to Malta intending to emigrate to any place in the New World willing to take us. A change in geographical location was going to allow us to leave the jumble of identities behind.

During the year we spent in Malta waiting for our emigration applications to be processed, my brother, born in Israel, and I were sent to a private teacher to be coached in English in preparation for our departure. By the time we left Malta, one of the first barriers to belonging, language, had been eliminated.

* * *

We were part of that huge wave of immigrants that had begun in 1947 in the wake of a programme drawn up by Arthur Calwell, the Australian Labor Minister for Immigration. His idea was to take in an unlimited number of displaced persons from war-shattered Europe in order to populate a land the size of the US, but with only seven million inhabitants. During World War II, the Japanese had failed to get even a small toehold in Australia, but white Australians felt that if their country did not increase its population it would soon be flooded by Asians.

Calwell was not an exponent of multiculturalism. Calwell's vision was fundamentally a racist one. He hoped that most newcomers would be of Anglo-Saxon stock, considering fair-haired Lithuanians more suitable as immigrants than dark-haired gypsies, and so the first shipload to arrive in Melbourne under his scheme was made up of what he described as 'beautiful Balts'. There were no Jews in that first contingent. The four hundred immigration officers sent all over Europe to recruit new settlers were told that Jews would have to be 'exceptionally good cases' to be allowed in.

My parents, brother and I were covered by the Maltese quota. When my father applied for a job in Sydney, he left the box marked 'Religion' blank in his application form.

'I see that you were born in Malta,' the personnel manager remarked. 'I take it that you are a Catholic. We don't usually employ Roman Catholics in this company.'

There was no anti-discrimination legislation in those days. But my father was not prepared to explain who or what he was.

Our parents' desire to avoid this trap of divisiveness, so insistent in

Europe, was one of the reasons that my brother and I spent our childhood with few connections to any new immigrant community. As we lived on the North Shore, we were anyway separated from most of Sydney's Jews, who congregated in the southern and eastern suburbs. Unlike our White Russian neighbours, who cultivated nostalgia for their homeland and kept a lighted candle before the portrait of the murdered Tsarevitch, we had no ties with any religious or national group. Which group would we have chosen? Most of Sydney's Jews were Ashkenazim. The Maltese community was solely Catholic. So was most of the Italian, whose language my parents had in common. My mother also shared a mother-tongue with the French expatriates with whom she worked. Culturally, she was even closer to her French-speaking Jewish colleagues from Egypt.

In my primary school, there were only two other Jewish girls. As it was not thought worthwhile to bring in a rabbi for three pupils for the weekly hour of religious instruction, we sat that period out. In high school there were almost a dozen Jewish girls so we did have the benefit of a rabbi, but my father actually asked for me to be exempted from what he considered to be 'indoctrination'. I defied him secretly, and with some sense of treachery, because I was lonely sitting out lessons in the playground, and it was humiliating to be asked by the headmistress to polish doorknobs (she found it hard to believe someone could have no religion at all). Still, I felt an impostor among those girls who knew their Hebrew alphabet, went to something called the 'Templymanuel' in Chatswood and celebrated Jewish festivals, which we did not.

In that assimilationist climate of the 1950s and 1960s, rather than speaking of ourselves as Greeks, Italians or Spaniards, we were all supposed to call ourselves 'New Australians'. Even if Croats and Serbs kept up their Old World rancours and, now and again, a bomb exploded in a rubbish bin on a Melbourne street, we were invited to make ourselves a *tabula rasa* and invent a new national entity.

My brother, aged only six when we arrived in Australia, hardly knew that he had been born a Jew. As a boy, he was more subject to physical violence than I was, although both of us endured taunts of 'reffo' and 'wog'. A local gang once tried to break his leg as he played in the park near our house. His need to identify with something was to turn him into what he thought of as a real Australian – monolingual, egalitarian, sporty, jocular and rough. In search for greater certainty, he aimed at merging seamlessly. So much so that he still refuses to believe that a neighbour whom he considered to be a close friend ever said she thought that his 'problem' was that his appearance was too Semitic.

'Your daughter is lucky,' the woman barged on. 'She doesn't look so . . . well . . . Jewish!'

'I'll give you just thirty seconds to get out of that door.' My father astonished my mother and me, witnesses to this incident, by allowing her even half a minute.

I knew this much about our Jewishness. When under attack we must defend it.

* * *

What better proof of how difficult, if not impossible, it is to disavow the past? As I moved from one country to another and re-invented myself with each move, I began to feel rebellious. My parents' idealism was too abstract. Rightly or wrongly, I yearned for more concrete points of reference.

This is what finally led me to undertake my journey around the small Mediterranean communities from which my family had come. Starting with my mother's childhood in Tunisia in a household dominated by her severe great-grandfather, Rabbi Jacob Arous, I was to discover a society in which identity was clearly defined – by religion. The same was true of the world of my paternal great-grandfather, another rabbi, Iusuf Tajar, who was born in Tripolitania when the Ottomans were still its rulers. Two generations later, for my father, Duggie, growing up in arguably the world's tiniest Jewish community, on the island of Malta, that sense of separateness was still there even if it was more difficult to sustain.

But for all these people, the whole of the Mediterranean was their pond. This is best illustrated in the story of my father's mother, Rachele, whose many brothers and sisters settled all round the rim of the Middle Sea, creating an intricate web of family connections. They went about their business, which had much to do with the pursuit of financial security, comfort and pleasure, and this placed them firmly among the new middle-classes of the world.

These were people who felt at home in a variety of cultures and languages. Not thinking of themselves in terms of nationality, they were true cosmopolitans. The life of my father's Egyptian cousins is an example of that and of the sort of finely balanced conviviality that once existed between Moslems and Jews in Egypt, the crossroads of East and West. The same can be said of the life of another of my father's cousins, Ninette, who stayed on in Tunisia after that country had gained independence from France.

Nowhere more than in Italy, however, were the Jews so assimilated. So that when the racial laws were promulgated in 1938, our family was brought face to face with other people's murderous ideas about who did or did not belong. Deprived of their livelihoods, they were reminded that the term 'cosmopolitan' contains the burden of the eternal outsider, suspect and despised.

After World War II, the same thing was to happen in the Arab countries in which our ancestors had settled after the expulsion of the Jews from Spain in 1492. The Jewish communities of North Africa and the Middle East did not suffer the tragic fate of the Jews of central Europe, but with the creation of the State of Israel and the growing Islamisation of these societies, they found they no longer had a place within new definitions of what constitutes a nation. Gradually, most of these communities were to see their numbers drastically reduced or disappear completely.

For many Jews, Israel seemed to be the only hope. My parents tried living there, but were to end up feeling that their place was not in the Promised Land either.

The theme of survival through geographical re-arrangement is at the heart of all these stories and is more potent than the experience of exile and loss. In North Africa and Malta, my ancestors became as much of the place as they had been in Spain and in Italy. In Paris, my numerous relatives may, like many immigrants, cultivate nostalgia for a perceived golden past, but they have also adapted to life in France. In turn, that country has had to adjust to them just as Australia has changed under the influence of each successive wave of migrations.

In the end, what displacement does is offer us all a tremendous freedom – to pick and choose from a variety of cultures and languages. It is pointless and even dangerous to crave for something simple and exclusive; all of us are made up of layer upon layer of identities, not just a single one.

If asked what I am, I should say that I am a Jewish Maltese Australian Englishwoman.

CHAPTER ONE

# the house on rue du lieutenant longello

For thirty years I have waged a silent battle with members of my mother's family. They would certainly deny this, pointing out that our lives hardly ever cross. But on the rare occasions we do meet, the tension between us is often palpable. None of us has ever articulated the source of our mutual antagonism, but I have come to realise that what we are fighting over is a perception of someone they are adamant they know better than I do. That someone is my mother, Lina Lumbroso.

The battle began in 1969, shortly after my arrival in Paris, where

most of my mother's relatives and some of my father's had settled in
the wake of Tunisian independence and the gradual exodus of the
country's Jewish population.

This was not the Paris of apartments with green-baize wallpaper
in the seventh arrondissement. Nor was it the city of my teenage
fantasy of *chanteurs*, writers and intellectuals philosophising in smoky
boulevard *cafés*.

It was Goddard's *Alphaville* with thin-walled apartments in tower
blocks hastily constructed for the tens of thousands of immigrants
pouring into the metropolis from France's colonies abandoned
with such bitterness. It was a city of cheap clothes bought in a tug-
of-war at Tati's (a North African success story, those Tunisian
relatives of mine kept reminding me) and of strange food from
diners and stalls in Belleville. Here, buyers and vendors shouted
orders in Arabic for *couscous, makroud, gnaouia, mloukia*, stomach-
burning *harissa* and those wonderful *casse-croûte tunisiens*, crusty
bread rolls filled to overflowing with tuna, olives and home-
pickled lemons, all those dishes which my mother, who had
learned her cooking not in Tunisia, but in a kibbutz in Israel, never
prepared for us in Australia.

It was a noisy, get-up-and-go world peopled by Attals, Boccaras,
Guezes, Attiases and Berrebys and not dispeptic Duchamps or
Dubois. Within the diaspora from Tunisia, people banded together
boasting that they were from Sfax or Sousse or Tunis. The group
from Tunis was splintered into tiny sub-groups made up of former
residents of its suburbs such as l'Ariana, Carthage, le Kram and La
Goulette. Those who came from La Goulette never failed to bask in
the glory of the disproportionate number of Jewish Goulettois who,
with their progeny, had made a name for themselves in France as
doctors, lawyers and leaders of industry and commerce.

They behaved as if they were still in a village and not in the capital of France. This meant not allowing any successful Goulettois to
get above themselves by denying their origins in that rundown seaside suburb next to Tunis's deep-sea port. There was always someone

in Paris who remembered that a father or an uncle had been a cobbler or a kosher butcher or a small-town rabbi.

This Jewish community, which I was only just discovering, had a long folk memory of exile and dislocation. You do not need to go back to the scattering of the Tribes of Israel; the expulsion of the Jews from Spain is a traceable starting point for many of its families. Having been driven out of the Iberian peninsula, their forbears had found their way to places all round the rim of the Mediterranean. My mother's ancestors, for instance, had first settled in Venice before moving on to Livorno. When Tunisia became a province of the Ottoman Empire in 1547, they joined the growing number of Sephardic Jews settling in North Africa. Here they benefited greatly from the Ottoman policy of ensuring conviviality between minorities. This tolerance, imposed from above, had only occasionally been interrupted since the time the Arabs, driving out the Byzantines, had advanced across '*Ifriqîya*' in the tenth and eleventh centuries. Although pagan tribes were forcibly converted to Islam, 'The People of the Book', that is, Jews and Christians, were considered to be Dhimmi or 'Protected People' and were allowed to continue practising their faith.

When the Gornim (the word is derived from the English word for Livorno – Leghorn) left Tuscany, they took with them their language, customs, traditions and dress. They established themselves very successfully. So much so that the local Jewish community, the Touansas, some of whom were the descendants of Berbers converted by the Jews driven into the hills by the Byzantines, became fearful of being submerged by the newcomers. This led them to break away. The divisions of the modern Parisian diaspora are not, therefore, a new phenomenon. The Touansas, feeling that their language and traditions were under threat, split to form a separate community.

Until I began this journey, I knew little of this history. So what if one of my ancestors was the Grand Rabbi Isaac Lumbroso? Pride in ancestry seems ridiculous to me. Perhaps if someone had been able to tell me that at the start of the eighteenth century he had tried to heal the rift between Gornim and Touansas, I might have been more interested. In 1969, I was caught up in arguing with my mother's family about my mother's entitlement to cut loose all ties with her past. They could not accept this and came to the only logical conclusion possible as far as they were concerned. My mother, they felt, had fallen under my father's spell and it was known that my father came from a family full of doubters and atheists.

'*As t'hab!*' they said in Judeo-Arabic patois. Then switching to French: '*Que veux-tu!*' What can you expect! They shrugged their shoulders and continued to mark my mother out as the Little Girl Lost from La Goulette. I had no doubts about the real Lina and sometimes became shrill when rejecting this notion of my mother – I saw her as a woman flying free of religion and closed communities.

*   *   *

Lina was only nine years old when she made a vow that, as soon as she could, she would escape from La Goulette. On Saturdays, always hoping that her great-grandfather, Rabbi Jacob Arous, would not hear her and call out, she would creep up the twenty-three steps leading from the street to the family apartment. This was located on the second storey of the building which Rabbi Jacob, when he married, had had constructed at the corner of the rue du Lieutenant Longello (now Emir Abdel Kader Street) and the rue Soliman (now Ali Trad Street). It was not arranged according to the Arab layout, with rooms around a central courtyard but, reflecting Jacob's wife's Livornese origins, was built in the European style. It covered almost a whole block and as well as a private dwelling it incorporated a synagogue, a *hammam*, or Turkish baths, and stables.

In moving to La Goulette, Rabbi Jacob had left behind the *Hara*, Tunis's crowded old Jewish quarter, and joined the many Tunisois now settling in the capital's new seaside suburbs. By the time of Lina's birth in 1926, La Goulette had one of the highest concentrations of

Jews in any place in North Africa. More Jews from Tunis poured into the suburb every summer, renting villas away from the heat of the capital's souks and avenues. On the Gulf of Tunis, in suburban La Goulette, the sea breeze dispersed the sulphurous stench of Lake Tunis, which hung over the city.

Lina knew that Rabbi Jacob was at his most vigilant on Saturdays. A stickler for observing Jewish law, on the Sabbath he kept the heavy street door open in case anyone was tempted to use the large knocker. For if sparks were ignited by the pounding of iron on iron, that would be deemed to be lighting a fire, a task forbidden on the Jewish day of rest.

Although as a French Protectorate, Tunisia, like France, required children to attend school on Saturdays, Rabbi Jacob did not approve of children taking lessons on the Sabbath. But if they must, then there was no question of their picking up a pen to write. This also constituted human labour.

Lina held her breath as she entered the cool sitting room. The windows of the house had no wire screens and a few lazy flies always hovered just below the ceiling. She set down her school satchel on one of the chairs lined up on opposite walls and reflected in the huge Louis xv mirror above the sideboard.

It was not only her great-grandfather she had to tiptoe past, but also the piercing black eyes of her dead paternal grandfather, Giuseppe Lumbroso, who had been the husband of Rabbi Jacob's only daughter. From his portrait, hanging between two carbines, he would watch her sneaking in from school and trying to cross the room to the kitchen or one of the bedrooms. In his lifetime, Giuseppe had earned parochial fame as a *bon vivant* and, more widely, as an amateur hypnotist. People of all religions travelled from many other towns to attend his séances. But in Rabbi Jacob's house, Giuseppe had been a shadow, even when alive, for his father-in-law, sole master of his house, had allowed him no responsibilities. Giuseppe might have been pleased to keep all his wages as a translator as mere pocket money, but every day he was reminded of his position in that household by the bread he ate which, to distinguish it from other loaves baked at the local bakery, was stamped with Rabbi Jacob's symbol of a flattened omega.

'Have you been writing in class today?' Jacob was standing there at the door to the sewing room, where all the Hebrew books were kept in glass-fronted cabinets, and he was glowering. He hardly ever wore European clothes. In his black *burnous* worn over a white *jellabah*, with a red *tarboush* on his head, he looked like an irate prophet.

Lina's stomach heaved. There was ink on the callus of her right middle finger. From under her Chinese-straight fringe her large brown eyes returned the old man's gaze. The blue of his eyes, inherited from some long-forgotten Berber ancestor, was a cold colour.

'The teachers don't understand,' Lina said, suppressing the hint of a whine, which might be interpreted as begging for her great-grandfather's understanding and make him feel her rebelliousness had to be subdued. 'There are twenty-seven other Jewish girls in my class and every single one of them writes on Saturdays. So why can't I?'

Rabbi Jacob was not used to disobedience. Simone, four years older than Lina, always did what she was told and did not even go to school on Saturday. The rabbi would make a show of rewarding Simone. When he summoned her to his room, Lina knew that her sister would receive five francs for good behaviour. Lina always pretended she had not heard Rabbi Jacob calling.

Her brothers, Jacquot and Dani, were too young to be expected to side with her. Jacob had already chosen a career as a rabbi for the studious Jacquot. Dani, whom everyone agreed was sweet-natured, was slow, especially when it came to learning Hebrew. For this, their great-grandfather would sometimes tease him cruelly. One Yom Kippur, having slaughtered the ritual chicken, he crept into Dani's room and waved the dead bird over the boy's head. Waving dead chickens over heads was a local custom, but it was not usually done over a sleeping child. Dani, suddenly sensing a presence, woke up and screamed in terror.

As far as Lina was concerned, practical jokes were just one more form of oppression, a source of anxiety not only for the great-grandchildren, but also for Jacob's sister who lived with him and his family all her life. A simple woman, she dressed in the oriental style which, in the era of the Sublime Porte, when she and her brother had been born, had been compulsory for Jews of North African descent. She always wore a wide-sleeved blouse, the *sûriya*, and baggy trousers, known as *saroual el Jaouiff*. Leading as cloistered a life as her Moslem female neighbours, she would promptly cover the trousers with a *foutta*, a kind of sarong, when visitors came to the house. Once Jacob folded the *foutta* in half and secretly sewed the edges together. It seems hardly imaginable, an old man with a white beard, secretly stitching a piece of cloth and chuckling with amusement. His sister was thrown into a panic when she discovered that she was unable to unfurl the cloth to cover herself.

If you saw Rabbi Jacob walking down La Goulette's dusty main avenue with its scraggly trees holding Jacquot's or Dani's hand, you might have thought him the very picture of a distinguished and respected patriarch. He was a man of property, the owner of his own synagogue, one of several in La Goulette. Clients of all religions frequented his *hammam*, which had cubicles to undress in, three rooms with varying degrees of heat and, outside, cushions and mattresses to loll about on. For a small fee, a woman attendant scrubbed backs with a loofah. For Jewish women, there was also a ritual bath, the *tebilah*.

As for the *Fondouk*, or stables, Rabbi Jacob rented these out to itinerant fruit and vegetable vendors who slept there at night, crowded into a single room alongside barrels of olive oil. These carters, poor men, would often leave pieces of bread in the trays under the barrel taps to catch the perennial drips. After a few hours, the bread was moistened and flavoured with the oil, which Jacob sold to supplement his income. As required by law, he kept a register of these lodgers. He also managed the market to which they brought their produce for distribution.

Most of the neighbourhood thought of Rabbi Jacob as a good

man. He was their *shochet*, responsible for the ritual slaughter of poultry and occasionally larger animals. He was the rabbi who gave his seal of approval to the lemonade prepared for Passover at the mineral water plant. And wasn't he also the one who, at the end of one Passover, invited them all to partake of *merguez* when their own had been stolen? They had hung these spicy mutton sausages at their windows and did not know that it was Rabbi Jacob himself who had taken them – for a laugh. They looked up to him.

As did the man who came knocking on his door one evening asking if Jacob could conduct a wedding ceremony straight away. Lina and her brothers and sister stopped bouncing on their beds when they heard Jacob's steps coming down the hallway. It wasn't physical violence they feared. If they were naughty, one of the grown-ups might chase them round a table and out into the street brandishing a fly swatter. It was their great-grandfather's moodiness they hated. They listened, in expectation of angry words because, in their horseplay, Lina had spilled coffee on the mattress. But when the slipslap of the Rabbi's *babouches* had passed, they put their ears to the door.

'Please,' they heard the stranger's voice at the entrance, 'the wedding has to be today. My ship is sailing tomorrow and God knows when I shall be home again.'

So the heat was off. This time, Lina, curious, did not refuse to go when Jacob summoned all the children. In the middle of the sitting room, watched by the hypnotic Giuseppe and the carved eagle above the sideboard, they were witnesses at a wedding.

Fellow rabbis visiting Jacob's house to discuss Talmudic texts considered him to be wise. Others saw him as the epitome of tactfulness.

'Go ahead and smoke,' he would allow as a perfect host, but always refuse any cigarette proffered. 'I myself only smoke on the Sabbath.'

As far as Lina was concerned, the humour eventually grew stale. Smoking on the Sabbath was yet one more item on the list of all that is forbidden to Jews.

Who in the four generations making up this household, bound by so many small prohibitions, would ever speak out against Rabbi

Jacob? They all depended on him. He not only provided the roof over their heads, but paid for their food and went shopping every day for it: crates of vegetables and fruit, sacks of flour, meat and spices. He had a close ally in his only child, Annette, the widow of Giuseppe of the scary sitting-room portrait. She who was in charge of all domestic matters. Unusually for her generation, Annette had completed her primary school education (certainly without ever going to school on the Sabbath), after which she had waited in her father's house for offers of marriage. As a young woman, she had been beautiful and elegant. And as befitted the daughter of a ministrant of religion, she spent a great deal of her time dispensing charity and first aid to the poor.

La Goulette was full of these. Not just Arab street beggars stretching out their hands when you passed and showing faces covered in flies and infected, watery eyes, but also poor Jews. They were not necessarily homeless men and women, but sometimes they were close to starvation. Every Friday night, they and poor Arabs and Bedouins would gather in the courtyard of Jacob's synagogue where he distributed food. On summer evenings, the smell of the poor would mingle with the perfume of jasmines while the rumbling of men galloping through prayers would roll in through the windows of the family apartment. If you listened quietly, you could also hear the waves slapping the sand on the beach a block away.

Annette's married life to the spirit-conjuring Giuseppe had been brief. When he died, she relinquished her *ingénue* name and was forever after known as Zia Nina. The ferocity she inherited from Jacob was then poured into her affection for her only son, Abraham, always known by the diminutive Mino. In a photograph taken when Mino was three or four years old, he is wearing lace-up boots and plus-fours with a matching jacket in pale satin. An extravagantly large bow tied round his neck matches the bow on Nina's hat. His hair is slicked into a kiss-curl on his forehead. Standing on a box to bring his cheek to the level of his mother's, he is hugging her. He is Nina's Little Man.

Although Lina loved Mino, her father, she could not look to him to have Jacob's Saturday writing ban lifted. Like his dead father, Mino had no authority in Jacob's house nor did he have any duties or obligations. For a while he went into business with a partner, but he had no heart for it. He preferred to work from home as it allowed him to take afternoons off to go to the cinema or to operettas, which were his great passion. Indulged by his mother all his life, he spent the money he earned as an accountant mostly on himself. You could see him at *la Jetée*, La Goulette's pier, every summer, dressed in a white linen suit and peaked cap. He could have been a dandy on any seaside promenade in Italy or in France. The local newspaper published during the summer months and containing all the parochial gossip caught something of his spoilt-boy panache in dubbing him *L'Amiral*.

Religion was the mainstay of Mino's life. People still remember him as deeply pious, always at prayer, even on the commuter train that took him to and from Tunis each day. Once the stationmaster held up the train for a whole minute so that Mino would not miss it and be obliged to recite the *Minha*, the afternoon prayer, on the platform. Fellow-passengers, Moslems in *jellabahs*, Christians in pin stripes and Jews garbed in either, grew used to seeing him *davaning* in the first-class carriage.

It was through religion that Mino was able to avoid all responsibilities, disappearing into comforting rituals whenever battles raged at the rue du Lieutenant Longello. These began as soon as he brought his new wife, Emma, back to his grandfather's house.

Emma Boublil was a woman of nervous disposition, sentenced to life as a wraith once she entered Zia Nina's sphere of influence. I have never seen a picture of the young Emma, one of six children from the first marriage of Joseph Boublil, known before he lost his fortune during World War I as *Le Roi du Sucre* (the Sugar King). The only image I have of her is one from years later in a photograph taken at Lina's wedding. She is seated next to Zia Nina and, though barely fifty, she looks lost and as old as her mother-in-law.

Emma must have once known joy. When her father married a second time and fathered five more sons and daughters, she was the centre of a cradling clan. But marriage exiled her from them. Though La Goulette was only a few miles outside Tunis, to her it was a backwater compared to the capital, with its wide avenues, fine shops and cinemas. In *cafés*, elegant people lounged about drinking *anisette*. They went shopping in the Galeries Lafayette or to plays and concerts at the Théâtre Municipal. In *pâtisseries*, they could choose from the range of cakes you might expect to find in France and not just Tunisian *yoyos*, *manicottis*, honeyed *briks* and *makrouds* with dates.

In La Goulette, every house was in need of a fresh coat of paint. When letters fell off shop signs, no one bothered to hoist them up again. The streets remained littered in the wake of vendors who charcoal-grilled sweetcorn in the open or sold *glibettes* (pumpkin seeds), pistachios and peanuts in paper cones.

Having a stepmother at home might have taught Emma to keep her head low before older women, but she could not have expected to come up against something as inflexible as the ties that bound Mino, her new husband, to his mother. Zia Nina was to make sure that her own adoration of her son would not be overshadowed by the love of a mere wife. To lock out her daughter-in-law, she insisted on speaking Italian to Mino, a language Emma, a *Touansa*, did not understand. Nothing could have rankled more than that Gornim propensity to give themselves airs, *elgrana issorbû elmâ belgarfû*, or drinking water with a fork, as the expression goes in the local Judeo-Arabic.

Taking a leaf out of her father's book, Nina allowed Emma no responsibilities, but supervised the housework herself and made and mended all the family's clothes. Even if Emma had been strong-willed, she probably would not have won the struggle. The small kindnesses that bind people to each other remained Zia Nina's preserve. It was she who cooked Mino's favourite dishes, allowing only Meiha, the deaf maid, to help.

Emma's days were empty even after the birth of her sons and

daughters, as Zia Nina also took over their care. When the plumber came past the house keening *P-L-O-M-B-I-E-R*, or the rag-and-bone man shouted *Roba Vecchia*, it was either Nina or Meiha or Rabbi Jacob who rushed out. From the balcony, Emma could see children whirling in ever-diminishing circles on their bicycles. The life they gave to La Goulette passed her by. She had no appetite for the thinly cut potatoes sold by the vendor who, from May to September, bellowed, '*Et voilà les frites Boccara!*' It was not her task to go out each morning to buy *Drôo* from the man who sold this green porridge from house to house. Since Zia Nina did all the sewing, Emma never spoke to the man who came by on a cart or leading a donkey laden with cloth and bobbins of thread. Across the rue du Lieutenant Longello, Madame Castel reflected Emma's emptiness as she stood waiting patiently by her front door for the travelling salesman who sold romances in weekly instalments.

Unlike Mino, Emma did not have religion to retreat into. Most women only knew their religion anyway through the food that was prepared for each holy day or festival, and in Jacob's house this was her mother-in-law's domain. Nina was the one who plucked the sacrificial poultry at Yom Kippur. There was a hen for each female member of the household, a rooster for each male. Although this sounds excessive, most of the birds were distributed to the poor. It was taken for granted that children did not fast on the Day of Atonement, but Emma's children usually made an effort to do so.

They killed their hunger pangs with quinces which, a week before Yom Kippur, they had studded with cloves and rolled into square pieces of cloth. On the day of the fast itself, they would carry these parcels around with them, sniffing them like smelling salts as they fought off feelings of faintness. In this way, they also advertised their virtue in attempting to abstain from food and water for twenty-four hours.

During Passover week, once the family apartment had been cleaned of all breadcrumbs, the Arous clan ate on the landing. This was done in honour of past generations. Eating outside the door of their home, they remembered the Israelites' willingness to make a hasty departure from Egypt. Throughout the week, lettuce leaves, green symbols of the approaching spring, were placed on beds and chairs in every room. When my mother was a child, it was her father's task to tap the children lightly on their shoulders with these leaves, a gentle re-enactment of the whipping of the Hebrew slaves in the Egypt of the Pharaohs.

For this festival, Jacob would slaughter a lamb for the sole use of the family, and for eight days, in commemoration of the exodus, everyone ate *galettes*. Different from the matzos we are familiar with in the West, their dough was moulded into concentric rings with holes evenly spaced around them. These biscuits were tough. Old people, afraid of cracking their dentures, would soak them in coffee or water.

Emma remains a shadow in these happier memories of my mother's childhood. With a succession of babies, one of whom died aged only a few months, she became nervous and depressed. Her sense of exclusion increased as Zia Nina did everything she could to ensure that she had little place in her children's affections. It became a commonplace in the family that Emma was 'mentally fragile'. But she did manage to extract at least one promise from Mino, who had little strength to protect her. He agreed to pay the rent for an apartment in l'Ariana, the district in Tunis to which, during the winter months, Emma removed herself, using as a pretext her fragile health. The sea air is known to be harmful to neurasthenics, someone had told her. For once, Mino stood up for her. After lunching with his children and his mother in La Goulette, he would visit Emma each evening. I can imagine Zia Nina pursing her lips as he picked up his hat after lunch, kissed her sheepishly goodbye and returned to Tunis.

If the house on the rue de Lieutenant Longello was a war zone, one of the battles Lina was intent on winning was that of writing on Saturdays.

'If you don't let me write, I shall give up school altogether,' Lina argued with her great-grandfather.

'*Lascia stare! Laisse tomber!*' Let it be, her sister, Simone, whispered to Lina in their home-brew of Italian and French, biting her lip in intense concentration over her homework.

'You'll go mad if you keep poring over those books,' Lina half-sang over a maths exercise that took her only a few minutes to complete but Simone hours and hours. It was the same with Hebrew, a language that Lina took no interest in. 'Let's go swimming. Or how about having another go at the *table d'esprits*? Let's get Jacquot and Dani.'

The three-legged *table d'esprit* was Giuseppe's greatest legacy. It stood in the centre of the sitting room.

With four pairs of hands flat on the table, Jacquot asked, 'Shall I die soon?'

'That's not allowed,' the others cried, shouting him down. 'And you can't ask if you're going to win the lottery either.'

But little Jacquot was persistent. 'When shall I die?'

The table thudded out the letters: *L'avenir est inconnu*. The future is unknown. But part of it soon became clear to Lina.

'I'm giving up school!' She would not cry or plead again for her great-grandfather to relent over the writing business.

He sighed and shook his head. It was hard to relate these customary signs of exasperation to the words he was now uttering. 'So be it. You can write on Saturdays.'

To protect Dani from these secular influences (Jacquot was, thankfully, an observant child), Jacob decided to send him to the Alliance Israélite school. He failed to see the irony of this, of course, for the Alliance Israélite Universelle had been established in the mid-nineteenth century with the precise aim of putting an end to the obscurantism that had so dogged the Jewish communities of the Ottoman Empire. Even though they administered a good dose of religion, the Alliance's schools were meant to offer entry into mainstream European culture. Dani found it hard to master Hebrew and could never keep up with the school's very high standards. After a year, he was withdrawn.

\* \* \*

'*Brobbi!* Oh my God!'

'*Ch'nouâ ekk el caprice*? What's got into her now?

The household was once again in turmoil. Lina had been to the carnival. Someone had given her a costume and she had joined in the festivities.

'Oh, you're really going to get it now.'

'Shut up, Simone. I haven't done anything wrong.'

But everyone at the rue du Lieutenant Longello was horrified. As far as they were concerned Lina had broken the boundaries of identity. It couldn't have been worse if she had announced she was going to kill herself. Not abiding by the laws of the Sabbath was one thing, but taking part in the rituals of another religion was another matter. Where else did a sense of self come from other than from religion?

It was all very well that La Goulette's Jews lived side by side with their Moslem and Christian neighbours and that their children attended the same schools. Each group influenced and was influenced by each other's language, customs, habits, cuisine and even music (although many Gornim affected to despise bleating Arab melodies, preferring concerts in Tunis where visiting artists like Boisard, Cortot, Thibaud and Casals performed). But venturing into other people's religious terrain, going to a carnival, was what had everyone rushing to re-assert their notion of self. More than angry, the whole family felt personally affronted.

'*Ya roukhi! Oh mon âme!*' Oh, dear God! they wailed.

Relations between the different religions might have been less strained if, as under the Ottomans, people's sense of who they were had not been clouded by the French colonial authorities. The latter were not averse to setting Moslems against Jews by disseminating the notion that Jews were intent on dominating the world through money and intrigue. This discourse was imported from Europe.

'I would have had more Moslem friends if there had not been so few Arab girls after primary school,' my mother maintains. She did have one Moslem friend, Mounira, whose father was a lawyer. In an increasingly bourgeois society, his values were not so far removed from those of most middle-class people of other faiths, but this set him apart from much of the Moslem community who considered him far too liberal and European. When he died, there was an attempt to deny him a Moslem burial, and a minor riot broke out at his funeral.

Lina's closest friend was Jewish. She was Zica, the dark, scrawny girl always pulling faces in class photographs. Compared to Lina, who looked neat in her pinafore and blouses tailored by Zia Nina, Zica was a scruff. Her parents, both schoolteachers, found it hard to make ends meet.

'*Oho! Le budget!*' Lina and Zica, on their way home from school, would exclaim in conspiratorial unison as they approached Zica's house. 'It's that time again.'

Once a month, Monsieur and Madame Jarmon went into a huddle over the household accounts. Out in the street, everyone could hear them as they shouted recriminations. Turning their heels, Lina and Zica would march over to the rue du Lieutenant Longello. There, in that perennially volatile atmosphere, they would find themselves in the middle of another explosion: Zia Nina trying to penetrate Meiha's deafness and the maid shouting back. Meiha had been a skivvy in the house since the age of thirteen, but she was the only one who ever stood up to Nina. Secretly, she was in love with Mino, and Nina was her rival, not Emma, the invisible wife.

Lina and Zica would turn back. Often, they found themselves toing and froing between family houses several times in a single afternoon, but there was nothing they liked better than each other's company. Zica gave Lina the sisterly affection she never wanted from Simone.

'I've given all my savings to the Weisses,' Simone announced one day. The Weiss family were refugees from Austria. They needed money to go on to Shanghai. Giving to the poor was a charitable act incumbent on all good Jews. Mino himself set aside one tenth of his income for charity. But Simone's nine hundred franc gift to the Weisses was really going overboard. Intensity now seemed to mark everything she did – labouring over schoolwork, trying to please their great-grandfather, being good. It was hard for Lina to feel any warmth for her sister. She knew that it was almost impossible to satisfy Rabbi Jacob and was always uncomfortable with Simone's craving for approval. I have a clear image of Simone as a child try-ing to build around her a protective carapace in the hope of warding off all that family bickering. Lina was much tougher.

The plight of the Weisses was a reminder of the growing turmoil in the world outside the Arous household. The end of the Civil War in Spain had brought a trickle of refugees to *La Petite Sicile*, the Ital-ian district down by the canal. In 1938, when the racial laws were promulgated in Italy, the Bonans, cousins living in Rome, returned to Tunis on the advice of the French Embassy.

In 1939, war was declared in Europe and Jacquot, the great-grandson on whom Jacob had pinned all his hopes for a rabbinical successor, fell ill. Because of the situation abroad, medicines could not be ordered from France to treat Jacquot's nephritis. The family doctor, drafted into the army, was miles away and could not be contacted. The only doctor in La Goulette was the French Army doctor who did not know how to treat a sick child. So Jacquot, aged only nine, died in great agony, watched by his help-less family. Apart from the image of his large soulful eyes, my mother says she hardly remembers him, but this might be her pro-tection against the pain of loss. Dani, who was much younger, has not forgotten that all the pupils from Jacquot's class came to the house with flowers for their dead school friend. Simone plunged into a deep depression. Rabbi Jacob was shattered.

When France fell and the Vichy regime was established, the former tennis star Borotra, now a government minister, came to

Tunis. A parade was organised for his visit. Only torrential rain after a scorching day prevented the capital's schoolchildren from marching. Caught up in their mourning, no one in Lina's family thought of telling her not to join in singing *Sauveur de la France* at school in honour of Marshall Pétain, the Saviour of France. As yet, most Jews were not in danger, but those Jews who, like Zica's parents, held civil service posts, now found themselves jobless.

\* \* \*

Meiha would not have heard them, but like everyone else she would have seen them. Coming out of the sky. Germans. Driven eastwards as American troops advanced from Morocco across Algeria, in November 1942, they arrived in Tunisia by the planeload. Lina and her classmates stood watching by the roadside, their hearts squeezed, their stomachs shrivelled.

'The war has been willed and prepared by international Jewry,' General von Arnim, Commander-in-Chief of the Axis Forces, announced in a decree dated 23 December 1942 and posted on walls in French, Italian and Arabic. 'The French, Italian and Moslem people of Tunisia have suffered greatly as a result of the bombings over the last few days. This is why I have decided to impose a fine of twenty million francs on the Jews of Tunisia.'

The Germans then began requisitioning apartments and houses, furniture and cloth. Fine carpets were removed from people's homes and were used to cover the glass of *café* façades so they would not shatter under aerial bombardments. As German soldiers sauntered up and down the avenue de Paris, machine-guns slung over their shoulders, people hurried past. At the Great Synagogue, the officiating rabbis, *shamas* and congregants were jostled out with unexpected brutality. In surrounding streets, all Jews – the old, the infirm, women and children – were searched.

'You'll soon learn how the SS deals with Jews,' Colonel Rauff said, before reportedly spitting at the Grand Rabbi, Haïm Bellaïche, and ordering his troops to convert the Great Synagogue into a warehouse.

After these insults, they turned their attention to deportations and arbitrary executions. The Grand Rabbi was summoned to the *Kommandatur* and allowed only one day to draw up a list of two thousand men to be placed at the disposal of the occupying army. These men were rounded up and put to work digging trenches, clearing rubble and repairing roads. There was little food on these forced labour assignments. Soap and water were in short supply. Within a few weeks, the men were plagued by lice and many had contracted scabies.

In this way, the preliminary mechanisms of the Holocaust in Europe were set in motion in a place where the Jews had lived since the days that Romans razed Dido's city to the ground and ploughed salt into the soil to ensure obliteration.

'All my subjects are entitled to my protection,' the Bey Moncef responded in defiance, 'whether they are Moslems or Jews.' In spite of German and Vichy propaganda, the notion of a Jewish conspiracy found little resonance in this part of the world.

'The fascists have merely begun with the Jews,' warned the Communist Party newspaper, *L'Avenir Social*.

La Goulette, as a seaport, was a prime target in the continuing air raids. Piling all their furniture into a cart, my mother's family moved to Le Kram to a house already occupied by one of Mino's clients. The conditions were crowded. Food and clothing were rationed. The rivalry between Zia Nina, Emma and Meiha became ferocious. The children were miserable. Mino tried to ignore it all. I have a photograph of him taken when he was in his early forties. His hair is already completely white and his shoulders are very narrow. He does not look strong enough to carry the burden of his disintegrating family.

Meiha was the only one with any means of escape from the chaos. She withdrew into her silent world. Late into the night she would scrub the dirty dishes with sand and croon to herself: *Papa va a Roma/Per comprar una corona*, dreaming that one day Mino would, as the song says, buy her a crown from Rome. As guardian of the keys to the cabinet where sugar, in limited supply during the war, was stored, she was able to make him his favourite sweet, caramel-coated almonds. She was the one who counted out the sugar cubes, which the children were allowed to dunk in rum as a rare treat.

The Germans now issued orders that all train services were to be suspended. It looked as if Lina and all the other children who travelled to Tunis each day would no longer be able to attend school. But Monsieur Ferlin, the Anglophile English master at the Lycée Carnot, came up with an idea. All pupils and teachers who lived on the TGM line, which runs from Tunis to La Marsa, would transfer to an aquarium at the *Institut Océanographique de Salammbô*.

And so my mother's playground became the marine institute's gardens, fragrant with orange blossoms and roses. In her free hours, she went swimming with her school friends, modestly dressed, obeying Rabbi Jacob's orders at least in this respect. Lessons were held in the old *Salle des Phoques*, now emptied of its seals. Here, and in the *Salle des Bassins*, it was easy for her mind to drift along with the fish and turtles in tanks, away from the beached diving suit that was straight out of Jules Verne. Away from the crowded house in Le Kram.

By now, however, Jacob was a weakened man. On Yom Kippur, he took to his bed. He had intended to fast, but had no strength to argue when the family insisted he drink some lemonade. He wept at the feebleness that prevented him from going to synagogue to blow the *shofar*, something he had done on each Day of Atonement for longer than most Goulettois could remember. Aged eighty-five, he turned his face to the wall and died.

Afterwards, people would say he had been fortunate. Simone would have broken his heart.

'We're very sorry,' the police told Mino, at long last the head of his own family – not that it was a role that he wanted or knew how to play. 'This is hardly the time to organise a search party for a wayward girl.'

Simone had disappeared from home. No one had noticed how silent she had become lately. She now went to ground so successfully that for six months no one in La Goulette even set eyes on her. Mino prayed. Zia Nina was frantic. No one thought to comfort Emma.

Crying. Howling. Keening. This is what faced Simone on her return.

'Where have you been? Didn't you realise how worried we would all be? What have you been up to?'

'Oh, nothing really. I was only keeping house for three German officers.'

For a good Jewish girl, this didn't seem possible.

'Look over there! Look!' Simone gripped Lina's arm as they walked down one of Tunis's avenues. 'There's Kristian. Kristian Khülen.'

To Lina's horror, Simone began waving her arms, shouting the German soldier's name, which would forever be branded on my mother's memory.

'He seems to know you.'

'Of course, he does. He was one of my officers. Did you think I was lying?' After all those years of trying so hard to please, something had exploded in Simone.

Lina was appalled and ashamed. If it hadn't been for the Allied advance, would Simone have stayed with those officers? The Germans only occupied Tunisia for half a year, but no one doubted that they would have eventually dealt with the Jews in the same way as they had done in all occupied territories, although the full scale of that murderousness was yet to be revealed.

Once the Germans had left, the family again piled their furniture on carts and returned to the house on the rue du Lieutenant Longello. Bravado and elation prompted one of their cousins to climb onto one of the carts and play the family's piano as they rolled all the way back to La Goulette.

Everyone here had already heard about Simone.

'Are you sure that all she was doing was keeping house?' aunts, uncles and cousins asked Mino. He did not know. He only wanted to be left alone to continue with the old rhythms of work, operettas and prayer.

'You can't let her go out alone again.' The relatives continued to assail Mino. 'You don't know what other crazy things she might get up to.'

So they locked Simone in her room. Her resulting frenzy was terrifying. And the anguish that followed even worse.

These days, my mother feels remorse for her lack of sympathy for her sister. But Simone's madness only increased Lina's desire to get away from the rue du Lieutenant Longello, from La Goulette, from Tunisia. Everyone about her seemed crazy. So she sought refuge at her cousins'. Here, the atmosphere was lighter. Seated round the dining table, all the children and some of their invited friends would do their homework, while Rosine, the mother, who was a piano teacher, played Chopin waltzes, Couperin or Mozart. In winter, they huddled round a *canoon*, an earthenware pot filled with hot coals, cheerfully warding off the cold damp of the Mediterranean house, with its thick walls and stone floors.

The war was hardly over when Mino's pains began, followed by nausea and vomiting. The doctors diagnosed stomach cancer. His skin turned grey. He was no longer able to eat *harissa*, that Tunisian speciality of chilli pepper paste with which, all his life, he had dowsed his food. It had stopped burning a long time ago; now that he was ill, it made him double up in agony. Once again, the rituals of religion were what kept him going.

To spare Dani, barely into his teens, the anguish of another death, the family sent him to stay with Emma's sister-in-law. There he was teased by his cousins for what they mistook as simplemindedness, not understanding his complete disorientation. He had already lost the ruling figure in his life, Rabbi Jacob, and a brother. His elder sister had become a mad stranger. Now he was losing his father. At the same time, Lina, suffering from typhoid fever, was frighteningly close to death.

Dani only came back home after Mino had died and Lina recovered. Simone, imprisoned in the house to stop her from committing other lunatic acts, sat around staring blankly. She could not be shifted from her melancholy. There were no sophisticated drugs to chase away the black mood that clenched her firmly between its jaws. For days, she would stare out of the window, unable to eat, not wanting to live.

In the end, the doctors decided to admit her to La Manouba. Although reforms to the highly centralised French system of psychiatric care had already begun, most of them had not filtered to the colonies where institutions were a case study in human misery. Whenever people speak of La Manouba, they do so in whispers, remembering that female patients were once forced to provide wardens with sexual favours. The family probably could not have acted differently, but their pained silence over Simone's abandonment to the horrors of the asylum remains to this day.

Lina became the sole breadwinner. Since Tunis University only offered the first year of a degree course, her ambition to leave La Goulette and complete her studies in France might have been realised had her father not died. She now took a job as a teacher at the Alliance Israélite School, but this lasted only one week. She shrugged off her dismissal. The Lumbrosos were Italian and if the French government suddenly decreed that only French citizens could teach in Alliance schools as these were now receiving state subsidies, it gave her a good excuse not to become a teacher. She had no patience with unruly children. But the bad faith of the French authorities was revealed when Dani applied for French nationality and was turned down. Not being of conscription age, he was of no interest to them.

Lina next found clerical work at one of her father's former clients, an ironmonger. Her wages were stretched tight to help feed the whole family. There was little hope that she would be able to get away from the rue du Lieutenant Longello. My father's sister, Yolanda, described the atmosphere there as being not unlike *Wuthering Heights*. The most bitter quarrels were still between Meiha and Nina, fighting now over a dead Mino. Emma remained cowed in a corner. Lina spent more and more time at her cousins'.

It was Yolanda, resident in Tunis for fifteen years, who came up with the idea of matchmaking her brother Duggie from Malta with Lina. She had not herself met the girl, but an aunt used to play cards with a cousin of Lina's. The only difficulty was to get Duggie to agree to an initial meeting.

'I know,' Yolanda grimaced as she put the deal to her younger brother who was in Tunis on holiday, 'the heiress was a bit of a disaster.'

'A bit of...' The rich man's daughter whom she had initially introduced him to had terrified him, most of all by her ability to spend money.

'Don't worry,' the girl's father had said to him, 'when you come and work for me, you'll be able to make lots of money and keep her in the same style.'

But Duggie had no ambitions to go into business.

'I'm told this Lumbroso girl is much nicer,' Yolanda said, not giving up on her marriage campaign. 'She has beautiful thick curls.' This is the way Lina's die-straight hair had re-grown after her bout with typhus. 'She also has a peaches-and-cream complexion.' While it was true that my mother had beautiful skin, prized in that society for its European whiteness, Yolanda, whose favourite novel was *Lorna Doone*, was exaggerating somewhat.

Duggie refused to listen. He decided he would leave his sister's apartment when Lina arrived.

'Nice to meet you. Sorry, but I'm going out.' One of the things that Lina was still to learn about Duggie was that he can be quite rude and then later bewildered when others are offended. He never intends to be hurtful. 'Where's my jacket? Excuse me, but have you seen where Yolanda put my jacket?'

His sister had hidden the jacket and, because he was wearing braces, something that would have made the locals hoot with laughter if he had shown them in the street, he was cornered. Lina wouldn't have expected such a tough-looking man, with such broad shoulders, to care about what strangers in the street thought.

My parents' courtship lasted just one week. Duggie acknowledged that he had been very lonely. That was why his mother had sent him to Tunis in the first place. She had worried that, newly returned to Malta from the army and India, he had shut himself up in his room listening to Beethoven symphonies. She herself only liked Italian opera. Besides, there was no reserve of marriageable girls on their tiny Mediterranean island.

The first step in my mother's journey away from her childhood began with the stroke of luck that had brought her a man who was not interested in a dowry. It was bad enough that she had a mad sister, people gossiped, but worse that her now impoverished family could not afford a dowry for her. Lina had resigned herself to being an old maid at home, forever looking after the old and sick members of the family. Now that there was a possibility of getting away, however, she agonised about abandoning them.

'Go!' Zia Nina said. 'Forget about us. Snatch this opportunity. I'll see to the dowry.' She then went out and pawned her jewels.

'But you're not buying a husband for your grand-daughter,' Duggie argued when he learned about the necklaces, rings and bracelets in hock. 'Anyway, you don't have the money to redeem them, do you?'

'Frankly, no.' Zia Nina lowered her gaze to her upturned empty palms. But she could not believe that Duggie wanted nothing. This was unheard of in her world. So she went to Monsieur Fitoussi's, the tailor, to borrow 50,000 francs to redeem the jewellery. Monsieur Fitoussi was kind and did not ask for collateral. But Duggie insisted that this money should also be returned.

This was my mother's first clear rupture with the world of her past. And when she married and Duggie took her to Malta, she took

the next step, which was to remove herself physically from the claus-
trophobic atmosphere and miseries of the house on the rue du
Lieutenant Longello. Settling in a kibbutz was meant to remove her
and my father from the restrictions of small communities, but it was
not until they got to Australia that they began to feel truly free of
their pasts. They left for Australia unburdened by possessions apart
from a few of the redeemed jewels that Zia Nina had, nonetheless,
insisted they should accept at least as a token dowry, and a few
clothes and bedsheets from the kibbutz.

The rare photographs that we had were not on display in silver
frames but kept in a thick envelope in a leather handbag hidden in
the linen press. So my brother and I grew up with hardly any images
of the world my mother had grown up in. It now occurs to me that
only those friends whose parents survived the Holocaust were as pic-
tureless as we were, stranded from their pasts.

When my mother came to visit me in Paris in 1969, I began to
see that there was more to her identity than the hard-working
career-woman I knew, able to lay on lavish dinner parties while
closely supervising her children's homework and spending weekends
at the beach body-surfing. In France, she met her family again for
the first time in more than twenty years. She seemed to discover a
longing for fried foods and the sickly sweet cakes favoured in La
Goulette. She joined in happily in the shouted conversations. She
met old friends again. But the very fact of her being able to immerse
herself in her first language, French, made my father and me feel
guilty. We realised that for all those years in Australia we had failed
to recognise that she had, after all, been labouring under a huge burden – that of speaking English. Although she speaks it perfectly, in
France she seemed to have become lighter, less anxious.

We were the ones who were jittery. When, one Yom Kippur, my
mother woke up and announced that she wanted to go to the temple to hear the *shofar* played, we hardly recognised her. Her old self
seemed to have got the upper hand. But she is the one who put
things in perspective, pointing out that these excursions into her past

are only temporary and enjoyable principally because of that. She will not be pinned down by her Parisian family's perceptions of her, but nor will she be restricted by ours.

*   *   *

When Lina left La Goulette, the disintegration of her family and former way of life had already begun. As she stood under the *chuppa*, it was to be the last time all Rabbi Jacob Arous's descendants were to find themselves together. Removing the drapes covering the mirror as a mark of their mourning for Mino, they ordered a few *canapés*, which is all they could afford, and fished out some wine from the stock Mino had collected from a bankrupted client. Simone was temporarily released from the asylum. In my parents' wedding photographs taken by a local photojournalist she is holding one corner of the canopy, watched by all the cousins, aunts and uncles and the sad-eyed portrait of the dead Mino. Zia Nina and Emma must have called a temporary truce because they are seated next to each other.

With Lina gone, Dani, aged fourteen, was now left to support the family – the only male descendant of Rabbi Jacob left to recite the Prayer for the Dead when Zia Nina and then Emma died. If he could solve the problem of who would take care of Simone, he would be released from the obligation of staying on in Tunisia, for life was becoming increasingly difficult for non-Moslems. Later, when he had married and had a young son, he joined the growing number of Europeans leaving North Africa in the wake of Tunisian independence. He placed the house on the rue du Lieutenant Longello in the hands of an agent who rented it out to a number of Arab families.

Over the years, it has fallen into severe disrepair in spite of acquiring a grand name, which it never had in Rabbi Jacob's lifetime – the Villa Arous. Arous being also an Arab name (meaning *fiancé*), no one living there these days knows that it once belonged to a rabbi. The synagogue was demolished, as were the Turkish baths. Brown sheep now graze in what was once the courtyard where beggars gathered for handouts of food on the eve of the Sabbath. The wooden door at its entrance has almost completely come off its hinges and is shored up by pieces of timber and lengths of rope. The amputated family dwelling has had many of its windows concreted in. The drainy smell of Lake Tunis still hovers in the air.

I went there a few years ago with my uncle Dani. I was hugely disappointed and not a little depressed for all I saw was decay. The mansion that my mother remembered seemed impossibly small. I felt like a mourner who had gone looking for, but found no grave to mark the existence of, a lost friend. The break with what had been and what now is seemed complete, emblematic of the Lina whom her Parisian relatives knew and the mother I now know.

*Article One: The Religion of Malta is the Roman Catholic Apostolic Religion.*

The Independence Constitution of Malta, 1964

CHAPTER TWO

# a view from the balcony

Travelling by train in Britain on a Sunday is not recommended. This is the day they do track maintenance. Cancellations and delays reach their peak. Trains get crowded.

A few years ago, on a Sunday journey from London to Manchester, the train I was on stopped for two whole hours in the middle of nowhere. Cupping my hands round my eyes to peer through the carriage window, all I could see was a black landscape over which the Hound of the Baskervilles might easily have been prowling.

Adenoidal apologies for this enforced stop, broadcast over the Tannoy, were met with a collective sigh. It was late and everyone was tired. Apart from the hiss leaking from a teenager's Walkman, for the next hour the carriage was enveloped in total silence. Some passengers dozed, others kept their heads down over a book or hid behind their broadsheet. This being England, everyone had a ploy for not looking strangers in the eye and starting up a conversation.

The tense hush was broken by the young woman with hair bleached to the texture of straw who was seated facing me. 'Ooh ah!' she sighed.

I looked up.

'The Maltese are terrible people,' she said.

'I'm sorry?' I swallowed.

'The Maltese. They're just awful.'

'But I'm Maltese,' I said, claiming Maltese identity on one of the rare occasions in my life. It was pure coincidence that this slur against my fellow-islanders had been uttered in my presence. This stranger had been thinking aloud and I felt I had to defend the Maltese.

'I don't mean you, of course.' She leaned towards me confidingly, though without lowering her voice. 'I mean that man in London. The one who takes most of me money.'

I could see other passengers coming awake. Soon they were straining to hear this waif's story as it quickly became clear she was speaking about her pimp. Three days a week, she said, she left her daughter in the care of her mother in Manchester to go down to London.

'You can make good money down there. On the game.' She didn't seem worried that everyone around us was listening. She was wistful rather than angry about the fact that her 'fellow' creamed off so much of her earnings.

In the 1950s and 1960s, the Maltese were notorious for their involvement in London's low life. Here we were in the late 1980s and she was telling me about a world of marginals with a Maltese man at its centre.

I suspect that, had my father been present, he would have tried to console this scrawny girl by telling her that's what happens to the

Maltese. 'They are like that when they get away from the island and the influence of the church,' he would have said. Although five generations of my family have lived on the rock, we still tend to speak of the Maltese in the third person. Especially when they are up to something bad.

On that stationary train, I had not picked the most glorious moment to declare that I was one of them. Because it makes things too complicated, I usually don't explain that I was born in Malta. To most people, being Maltese is synonymous with being a Catholic. In Malta, you cannot get away from it. But when I give my name to inquisitive old people on the island, some of them remember that there's something unusual about our family even if they have forgotten it is our religion. Since there is only a small pool of surnames on the tiny island and the rest of its archipelago, others immediately remark that our name is not Maltese. When they infer that we do not quite belong, we fall back on a pride in being Jewish, even though most of us have not been to a synagogue service in years. Unfairly, one of us is sure to mention the Maltese mixed up in London's underworld.

But when the Maltese are under attack, perversely we feel Maltese.

\* \* \*

'Down to our subconscious,' my father, Duggie, might add. For the first ghost he ever saw was the ghost of a priest. Dressed in a red soutane, he was ringing a bell as he skimmed down the steep steps of Valletta's Strada Zecca, Old Mint Street.

During my father's childhood, living priests used to do this, come out ringing bells when summoned to the home of a dying parishioner. Duggie, his elder brother, and their five sisters were sometimes woken by the clanking of bells followed by rapping on doors. From their shuttered green balcony, seven pairs of eyes would peek through the green slats as surreptitiously as ladies in a *zenana*. They watched silently as the cleric zig-zagged from one house on one side of the street to another on the other side. In apartments all along his route, mothers chivvied children out of beds and prodded them down narrow hallways to front entrances. Solid doors creaked open.

'Go! Follow the priest!' The women would thrust a lantern into the hand of each glue-eyed child.

Maltese children, still in pyjamas, would straggle behind the priest, casting eerie shadows on the high walls of the baroque Archbishop's Palace across the street from my father's family's apartment building. To tag along was a Christian act of piety for which the processioners earned points for a place in heaven.

'That is what *they* believe,' Duggie's mother, Rachele, used to say clicking her tongue and rolling her eyes. 'Not only that. *They* also believe in the Virgin birth.'

This greatly puzzled Duggie. Although exempted from compulsory religion at school, he had heard about the Virgin birth. By a sort of process of osmosis with the surrounding community, he was even able to recite all of Mary's titles: Gate of Heaven, Tower of Ivory, Stella Maris . . .

'How can it be? A woman who's a mother and a virgin?' Eventually, he wound up the courage to ask the priest at his school.

'Let's say it's a mystery and should not be examined too closely.' The Jesuit winked in complicity.

Duggie did not ask how it was that Mary was also the Ark of the Covenant. This epithet was the most confusing of all to a Jewish boy.

Once a year, a man climbed up a ladder and balanced precariously above the well which stood at the bottom of Strada Zecca, where Duggie and his family lived on the top floor of number 69C. On her Saint's Day, the man would tenderly lower the Virgin from her sandstone niche after the sun had turned Valletta's massive curtain walls to a coralline gold. She was carried along the streets, a line of swaying torch-bearers following. It was Ondina, the second eldest of Duggie's sisters, the clever one, who invented the game of huffing and puffing to try to blow out the flames. Because she had a large mouth, they nicknamed her *Karus tal Germania* after the clown-head moneybox into whose huge mouth her brothers and sisters plopped pennies. Their father, Banino, was furious about her lack of reverence.

'How can you expect the Maltese to respect you, if you don't respect them?'

'Tell that to your eldest daughter,' their mother muttered.

Duggie wondered how his mother did it, drawing in her small neat features as if she were pulling in the strings of a reticule. His father, sucking his pipe, looked puzzled.

Yolanda, their eldest, had just had her hair bobbed. '*L'ultima moda*,' she declared in Italian as she paraded her modern haircut. It was so much better than long hair which, when pulled back, had made her look weak-chinned.

Duggie hoped this was the end of fashion. He understood *l'ultima* to mean the last rather than the latest and was relieved. Fashion only meant trouble.

Arguments at home, to begin with. When Yolanda took her father's best *borsalino* and cut the brim to make a modish *cloche*, he was not pleased. Banino was meticulous about his appearance and liked his children to be well dressed too. This is why he cut suits for all his family, doing so as skilfully as a master cutter at any grand couturier's. Visiting British nobility regularly went to his shop on Palace Square to have suits made from the English worsteds, serges and tweeds displayed in the window. Clients liked Banino's cultivated manner. He read widely and in the short stories he wrote enjoyed creating pastiches of famous English and Italian authors. When customers sighed for England's greenness, he empathised because he had served his apprenticeship in Croydon, still a village on the outskirts of London at the turn of the century. Pretty ladies sat on the wooden horse upstairs in the shop to have their leg measurements taken for riding breeches. Yolanda reported this to Rachele who often sent her round to Palace Square to see what Banino was up to.

Yolanda never forgot the row between her parents on the day of

Duggie's *Brit Mila*, literally Covenant with God or circumcision. Banino, summoned home for the ceremony, had been so flustered that he had accidentally locked one of his female clients in. The woman had to climb out onto the balcony to shout for help. To Rachele, this had been a public humiliation. Once the rabbi, who had been brought to the island from Sicily for the occasion, had sailed back home, there were black recriminations.

Duggie remembers that the incident with the *borsalino* ended with tears, but Yolanda soon picked herself up. She was, as her little brother had heard her say, the Heroine of the Bread Riots of 1919. 'Foolish girl. You could have been injured,' Banino had bellowed when he learned what his eldest daughter had done. He had watched the rioting from his shop.

After bread prices had soared following the end of World War I, a mob had turned out in the streets, calling for the blood of the millers. Banino had seen the demonstrators hurling a printing press from a window at the offices of *The Malta Daily Chronicle*. Then they marched up the Strada Reale to the millers' grand houses, across the street from the even grander Opera House. Eleven-year-old Yolanda went with them and cheered as the rioters threw stones at the millers' sealed shutters.

Foolhardy still, Duggie thought, when the teenage Yolanda, who had grown tall for a Maltese girl, stepped out in her new-style sleeveless dresses and home-made hat. People noticed her. From pulpits, priests had railed against the modern woman, shamelessly displaying her bare arms. So that when Yolanda passed down the street, men and boys would shove burning cigarette butts at her, trying to stub them out on her arms.

'The girls will all have to learn to box,' Banino announced. 'I'd like you to teach them,' he said to his trainer who, for two shillings, sparred with him each morning at home. All that feinting and jumping about threw Banino's twin canaries into a fluster. And the chickens, which Rachele kept in a cage on the balcony, became agitated.

Banino was not always prepared to creep round other people's religious sensibilities, especially when it was a matter of principle. What made Rachele nervous, this refusal to toe society's line, was the thing my father admired the most about his own father. When the works of George Bernard Shaw were placed on the Papal Index, Banino ordered a complete set of his plays from a bookseller in London.

'Is father a Freemason?' one of Duggie's sisters asked her mother. A maid had tugged at her arm as they had passed the Brotherhood's headquarters and whispered that Banino was one of those wicked people. The girl had confused Judaism with Freemasonry.

'Who is Mohammed?' Duggie wanted to know. 'Is he one of our prophets?' He had come home bruised and dishevelled after a fight with a fellow pupil.

'Don't be ridiculous.' Rachele always dismissed the children's questions. She loved them as babies, but became impatient with them as they started to grow. Duggie had been seven years old before she had agreed to have his golden curls cut. His mother could hardly believe that, among all her dark-haired children, she had produced such an unsouthern-looking wonder. It was a shame, she thought, when he had to wear those thick, horn-rimmed glasses. The kids on the block made fun of his spoilt brat's appearance and he soon learned to hit out.

'Can I play with you?' Duggie, aged six, asked a neighbour's daughter the same age as him.

'Don't be silly,' she replied. 'You're a boy.' Dressed in the pinafore that Miss Linda, his kindergarten teacher, required all her charges to wear, made it hard to tell. 'Boys don't play with girls, don't you know? Besides, you're a Jew.'

It was a small community, the Jewish one, rarely numbering more than one hundred. Most were middle-class. Some were poor. Like the Mizrahis. Mr Mizrahi sold trinkets on the street.

'Rosaries from Rome! Watches from America!' he would call from his patch on the pavement. When he was tired and hungry, it became, 'Watches from Rome! Rosaries from America!'

They were not the only community of outsiders. My father's

family's Greek neighbours were also different. On Orthodox Easter, celebrated on a different day from Maltese Easter, they threw plates out of their window.

'Stop that racket!' Rachele would call, shaking her dumpy arm at them from her balcony as crockery smashed on the stone pavement.

'And you up there, stop drenching our clothes,' the downstairs neighbour shouted at Rachele. The woman had hung out all the costumes from Carnival on the clothesline. Rachele, watering her jasmines, had not noticed that the water was dripping onto the balcony below. 'I know,' the woman below called out. 'They offend you, these costumes, don't they? Because they're part of our religion.'

Religion was just one thing that set my father's family apart. Language was another because at home they spoke Italian.

'*Ci, ci, Macaroni,*' the kids on the street would tease. My father's sisters loved to join in as these urchins followed the water cart. On hot days, they cooled their feet in the water leaking from the tank. But as you were not allowed to go to school barefoot, many of these children received no education at all, their families too poor to afford shoes.

'Look, look,' the Strada Zecca girls would call out, 'there go those boys again.'

'Those boys' were two brothers who between them had just one pair of shoes. So, every day, they went to school wearing one shoe each. On the other foot, the first brother wore a bandage, while the second hobbled along with the lint unravelling from his unshod foot.

They were not the poorest of the children from the slums of the Manderaggio, the district by the shelter pen which had been gouged out of the rock three centuries before to create a haven for the galleys of the Order of the Knights of St John. At the Jews' Sallyport, below Strada Zecca, the most pinched of the boys who did not go to school would hire out bathing suits for a living. If you threw a coin into the sea, they dived in to retrieve it. The water was so deep that it was more black than blue. Sometimes, the boys would bob up brandishing sea urchins.

'*Giorgio! Giorgio!*' other kids would croon to George, Duggie's closest friend and double cousin (his mother was Banino's sister, his father Banino's first cousin).

'*Ti vogliono!*' children in the street would sing, mimicking chubby Vita, George's crippled sister, sitting by the window, calling out in Italian rather than Maltese. 'Come back in. Mother and Father want you.'

'Poorvita,' all her cousins called Vita. During the great influenza epidemic of 1919, she had almost died. To save her life, doctors had amputated a gangrenous foot and the family had changed her name from Rina to Vita. Name-changing was an old Jewish custom, intended to deceive the Angel of Death, so that when he came looking for a sick child called Rina, and her name had been changed to Vita, he would not find her.

'*Ti vogliono!*' Vita would keep up the refrain until her brother came back indoors.

'*Ti vogliono*' is what his cousins dubbed George as one of them grabbed his arms, another his legs, and dragged him down the stairs, his bottom bumping every single step. Duggie was sometimes the ringleader, but it was the revenge of all seven cousins because George's father was rich and George always had much more pocket money than they did.

The Italian spoken in my father's home and the cause of so much teasing by other children was the legacy of his grandmother, Corinna, and not an affectation or a political statement against British rule of the Maltese islands. Nonna Corinna lived on St Christopher's Street. Before her marriage, Corinna Coen had run a Dame's School for Jewish girls in Florence. She had arrived in Malta with a trousseau of solid oak furniture and ceiling-high, gilt-framed mirrors, all listed in the shipping gazette, *Lloyds Maltese*. The gazette recorded the names of everyone leaving or arriving on the island: English ladies with their maids; merchants from Tripoli, Algiers or Smyrna; pashas with their harem (individual members of which remained unnamed).

Corinna had also brought an education with her. She had decreed that all her children and grandchildren were to learn reams of Dante by heart because the Divine Poet was her speciality. Maltese scholars sometimes came to her to ask for explications of obscure passages, but they never acknowledged her contribution in their dissertations. Her grandchildren remember her as straight-backed and with a predilection for hats with stiff-stemmed flowers. These concealed the thin hair, which even, as a young woman, was the bane of her life.

Just before Duggie's last and youngest sister was born, the family had sent Yolanda to live with Corinna to ease the crowding at Strada Zecca. To Duggie, aged two at the time, the departure of his eldest sister was eased by the fact that she was living only two blocks away. Still taking on some of the burden of looking after her younger brothers and sisters, she would come round to pick up Duggie on her way to a matinée at the opera. This is how, at a very early age, my father learned all the libretti of both famous and obscure operas and operettas.

Opera was fun. Duggie remembers the occasion when Manrico's visor got stuck in 'Il Trovatore'. The audience howled the singer off the stage. Opera was also confusing. When Pagliaccio sang '*Vesti la giubba, la faccia in farina*' (on with the motley and white up the face), Duggie thought he was singing '*Vesti la giubba, facciala farina*' (put on the motley and squish it into flour).

Explaining why Yolanda did not live with them, my father's parents said: 'Crowding causes diseases. Diseases kill babies.'

'Only seven children!' School friends were amazed, counting my father's brothers and sisters. Just one school friend came from a family with fewer children, two survivors out of a total of eleven births. Seven children and no deaths – it was almost unheard of.

Yolanda had not wanted to leave.

'Remember the scarlet fever?' her parents had reminded her. When a member of the family downstairs had caught the disease, that family's apartment had been cordoned off for forty days and

forty nights. A policeman had kept vigil at their door, stopping anyone from going in or going out.

Five years later, it was Malta Fever. Duggie contracted it from
goat's milk.

For a whole year, he was confined to his bed, his temperature
soaring during the day and returning to normal at night, in a cycle
the exact opposite of other fevers. Though he had no cure, the doctor had called each day just to keep Duggie company.

'But Malta Fever is not contagious,' Yolanda was able to argue. It
was because the milk was unpasteurised. The goatherd, who walked
with his flock all the way from Hamrun to Valletta, milked each goat
in front of people's doors. When it rained, however, he left his flock
at home and lugged full churns into town. Sometimes, he thinned
the milk down with warm water supplied by his friend, the *café*
owner. From the balcony, one of Duggie's sisters would lower a basket containing a canister down to the pavement and haul the milk
up.

'Quick, quick. Fish out the goat hairs!' Ondina, the sister Duggie
loved most for her sense of fun, would send a *frisson* of horror down
her prissier sisters' backs. Such a pretty, wide-eyed child and so
mischievous.

'Think of going to Corinna's as company for your grandmother.
You'll have a room of your own,' Rachele and Banino, trying
another tack, said to Yolanda.

But to their eldest, it was like being expelled from Paradise. She
missed her brothers and sisters, the early morning scrum for a turn
in the bathroom, her father testing his vocal cords, Duggie whirling
on his bike round the living room while blowing on a harmonica
and crashing into furniture, the neighbours banging on the ceiling.

When they came home from school, blind Uncle Clemente, who
lived downstairs, was always there to meet them. He recognised the
footsteps of each of the seven children and would stop them to pat
them on the head. Duggie remembers his gentleness. Clemente was
not only a familiar figure to the Strada Zecca children. Many

people in Valletta grew accustomed to seeing him, the *Olio Sasso* rep, on his rounds about the capital, stepping carefully up and down the slippery stairs of its narrow streets. He paid a boy to lead him. At Strada Zecca, Clemente's special place was on the flat roof, among the flowers planted by Duggie's brother. Clemente used to sit there for hours, his face turned to the sun.

'I've heard that the sun's rays can restore vision,' he explained to the children.

At Nonna Corinna's, it was silent. Leaning out of the balcony, Yolanda would stare for hours at the shadowy street below, behind whose high walls lay dank inner courtyards. Across the bay, she could see the seaside resort of Sliema drenched in blinding sunlight. Dark and light. Light was reflections on water. Dark was her grandmother's apartment where the only other company was the tubercular maid.

'Now, take care. Never drink from the same cup as her. Or eat from the same plate.'

Gradually, however, Yolanda adjusted. Corinna was firm, but not as stern as she had expected. Her unsmiling face was a mask acquired from years of putting up with her husband, a drunkard. She could be bawdy, teaching her grandchildren songs in Italian about priests breaking wind or doing something that Yolanda didn't quite understand. For sex was the 'great unmentionable', especially at Strada Zecca. When Banino caught Ondina chatting to a boy on their front doorstep, he pulled her in by her pigtails. Rachele slapped her when she repeated something about a neighbour's difficult labour although Ondina hadn't understood what labour meant.

In 'exile', Yolanda's closest friend became her Egyptian-born cousin Ida, the only child of a widowed mother. Initially, she had thought Ida spoilt. As Ida grew into a beanpole, all her underwear, beautifully embroidered by her mother, was handed down to the resentful Strada Zecca girls. When one of Banino's many cousins came home on leave from his post as British Consul in Sana'a, Ida alone received a gift of a watch, which she kept waving about. It was really to reassure herself, but Yolanda and Duggie's other sisters saw it as showing off. Collectively, they were only given a box of stale English biscuits, which they knew to have been an afterthought.

In the end, Ida was too sweet-natured to be seen as an opponent, and she and Yolanda became inseparable. Sometimes, they shared Uncle Clemente's box at the Opera House and tried to remember what Rachele had whispered at home about the opera stars to whom he sent lavish bouquets. Had he gone blind because of one of these women with loose morals?

What really made Ida 'one of us' was that her mother was not well off, unlike their other cousins. The habit of dividing up the world, begun with the Maltese, was carried on within the family. Banino could not help his resentment against its wealthier members. He knew it was ungenerous, but he nonetheless infected his children with his rivalry. For he might have been rich had it not been for the 'Man at Barclays'. Guessing that revolution was brewing in Brazil, Banino had instructed the bank manager to sell all his Sao Paulo stocks and shares. But the manager had taken no action, claiming afterwards that he had no record of such instructions. Banino came home, removed his hat and sat down at the oak table, which had once been part of his mother Corinna's dowry.

'Yesterday, we were rich,' he shook his head. 'Today, we are poor.'

For months afterwards, he complained of a rash and by the end of the year he was diagnosed as suffering from diabetes.

He measured his poverty against his cousin, George's father, who was a success. The latter always seemed to overcome financial crises. Before World War I, he had lost a fortune when the bottom fell out of the ostrich feather market. He, his wife and his brother, Blind Clemente, had all had to move into a single room at Corinna's.

'Just because we are poor now,' he reminded everyone, 'it doesn't mean that you can come barging into our room. Kindly knock if you wish to enter.' As he spoke, his nostrils quivered and his manicured Van Dyke beard suddenly appeared more dapper. Putting on his riding habit and with crop in hand, he would stride round Valletta's city walls and down the Strada Reale, its broad main avenue, every morning. Dressed up like this, he hoped people would still believe he was a man with a fortune.

He soon recovered, however, and, in 1929, managed to survive the Great Crash while the last of Banino's investments in European princedoms turned to dust.

'Zia Rachele,' the rich cousin's son, molly-coddled 'Ti vogliono' George, would turn up at Strada Zecca and stick his foot in the door. 'Is Duggie there?' he would ask. If he was persistent enough, Duggie might be allowed to come out and race him on the roof. Duggie was mad about running and hoped that by the next Olympic Games in 1940 he would run for Malta.

'Not today. He has homework to do.' Rachele would try to squeeze George's foot out of the doorway. Through the crack, he could glimpse all the seven cousins seated round the dining table, noses buried in books: *Orlando Furioso, Gerusalemme Liberata*, the poems of Pascoli, Tennyson, Shakespeare and Dante. Those books were handed down from sister to brother. By the time it was the youngest daughter's turn, the spines had been repaired over and over again and it was hard to see the printed text for the pencilled notes between the lines and down the margins.

To keep George out was one of Rachele's minor victories over his rich father. 'They may be wealthy, but our children are cleverer than theirs,' she would say. Better at sports too because by now Duggie had a cabinet full of trophies; George could only boast one tiny silver one, the size of an eggcup.

Banino too had his triumph one holiday at Marsascala. Every summer, he rented a villa in this isolated fishing village. When Valletta's breathless heat became intolerable, the family would load all their furniture onto carts and, with their two maids, climb into two horse-drawn *karozzin*. These would carry them up the hill and then down the steep slope to the ferry. On the other side of Grand Harbour, another two *karozzin* would pick them up. With the furniture cart, which had gone by land around the harbour, following behind, they travelled slowly past the bleached drystone wall enclosing the market garden.

These days the area round Marsascala has passed through the hands of developers. When Duggie was a boy, there was no road along the bay and the children had only to pick their way over the rocks to be able to splash straight into the water. The sole shop in the vicinity was a bakery, to which Rachele sent them, or the maids, to buy crackly crusted bread to make *hobs b'zeit*. Their brown skins glazed with water droplets and their lips stinging from seasalt, they would wolf down thick slices of this crusty bread flavoured with crushed tomatoes, olive oil and the capers that are Malta's most abundant crop.

Once the sun set, neighbours dragged out tables into the street and there was music and dancing to the hot blue light of paraffin lamps. Banino would stretch these holidays until long after the first rain showers had broken the trance of summer and it was time for the children to prepare for the new school year.

'Why don't you buy our rowing boat?' Banino said to George's father who had also decided to rent a summerhouse at Marsascala. Banino and all seven of his children stood lined up on the rocks as their rich uncle prepared to board. He was a fat man but carried his weight with grace and dignity. He climbed into the boat and picked up the oars. The boat began turning slowly in a circle. Then it started to fill with water. Soon he was knee-deep in seawater. All seven children burst out laughing, for which neither they nor their father were ever forgiven.

\*   \*   \*

In addition to the lines separating the Maltese from our family and the rich relatives from the less well-off, there was a divide between those family members who were more assiduous about observing the laws of Judaism and those who were less conscientious. The island did not always have its own rabbi. The rules of *kashrut* were hard to observe. Whenever the *shochet* was on holiday, the observant cousins ate fish with a sense of superiority over the Strada Zecca horde. The rabbi, brought from Sicily for one day to officiate this time at Duggie's *Bar Mitzvah*, sailed home in the evening without having supervised this rite of passage. Duggie had absconded for the day and could not be found. But Banino was not terribly strict about enforcing observance.

George's father, a good and pious man, gave money to a home for indigent Jewish men in Palestine. His portrait hung in each of the dormitories.

'He's a fool,' Banino slapped the newspaper he was reading. 'Look what he's done.' George's father had written a letter to the editor praising Mussolini's regime.

'He seems to have forgotten the invasion of Corfu. Does he think that Mussolini will stop at just one island?'

Since the 1923 occupation, Banino had been keeping a close watch on events in Italy. The savage Italian invasion of Abyssinia in 1936 had forced him to take a stand. The League of Nations was powerless, but he could protest in his own way.

'In this house, we will no longer speak Italian. From now on only Maltese is allowed.' Though, of course, English continued to be the language at school for his children.

Like many Maltese, Banino was an Anglophile, but the banning of Italian (his mother tongue) from Strada Zecca had more to do with the injustices and brutalities of the fascist regime than with a rigid allegiance to British rule. The British colonials did not always treat the Maltese as a people but saw them as inferiors, the native inhabitants of a fortress strategic to their Empire. During Count Gerald Strickland's premiership in the 1920s, 'cultural nationalism', especially where it took the form of pro-Italian policies, was ruthlessly suppressed. Because Malta was seen as a key to Britain's sea power, Strickland's aim was to make the Maltese as English as possible.

'Stafford: listed in the Domesday Book. Stoke-on-Trent: known

for its fine pottery. Leeds: famous for its fine cloth.' Like every child
of the Empire, my father learned this litany from *Our Island Story*.
But 'our island' was not our island. The history was another nation's.

By the 1930s, the preferment given to those with an English education bitterly divided local political parties. The issue of Maltese
identity was hotly debated. Strickland had even put it about that the
Maltese were Aryans, closer to the English race than to Latins or
Semites. But a large number of Maltese nationalists opted for a policy of *italianità*, arguing that by tradition, religion, culture and
historical continuity Malta was of the Latin Mediterranean world.

'Do you have a second name?' Duggie's headmaster asked him one
day.

'Yes, it's Albert.'

'Good. From now on we will call you Alberto.'

'That's what he thinks.' Banino picked up his jacket and hat and
marched to the governor's residence to lodge a complaint with his
secretary. With his broad frame and bullet-smooth head, my father's
father looked as if he would always win a fight. Within a week, Duggie was Duggie again.

In Italy, Mussolini continued to rant against the British for not
encouraging the use of Italian in Malta. He offered scholarships to
Italian-speakers living abroad.

'That is out of the question. Duggie is not taking up a fascist
scholarship,' his father said.

Anyway, Duggie was not doing very well at school. He was completely absorbed in running.

'You don't imagine there are going to be Olympics in 1940, do
you?' Banino could see war on the horizon. The 1936 Games had
opened his eyes to the way events were unfurling. When a German
Jew jumped ship in Grand Harbour and the authorities sought to
deport him, Banino strode to the German Consul to demand that
deportation procedures be halted.

But George's father still insisted on speaking Italian at home. The
family was now divided along linguistic lines.

At 69C Strada Zecca, they had discovered a new loyalty to the Maltese language. Ondina started writing wistful short stories in Maltese. She joined the committee set up to devise a standard orthography for the language. When language became a cause and a sign of belonging, Banino and his children were quite clear where their loyalties lay.

* * *

On 10 June 1940 Italy finally declared war on Britain and Malta. When the aerial bombardments began, the family was evacuated from Strada Zecca to Balzan. Duggie joined the British Army.

'As you are an Italian-speaker,' the recruiting officer said, 'we will be posting you to India to interrogate Italian prisoners-of-war.' They were being held in detention camps throughout the subcontinent.

Seven years later, Duggie returned, not to the apartment with the enclosed green balcony, but to the seaside house in St Julians, which had replaced the villa at Marsascala. It was now the family's permanent home.

Duggie's war had been an easy one compared to that of the people left behind in Malta. With the blockade of the island, the Maltese had all almost starved to death as successive convoys failed to get through. The little food left on the island had had to be prepared on a communal basis in Victory Kitchens. When, in August 1942, two transport planes had managed to fly out some of the sickest women and children to Cairo (where Duggie was now stationed with his Indian regiment), tough Allied soldiers at Almaza actually wept to see them so emaciated and covered in sores. Back on the island, pneumonia and other respiratory diseases were rife in the unsanitary conditions of the air raid shelters and an epidemic of polio encephalitis had broken out. Thousands of buildings were destroyed.

The end result, after the war, was the hardening of Maltese resolve to assert their separate identity.

'We are not British,' Banino said, echoing the feelings of many Maltese who, over the 145 years of British occupation, had accepted English as their official language. So much so that many middle-class parents even took to speaking English to their children. 'Nor are we Italian,' Banino continued, although in his youth he, like other Maltese, had considered Italy and the Italian language as a source of culture.

'*Malta Maltija*' (Maltese Malta) now became the watchword for many islanders. It had been so at Strada Zecca for quite some time. In abandoning Italian and opting for Maltese, my father's family had clearly shown where their allegiances lay.

My father left the island long before Maltese independence in 1964, as did three of his sisters. But since there are still members of the family living there, none of us can say that we are free of our ties with the place. Year after year, many of us return to Malta. Not just to see our ageing uncle and aunts, but because it is, after all, the one place in the world about which we feel we can say quite clearly, 'This is where we come from.'

All this might have been hard to explain to the girl on the London to Manchester train.

*Neither Jews nor rats can exist in Malta. The Maltese are too much for either.*

LORD FISHER, *First Sea Lord* 1904–1910

## CHAPTER THREE

# rabbi josef's island minian

In his portrait, my father's great-grandfather, Rabbi Josef Tayar, looks gentle. I wonder how his warm expression might have changed had he been able to see ahead to the watered-down sense of Jewishness of his heirs. He could never have imagined how scattered we would all become and that some of us would grow up not even knowing how to recite the *Shema*, the central prayer of the Jewish liturgy. What does it mean to say you are Jewish, he might argue with me. I can only agree with the writer J.B. Yehoshua, who says that this is not a question to agonise over. That not even the *Halacha* requires a belief in God. That a Jew is simply someone born of a Jewish mother.

I am enchanted above all by Josef's oriental appearance. Here is a man who has sat for an anonymous portraitist wearing a black *stambouline*, or frock coat, and, wound a black turban around his red fez. In 1809, the year of his birth, the Karamanli dynasty, which ruled his native Tripoli, would not have allowed even that small touch of red. Black was the colour assigned to Jews. Their black clothing and headgear was what distinguished them from Arabs or Greeks or Armenians, all of whom had their regulation colours under the Ottomans.

In 1846, the year of Rabbi Josef's arrival in Malta, he bore a name that would have made it difficult for most to distinguish him from an Arab – Iusuf Tajar (the change to Josef he made himself; the *j* in Tayar became a *y* a couple of generations later). My father always jokes that Iusuf was the descendant of owners of a caravanserai who used to take foreign merchants all the way from Tripoli to India. One of our late cousins was sure that the family came originally from Turkey. In the registers of the Maltese Jewish community, Rabbi Josef listed himself as a French national.

I can only guess that this nationality was obtained under the system of Capitulations. Originally intended to protect foreign merchants working in the Ottoman Empire, with a view to fostering trade, Capitulations were the equivalent of a *laissez passer* granted by foreign consuls to non-nationals. Holders of Capitulations came under the jurisdiction of the European country granting them and were able to move about freely and practise their religion.

In Tripolitanian history, however, we find Tayars described as Livornese as far back as the sixteenth century and not associated with camel drivers. In the eighteenth century, a Rabbi Shabbetai Tayar wrote a *piyyut*, or liturgical poem, to commemorate the 1705 siege of Tripoli by the Tunisian despot Ibrahim al-Sharif. The *piyyut* was still sung in Tripoli's synagogues until the last of Libya's Jews were driven out following the Six Day war between Israel and Egypt. Shabettai's father, Rabbi David, is known to have been a member of the kabala. The relationship with Rabbi Josef, however, is unclear.

Usually I associate severe black clothing and long black beards
with the Chassidim, whose stagnant religiosity in this day and age is
something I feel has no connection with me. But I start to connect
with Josef, this man from another era and another place, when I picture his arrival on the island of Malta because I have several times
returned to the island by sea. Although Josef and his family had travelled only a couple of hundred miles from the Barbary coast, Grand
Harbour must have seemed an awesome sight. High above the water
stand the curtain walls of Valletta's fortifications with their corner
watch turrets. The domes of churches glint in the sunlight. As ships
slide into harbour, to the starboard they pass the Fort St Elmo light-
house, to the portside Fort Ricasoli.

All these great structures were the works of the Knights Hospi-
taller of the Order of St John, not known for their friendliness
towards Jews. Driven out from the Holy Land by the Turks, the
Knights had been forced to move to Cyprus and then to Rhodes.
Their headquarters had also briefly been in Tripoli. When, in 1524,
the Emperor Charles V offered them Malta as their new base, they
had not been greatly impressed. But faced with little alternative, they
set about building a city and fortifications to replace Mdina, Malta's
old Arab capital. Whereas Mdina is a town of the East, with narrow
lanes and buildings congregated on a cactus-spiked hilltop and huddled silently against the sun, Valletta is a microcosm of the great
Baroque capitals of the Western world. The symmetry of its layout
and the massive scale of its constructions are a reminder of the
Order's past authority. The island's numerous churches, with their
Rococo encrustations, as rich as sea life, symbolise the power of
Roman Catholicism from which, even now, there is little divergence
in Malta. The Maltese historian, Godfrey Wettinger, has described
Maltese society as possessing a hardened and fossilised xenophobic
brand of Christianity.

Even the topography of the place seems hostile. The tiny island
looks like a moonscape oddly thrust out of the sea. The bleached
honey colour of its countryside is of a piece with the towns, which

resemble nothing so much as clusters of uneven coin stacks. Where parallel fault lines occur, there is a succession of deep depressions and high ridges on one of which the Inquisitor's Palace still stands. Thin layers of soil nourish brittle vegetation. Any greenness is sucked out by the sun that pounds the globigerina and coralline limestone from which the Maltese archipelago is formed and its buildings constructed.

Josef was not only a rabbi, but also a merchant, so he may have already been familiar with the island. The Jewish community certainly knew him. By the 1840s it had grown large enough for the Chancellor and Board of Governors of the Strada Reale Congregation to feel they could afford a rabbi, if only a part-time one.

Standing on the deck of his ship with his wife, Smeralda, and their sons, Saul, Jacob, Moïse, Cesare (my great-grandfather) and their daughter, Rachella, still a babe-in-arms, did Josef feel any qualms about coming to this island? For in leaving Tripoli, he and his family were exchanging one Jewish community that lived more or less peacefully with the majority Moslem population for one with only a precarious hold in a rigidly Catholic society. Engaged principally in trade, Jews travelled freely throughout Tripolitania and Cyrenaica and were often the sole link between scattered outposts and the towns and cities of the regions. It was not as if there was no sense of difference between them and the Arabs and Berbers. For centuries, however, any incipient hostilities were kept in check by Tripolitania's Ottoman overlords. The Ottomans mostly get a bad press, but they must be credited for the relative peace they were able to maintain for centuries throughout their empire. Nowadays, when Serbs and ethnic Albanians are murdering each other and when Arabs and Jews are reluctant to negotiate, the Ottoman formula should not be forgotten. Communities were kept separate, but a greater authority was always there to stop them killing each other.

In my great-great grandfather's Tripoli, the Ottoman regime, which had kept a relative balance between its different ethnic and religious communities, was in serious decline, but had not yet completely crumbled. And modern ideas of the nation-state and European concepts of race had not yet forced Jews to choose between the European and Arab camps.

\*  \*  \*

Eighteen centuries before Josef, another Jew, a shipwrecked Saint Paul, described the inhabitants of the Maltese islands as a bunch of pagans. But a *menorah* painted on the wall of one of the island's many catacombs points to a Jewish presence thought to date as far back as the days of the Hebrew seafaring tribes of Zebulun and Asher.

That presence was continuous under the Romans and Byzantines who were, in turn, succeeded by the Arabs. The latter occupied the Maltese islands from 870 to 1090, eradicating the Phoenician language and giving the Maltese a language based on Arabic.

When Josef arrived in Malta from the Barbary Coast, he was coming to a place whose Semitic dialect, peppered by the nineteenth century with Italian and French words, he largely understood.

In 1090 the Normans drove the Arabs out and Malta became a dependency of the Kingdom of Sicily. During the three hundred years of Norman rule, the Jewish communities on the islands of Malta and Gozo were to peak to levels, which to a rabbi in Josef's day would have seemed incredible: approximately five hundred members in Malta and three hundred and fifty in Gozo. As elsewhere in Europe, they were treated with contempt, which sometimes erupted into acts of violence. The Jews of Malta specifically were expected to provide banners for the royal galleys and lamp oil for the loggias of Sicilian palaces. A venal queue of Christian office-holders lined up each year to demand expensive gifts from them.

These assaults on the Jews as a group choosing to set itself apart did not discourage them from adhering stubbornly to their faith. What made the authorities uneasy, however, were the links Jewish traders maintained with the Moslem communities of North Africa. (More than six centuries later, Josef was to supplement his income through trade with Tripoli, thus resuming these historical ties.) When the Lateran Council of 1215 decreed that Jews were to wear a wheel-shaped badge as a sign of their religion, their separateness was enshrined in this visible manifestation.

At the beginning of the fifteenth century the Crown of Sicily was combined with that of Aragon. So that what was happening in the Iberian peninsula was also to have an impact on Malta. In Spain, hatred for non-Christians (the peninsula also had a large Moslem population) had been simmering for a couple of centuries. In 1348, it was rumoured that the Black Death had been caused by Jews. In an atmosphere of panic, Jews were massacred throughout Spain. Fearing for their lives, one hundred thousand of them converted to Christianity. Most Christians did not consider this conversion to be genuine, however, and Jewish converts were to remain an object of profound distrust.

In Spain the net gradually closed in on these *Conversos* while, in Malta, measures were taken in 1485 to prohibit Jews from peddling their wares in the countryside and in the suburbs of the capital. They were ordered to confine their activities to a single quarter, the *Giurucca*, so as not to contaminate Christians with their 'pernicious propinquity' as one of the fascicules of the *Codice Diplomatico dei Giudei di Sicilia* describes it. Jews living near a church were ordered to sell their houses and move into the ghetto.

In 1492, Ferdinand II, encouraged by his wife Isabella and her confessor Torquemada, issued his infamous Edict of Expulsion, banishing all Jews from Spain and its dominions. Both my mother and father trace their ancestors back to these expelled people whose journeys were to take them to North Africa, some directly, some via Italy and Turkey (Rabbi Josef's forbears probably chose all these routes). The Moslem states welcomed the exiles for the knowledge they brought with them in areas ranging from printing to mapmaking and medicine to diplomacy – many Sephardic Jews were great linguists and as such had been useful emissaries. To the Ottoman Empire the Jews of Spain and its dominions also took their tradition of rabbinical leadership. In this model, the rabbi as scholar had as much say in running the community as the mercantile classes. Rabbi Josef, a scholar (his title was *Hakham* meaning Sage) and merchant, was to combine both authoritative functions and was not unusual in doing so.

Although the Royal Council argued that Malta was a special case, since expulsion would radically reduce its total population, the edict was applied mercilessly. All Jewish property was sequestered. Money, precious metals and stones, all livestock were confiscated. Businesses owned by Jews were sold for a pittance. Not only did Jews lose everything they had owned, but they also had to pay the crown compensation for the loss of tributes caused by their departure. Each person was allowed to take just one suit of common clothing, a mattress, a pair of worn sheets and a little food for the journey. The twentieth century was to invent nothing new in heart-rending departures. Cecil Roth, the historian of Italian and Maltese Jewry, imagined that some of these exiles' Christian neighbours must have done what is recorded the Christians of Sicily did. They climbed on their roofs and waved the Jews sorrowfully goodbye.

No one knows where Malta's Jews went to, but they may have become part of the Sicilian community, which remained a separate group throughout the Levant. In the Maltese archipelago, the only echoes of their presence were in place names like *Gnien Lhud* (Garden of the Jew) or *Bir Meru* (Meyr's Well). Near Zebbuġ, *Hal Muxi* reminds us that a certain Moshe once owned a farm here.

In 1530, against the payment of an annual rental of one white falcon, the Knights of the Order of St John replaced the House of Aragon as rulers of Malta. From the heart of the Mediterranean, they saw their mission as waging war against the infidel. They developed a lucrative sideline in seizing ships and holding passengers and crew to ransom. Among these captives, there was always a high proportion of Jews. They were taken back to Malta and kept as prisoners until money could be raised for their release.

To deal with these depredations, Jewish Societies for the Redemption of Captives, known as the *Pidion Shevuim*, were now given a more formal status than had been the case during the Middle Ages. In Venice, Livorno and even as far away as the Sephardic communities of Amsterdam, these fraternities acted by sending an agent to ascertain if there were any Jews among the Knights' captives. He was empowered to pay the prisoners a small allowance to cover their immediate expenses. The *Pidion* then set about bargaining for their release, transactions sometimes dragging on for months, even years. The Knights practised a form of extortion, holding out as long as possible to obtain the maximum amount of money for each of their captives. Coming from Tripolitania, Rabbi Josef would have known of such practices. Barbary corsairs had been doing the same sort of thing for centuries. The siege celebrated by his ancestor, Shabbetai, in his famous *piyyut*, had begun with the hijacking of a merchant ship carrying gifts from the governor of Egypt to the Bey of Tunisia.

In modern history Malta became unique in having a community made up solely of Hebrew slaves. One can only marvel at the tenacity of their faith. From his palace in Vittoriosa, the Inquisitor issued orders that they were to be exempted from work on their religious holidays. If their number fell below that needed for a *minian*, the *Pidion* agent was required to remove the Scroll of the Law until such time as a quorum for prayer could be constituted. The formation of *minians* was to be a constant problem well before Josef's arrival as well as during his rabbinate and afterwards.

Free Jews were not welcome in Malta. If they wished to make the island a port of call, they had to seek permission from the Grand Master of the Order. If this was granted, they were only allowed to enter Valletta through what is still called the Jews' Sallyport, below Strada Zecca, where my father lived as a boy. At all times, men and women were required to wear a yellow piece of cloth sewn onto their headdress.

Malta had no official rabbi, although a number of reluctant rabbis did occasionally find themselves stranded there, having to be redeemed. In 1666, a whole pod of rabbis was captured and imprisoned on the island.

The Knights ruled Malta for more than three hundred years. In 1792, their possessions in France were confiscated in the wake of the French Revolution, which was also to see the emancipation of European Jews. In 1798, Napoleon expelled the Order from Malta. When, less than two years later, the Emperor's troops were in turn driven out by the British, free Jews were able to settle in the Maltese archipelago.

The way was open for Rabbi Josef and his family. To some extent, they were economic migrants, that term which, these days, is used so disparagingly. To emigrate one now needs to have better credentials, to be the victim of political persecution solely. But this criterion usually comes with the other.

For Josef, however, Malta was hardly a promising new homeland. Most of its inhabitants were extremely poor, water was scarce and even the land-owning classes found it hard to maintain hygienic living conditions. Trachoma, cholera and the plague were more or less endemic and Undulant fever was so common that it became known as Malta fever. Visitors to the island speak of an ill-fed and poorly educated people.

Infant mortality remained close to fifty per cent. Baby Rachella was soon to become part of these statistics, although the exact cause of her death is unrecorded. Aged twenty-four months, she died a year after the family's arrival. The birth of Josef and Smeralda's first Maltese son, Rahamin Clemente, helped soothe the family's sorrow over the loss of their only daughter. Other more sturdy children followed: Abram, Gabriello Vita and finally another daughter Diamantina.

When Josef and his family took up residence within the precincts of the Strada Reale synagogue, the modern Jewish community had not been long established on the island. In 1835, Sir Moses Montefiore and his wife, on their way to Jerusalem, had stopped in Malta and found just six Jewish families living there. Only with the help of Moroccan merchants were they able to form a *minian*, but Lady

Judith sat alone in the women's gallery. 'A Narrative of a Mission of an Enquiry to the Jews from the Church of Scotland of 1839' describes the community as being wretchedly poor, no different, therefore, from the general population.

I so want the story of the family *minian* to be true. I have added up the number of Josef's sons over and over again. I have searched the registers of the Jewish community, the keeping of which Josef himself instituted. I have looked in vain for one more son because it is one more instance of the problem of forming quorums for prayer, which has from the Inquisition to our own times dogged the Jews of Malta. It also encapsulates the difficulties of keeping up religious practices in a place where, during Josef's tenure as rabbi, rarely more than twenty-five Jewish families lived. It demonstrates the tenacity of past generations in maintaining their separateness.

According to family lore handed down over five generations, since it was always difficult to form a *minian*, Smeralda, the matriarch, was granted the honour of becoming the tenth member of the quorum whenever ten men could not be mustered. This was the only way of getting round the perennial problem of finding enough Jewish men to make up the necessary number. It was also a sort of reward to her for producing so many sons. But what is missing is proof of the birth of one more son to sit alongside Josef, Smeralda and the other boys.

I do not want to let this story go. I tell it every time I meet other Jews, who are amazed that there is a community in Malta, because the Maltese are known only to be Catholics. Most Maltese themselves do not know that there are Jews among them, and those who have Jewish names e.g. Ellul (which is the sixth month of the Jewish calendar) do not often know of their own Jewish ancestry.

Being Maltese-born, I am an exotic not only among Maltese but also among Jews. I can choose to have allegiances to both, to either or to none. And I am never more self-protectively Jewish than when I see fellow travellers at Brussels's Zaventem airport staring hostilely at Chassidic Jews from Antwerp with their medieval appearance. These religious Jews might not choose to classify me as one of theirs, but I want to distance myself from the rude gawking strangers by calling out that I am the descendant of a long line of rabbis.

An identity is never just one single thing. It can go on being divided and sub-divided. The danger is when people start believing that there is a principal, superior identity based on race or religion or some other criterion.

Life was never easy for the Jews of Malta. The community was too poor to be able to engage Rabbi Josef other than part time. He supplemented his income of fifteen *scudi* a month (one *scudo* was equal to 2/6) as *shochet*, or ritual slaughterer, and *hazzan*, or cantor, by keeping his hand in trade. Under his contract, he also received one *soldo* for each pound of poultry slaughtered.

Josef was responsible for the pastoral care of the Jewish families permanently established on the island, and for the needs of a large number of Jewish travellers. In 1848, the year of revolutions in France, Germany and Hungary, many people fleeing persecution passed through the island. Assisting the Jews among them greatly strained the community's limited resources.

The administrators and Josef had to appeal continually for funds from the Rabbinate in London. That old standby, the Livornese *Pidion*, still in existence half a century after the departure of the predatory Knights, also stepped in from time to time to help the Maltese community. When the Torah and ornaments were stolen from the synagogue, the letter sent to the Ransom Society reminded it that the Maltese Congregation, the *Università*, owed its existence to the Jews of Livorno and appealed for help to recover the burgled property.

But by 1851 something happened that prompted Josef to leave the island and return to Tripoli. A letter dated 22 October and co-signed by Jacob Abeasis, the chancellor, and other members of the Strada Reale Board, speaks of his sudden departure. He had been experiencing business difficulties. An outbreak of cholera might have been the last straw.

Here, perhaps, is an opening for the birth of that other son, the missing eighth. Smeralda might have given birth in Tripoli and this might explain the omission in the Maltese registers.

With Josef gone, the board described the community as feeling 'leaderless and directionless'. They had obviously grown used to this solid figure with his large black eyes and hairy face. But in November he was back. The community, by now numbering 130, had undertaken to engage him full time. They drew up a contract in imperfect Italian and Josef signed his name in both Hebrew and Roman script. Abraham Masliah, appointed *Shamas*, was to help him.

His tasks included teaching Hebrew. One of the clauses of the contract stated that if children misbehaved in class, no coercive measures were permitted. The community felt that corporal punishment was shameful and would damage their reputation. In an age when beating children into submission was accepted as necessary, this was an unusual stipulation. Only the chancellor of the community was entitled to punish children for disobedience on the proviso that he consulted others first of all.

Josef's story is not one of dramatic departures and losses. It is a typical tale of Jews moving from one part of the Mediterranean to another and going about the business of living as best they could. Josef's principal anxieties were related to the day-to-day running of the synagogue. Immediately after his appointment, he and the governors of the synagogue sent a letter to the Consistory of the Israelites of London asking for money to enable them to rent better premises. Josef also co-signed a letter to Sir Moses Montefiore requesting help in the search for a new location for the synagogue.

The steady stream of appeals shows a community not always at ease, a congregation anxious to keep its head down in order to survive. Maltese society was still governed by a religion that had always been relentlessly hostile towards them. Half a century after Josef's arrival, Lord Fisher was still able to utter the following brutal words, offensive to all parties concerned: 'Neither Jews nor rats can exist in Malta. The Maltese are too much for either.'

Still, these were not the days when the Spanish ruled and the

Jews feared for their lives. They knew that ultimately they could rely on Britain to protect them. When, in January 1852, the Chief Inspector of Police ordered a census of all the Jews present on the island, the community board wrote to Earl Grey, Secretary of State for the Colonies, asking him to intervene. They were at the time deeply depressed by their failure to find new premises for the synagogue and seem to have panicked over the police chief's order. They saw it as the first step towards having non-British Jews expelled from the island. Josef would not perhaps have been able to remain in Malta.

It became clear, however, that, even if the authorities seemed to be trying to harass them, the ordinary Maltese were not terribly aware why this should be so. And in the end even the authorities came good and offered the community a lease for premises on Spur Street. These now became the island's new synagogue.

By this time, Josef was firmly established as rabbi. He handed over his commercial activities to his sons. Because they drank heavily, Saul and Cesare were not terribly successful, but Jacob grew rich on trade with Tripoli, his birthplace. The cover of Renzo de Felice's history of the Jews of Libya shows a bill of lading addressed to Jacob di J. Tajar, proof of the importance of the family's continued connections with Tripoli. Unable to find wives within Malta's Jewish community, two of Josef's sons married Tripolitanians. Another married an heiress from Morocco and my own great-grandfather the head of a Dame School from Livorno. He opened a leathergoods store in the building that had once been the Treasury of the Knights of Malta. In the late nineteenth century, the top floor was part of the Grand Hotel. Its corridors must have housed some knightly ghosts made restless by the fact that on the ground floor, on the Palace Square side, there was a shop owned by a Jew.

All these marriages reinforced the family's connections throughout the region. Diamantina first married a Tripolitanian, but spread her wings in her second marriage. Chaim Pelischke, her new husband, was a Polish Jew from Calcutta, a man with a true jumble of origins. When Josef died in May 1863, Diamantina was, however, still a small child.

The mystery of the eighth brother remained. When first on his trail, I came across a *carte de visite* that Diamantina had sent from Livorno. The studio photograph of Josef's youngest, taken in the 1880s, shows a plain, slightly plump young woman. On the back, Diamantina wrote 'To my dear brother Alessandro'. Against any other definitive proof, I thought initially that this must be the solution to the puzzle and that the eighth brother was someone called Alessandro.

In February 1997, however, I received a letter from a French officer stationed in the naval base at Toulon in the south of France. He claimed that his wife's great-great aunt had married a certain Nissim Tayar in a village outside Paris. The registers of the Municipality of Queue-en-Brie record the marriage of Agathe Christine Pappens to Nissim de Joseph Tajar, born in Valletta in 1851. There could be no doubt, therefore, that this was after all the missing son.

In 1851, Josef was forced to leave Malta. In the upheaval, had he forgotten to list the birth in the registers that he kept for the community? Or did someone, copying the registers, deliberately leave Nissim out? This son was twelve years old when Josef died, and his marriage to a Christian was still in the future. If Josef could have foreseen that one of his sons would 'marry out', he would perhaps have crossed Nissim off the list of births himself. Nissim was to break one of the strictest taboos for a religious Jew. In the eyes of his family, he would have become a dead man.

In its early days, Judaism was not averse to proselytising and recruiting new members to the religion. But with the scattering of the tribes of Israel, exclusivity became more important. How else were the saved to be identified when the Messiah finally came? Jewish society could only be maintained by belief in a common ancestry and by adhering strictly to a common faith. Israel would never have been created without this sort of doggedness. Nothing worse could befall a Jewish family, therefore, than to have one of its sons marry a non-Jew.

I am both drawn and repelled by this rigid adherence to exclusivity. A world without cultural differences is unattractive, but a world where these differences lead to murderous conflicts is equally appalling. Assimilation has not always worked. The assimilated Jews of Eastern and Central Europe died with the realisation that no matter how integrated they considered themselves, the anti-Semites despised them for trying to pass themselves off as fellow-citizens (one need only think of Marx, Trotsky and the poet Heine). The Ottoman model of separate existences was not a perfect solution either although there was always room in it for people to travel freely over a vast area covering much of the Mediterranean region and the Middle East.

In this generation, many of Josef's descendants are married to non-Jews. In his and his children's generations, this was rare. Only Diamantina seems to have kept in touch with someone called Alessandro who might possibly have been Nissim. He, the phantom brother, that missing member of the Rabbi Josef's *minian,* had found a new life and a new identity for himself in another place and among other people.

*This is not a place, but a pattern of relationships . . .*

NEAL ASCHERSON, *Black Sea*

CHAPTER FOUR

## jacob's children

'Have you asked for a medical certificate?'

On the eve of Duggie's wedding to Lina, an acquaintance put this question to my father.

'What for?' my father replied. 'Well, the sister is in an asylum. Madness might be hereditary. Before you marry that girl from La Goulette, you ought to find out.'

No one thought of delving into the mental balance of my father's family. The notorious rages of his Greek grandfather, Jacob Israel, were part of family lore. But they were presented as amusing anecdotes to his descendants. When Jacob was displeased with a meal that Julia Zanzuri, his wife, set before him, he would give a sharp tug to the tablecloth. My father's mother, Rachele, who was Jacob and Julia's sixth child, spoke of a cascade of crockery and cutlery crashing to the floor. Julia and the children would scurry to pick up the pieces. I wonder if they worried about their exposed backs. Because in synagogue Jacob would bring his walking stick down hard on the back of congregants he spied picking their toenails or nose.

These fits of rage were just part of his general eccentricity. Oh, funny bad-tempered old Jacob, we, his descendants, now say. If any of us displays similar petulance, Duggie is sure to mention The Shattering of the Dishes. Time has given Jacob's wrath a certain aura, which also tinges the rumour that he had fled his native Corfu after almost killing a brother.

No one classified Jacob as mad. On the contrary, the Maltese Greek community was immensely impressed by his good character. After he had lived in Malta a number of years, they issued him with an affidavit attesting to his good citizenship. Mr Karalambis, the Greek Consul, and thirty other dignitaries of Greek descent signed this testimony on parchment, praising Jacob's acts of charity. It was only in the family that people whispered about a murder. Three generations later, it adds to the mystery of Jacob's earlier life on the island of Corfu.

Little is known about the thirty-one years that preceded his arrival in Malta in 1865. Was it, as was the case with many of Greece's departing sons, a longing for prosperity? Or was it something sudden and dramatic that had propelled Jacob to leave? He uprooted himself at an age when many might have ceased to dream of making a fortune in another country. But as the Germans destroyed all the records of Corfu's Jews during World War II, no trace of his past remains.

Behind him, Jacob left one of Greece's thriving Jewish communities. By establishing himself in Malta, he spun another thread in the multiple webs laid down by each generation of my family as they moved backwards and forwards across the Mediterranean. The networks that were created in this way were typical of many Jewish families. When Neal Ascherson describes the Black Sea as not a place but a pattern of relationships, he could just as easily be speaking of people like us.

✳   ✳   ✳

In marrying Julia Zanzuri of Sfax, Jacob Israel's pattern of relationships also opened out to the Jewish communities of the south of Tunisia. Julia was only thirteen years old when he first set eyes on her in the synagogue in Valletta. She was sitting on a bench, dangling her legs and munching peanuts. Soon, Jacob was making enquiries about her.

'You mean the daughter of Rabbi Samuel?' others in the congregation said. 'Of course, you know how they got here, don't you? Remember when the tribes in central Tunisia rebelled against the Husseinite Beys and all Europeans had to be evacuated? Well, Rabbi Samuel, a widower, came to Malta then, bringing with him his small daughter.'

There were few marriageable Jewish women in Malta from whom Jacob could choose. The thirty-year difference in age was an obstacle that had to be overlooked.

In the registers of the Maltese Jewish community, the record of Duggie's grandparents' marriage is followed by the names and dates of birth of eleven children born in unrelenting two- to three-year intervals between 1870 and 1895: Samuel, Abramo, Rebecca, Giuseppe, Victor, Rachele, Raphael, Mary, Elise, Daniel and Emilia. Only Abramo and Giuseppe did not survive beyond infancy.

The youngest of the children never knew her mother as anything but a woman broken in health by the succession of pregnancies, births and probable miscarriages. Rachele, my grandmother, may not have directly witnessed the births, but she surely heard her mother's groans and watched midwives hurrying in and out of the bedroom, bloody rags or bedpans in their hands. It must have seemed a messy and unnerving business to a young girl. Secrecy must have made it more frightening.

There were many burdens placed on her mother. Shielding the children from their father's explosions of temper was one. Acting as his interpreter, another, because Jacob never learned to speak any language well other than Greek. Rachele, who for most of her teenage years shared the care of the family's babies with her mother, watched and told herself that she would not be trapped in the same way.

'Jacob Israel, Army Contractor Agent' his rubber stamp read. A photograph taken at the beginning of the twentieth century shows us a distinguished-looking, even handsome, head of family, with soft white hair and beard. I have stared and stared at his face, but do not see someone prone to violent rages. He is wearing a three-piece suit, the waistcoat of which is stretched over his paunch, and looks like any other complacent bourgeois of his era, his family at his feet.

Perhaps the expression on the faces of the four daughters who are flanking him gives the clue to his character. Rachele, Emilia, Mary and Elise look sullen, as if their father has just clipped them on the ear to get them to sit or stand still for the photograph. A couple of years ago, I asked a friend to blow up each of the faces in this family portrait. I was hoping for more tell-tale details of the subjects' state of mind and thought an enlargement might bring these people to life. I only ever knew my grandmother, Rachele, as a mistrusting, puritanical and bossy old lady. Perhaps the photograph could give me an idea when the capacity for joy started to seep out of the young Rachele's life. Her sisters seem to be swallowing a defiant giggle in their puffed cheeks. What the close-up of my grandmother shows, however, is the beginning of that tight-lipped sulk that would later become a habit with her. Julia sits in front of her husband, her body round as a Russian doll's, at her feet Daniel, the last of their sons still living at home. She looks worried, harassed and in pain.

By the time of this studio portrait, Jacob had grown wealthy from investments in warehouses and land not only in Malta but also in Tunisia. Jacob had started out by selling surplus military clothing. In doing this, he perpetuated the most traditional Jewish trade of his homeland, which was dealing in textiles and clothing. In Greece, the Jews of Salonika had at one time paid their taxes to the Sublime Porte by manufacturing uniforms for the Ottoman army.

The Ottomans had kept a close eye on Orthodox anti-Semitism. Among their subject peoples, collecting taxes was their main concern so that any disruption caused by ethnic or religious conflicts was quickly suppressed. In 1840, when Jacob was only six years old, the Blood Libel, that centuries-old slur that Jews killed Christian boys so that they could use their blood to make *matzot* for Passover, was once again cast against the Jews. Greece's Ottoman rulers promptly intervened to quash this cyclical rumour, issuing a *firman* to dismiss the accusations.

In 1890, it is not hard to imagine how Jacob felt when he saw people once more resorting to the Blood Libel. That there was no such thing as progress. That one could never be free of prejudice. That Jews must always be vigilant. His heart must have felt squeezed when he learned that the Archiepiscopal Palace in Valletta had placed its seal of approval on a pamphlet entitled 'The Blood of Catholics Shed by Jews'. As the Maltese Jewish community held its breath, the Chief Rabbi of London called upon the Roman Catholic Archbishop of Westminster for assurances that Malta's Jews would not be molested. But without waiting for orders from above, the colony's police intervened spontaneously and banned the pamphlet. A gap between the attitudes of the religious authorities and ordinary people was shown to exist.

But this did not stop Jacob from clinging to mistrust and diffidence. 'When you see a religious procession, just run!' was the injunction he issued to his children. He managed to frighten at least the daughters.

'He wanted me to kiss the cross,' Rachele said once when she came running home after a priest had stopped her in the street and pressed a crucifix to her lips. 'But I spat after he'd gone,' she added victoriously.

By observing her mother, Rachele's first lesson had been that the world was a hard place for women. Her second was that it could be an unfriendly place for Jews. But she was young and courageous. It must have been gradual, the realisation that wives and daughters are vulnerable.

Acts of charity are incumbent upon all Jews, but Jacob's charity was sometimes expressed at the expense of his children. When the *Gregale*, the Greek wind that sweeps all the way from the Balkans, began battering the Maltese islands, the girls would begin the ritual of folding their cotton blouses and linen skirts. Unlocking the trunks in which their winter clothes were stored, they prepared to pull them out and smooth the summer clothes in their place.

'*Mamma*, I can't find my shawl,' Rachele would howl. 'And Emilia can't find the blue sweater you knitted for her last year.'

Poor Julia. On that inflated body, she could only have been able to waddle into her daughters' room to find out what had happened.

'Look right at the bottom of the trunk. He can't have given them away,' she would say to try to calm the girls.

But they all knew that this was precisely what Jacob had done. When beggars came to his door, he could never send them away empty-handed. They always left with a loaf of bread, a few potatoes and often the best of the children's clothes.

The same high-handedness led Jacob to impose a 6.30 PM curfew on both daughters and sons.

'What is that bandage on your wrist, *Signorina*? Jacob said when he stopped Rachele as she tried to creep past him.

'Oh, it's nothing,' Julia piped in before Rachele could think up an explanation. 'She was helping the neighbours clean their windows. And she fell.'

Subterfuge was the only way to avoid Jacob's wrath. Coming home after curfew, Rachele had hurt her wrist climbing in through a window on a ladder set against the neighbours' wall.

'Where is Raphael?' Jacob boomed as he strode towards the door of his fifth son's room. Julia looked away – she knew that Raphael was not at home. But his trick of plumping up the pillows into a human shape before sneaking out had worked. Jacob, having peeped in and surveyed the room, quietly shut the door.

Sons, of course, could leave home more or less freely whereas daughters, Rachele noted, had no choice. Her eldest sister, Rebecca, was able to escape only through marriage, leaving first for Tunis and then for Cairo.

Samuel, the eldest son, made the short sea-journey to Sfax of his own volition. There, he was able to take advantage of family connections, lodging at the house of Julia's brother. But he could only find work in Skirra, thirty-five kilometres away, which meant he came back to his uncle's home just for the Sabbath. Breaking loose from all the inhibitions and prohibitions of family, Jacob's first-born turned to drink. He was a weak man and very lonely.

'I knew it was a mistake to give him all his inheritance,' Jacob grumbled when he was informed of Samuel's dissipation. Before Samuel's departure, his father had given him £7000, which in those days was a fortune.

But Samuel's failure, away from Jacob's influence, might act as an object lesson to his other sons. For Victor too was beginning to defy his father's authority. At the age of eighteen, he won enough money in the national lottery to set himself up independently in business. With this windfall, he bought a consignment of wheat, which he stored in one of Jacob's warehouses. When the price of wheat began to plummet suddenly, Jacob did not consult his son, but decided to sell the bales in his keeping immediately.

This time, it was Jacob's turn to duck the blast of someone else's fury. 'I did it for you,' he argued. 'You would have lost all your investment.'

Feinting to dodge a son's anger was not a pleasant experience.

Victor was unforgiving. He bought a passage to England. It was the height of the Boer war and he seethed as he watched wheat prices soar while he worked as a poorly paid clerk for Gotchens of London. In 1901 he answered an advertisement put in a newspaper by an import-export firm looking for an agent for their offices in Peru.

Iquitos was as far away as Victor could get from Jacob. Nonetheless, when he met his first wife, he wrote to Malta to ask for his
father's permission to marry. Still rather afraid of Jacob, he chose not
to mention that Georgina was Catholic, knowing full well that her
surname, Medina, would be taken for a Jewish one.

From Iquitos, Victor wrote to Raphael to offer him a partnership
on the banks of the Amazon. Neither Julia's tears nor Jacob's
counter-inducements could hold their third son back. From their
rubber plantations, Victor and Raphael sent postcards home of their
steamboat. With a magnifying glass, Rachele could pick out Malta's
Latin name *Melita* on the prow. Other photographs displayed the
brothers' mock-Renaissance offices with their single and double
pedimental windows, curved gables and tile-clad façade. What better way of displaying the success they had achieved against their
father's forebodings that they would fail if they left Malta. This really
was thumbing their noses at Jacob.

It must have set Rachele dreaming. She could not help feeling
envious of those brothers who had got away. She longed to travel
too, but her only chance to do so was as a companion to her mother.
Worried about Julia's bad health, Jacob would regularly send his wife
to spas in Italy, usually accompanied by Rachele. In foreign resorts
Rachele had her first and only taste of what being free of her father
and the younger children was like. I cannot attribute feminist long-
ings to my grandmother. But if she'd had a choice, I suspect she
would not have minded her life continuing like this: Mamma's good
little girl taking afternoon teas and dinners in elegant dining rooms
with palm court orchestras playing excerpts from her favourite Italian operas. This was the world of the new middle classes into which
Jews were now being assimilated.

But anxiety was never far away, a habit easily ingrained in the children of parents prone to violent changes of mood. Before her eldest
sister married and left for Egypt, Rachele had shared a room with
her. Anxious about being alone in the dark, she would plead for a
light to be left on whenever Rebecca and their parents went to the

opera. Thunderstorms also made her nervous. And she could not share the playfulness of her younger sisters when they had themselves photographed in pussycat poses imitating those of music hall *soubrettes*, unafraid of showing expanses of soft, delicious flesh. Rachele, in blouses buttoned up to her chin, held herself aloof. In her early twenties she still looked like a child. While her younger sisters had begun flirting with boys, she seemed to be holding herself back from turning into a woman.

I believe she would have liked family life to have been captured forever in a capsule of sun-drenched summer mornings – when she and her sisters would make their way down to the pools below Valletta's fortifications and laugh and squeal as attendants in the bathing cabins dunked them in the water.

In the afternoons, their best friends, the Critiens, joined them for a stroll down the Strada Reale, past its Baroque façades with their enclosed wooden balconies. The Critiens and Israels were such good friends that when the Israels moved to Tramontana Street, the Critiens moved as well. Each Israel girl paired up with a Critien girl as they promenaded past the Knights' old headquarters on Palace Square. Leaning on the parapets of the Barracca Gardens, overlooking Grand Harbour, they would surreptitiously glance over their shoulders at couples courting in the shade of the oleanders and jasmine vines.

Rachele had no wish to be one of those women being wooed. Remembering how she always wiped her cheek after I kissed her, I wonder if kisses were repulsive to her even then. She raged when Jacob insisted that she should be polite to a young man who had started calling on her. She was not impressed by Abraham (Banino) Tayar and felt he was being forced on her by her father. I suspect that she also felt disturbed by his sensuality, which every photograph of the young Banino still exudes. His shoulders are bullishly broad. There is a pent-up energy to him. He is dressed so impeccably that you can almost smell the cologne.

Rachele never spoke of falling in love with the man who was to become my grandfather. But she cannot have been unaware of the power of sex for she gradually grew watchful of other women and how they behaved in Banino's presence. To begin with, however, she still hoped that she would not be forced into marriage.

'He's from a good family. The grandson of Rabbi Josef Tayar,' everyone told her. 'And he owns his own business.'

Rachele must have often passed his shop on Palace Square. Here, he sold lengths of fine English cloth. Trained as a cutter in England, he had returned to Malta and converted his father's leathergoods business into a tailor's shop in the building that had once housed the Treasury of the Knights of Malta.

Handing Rachele over to the marriage bed was her father's great betrayal. Worse, however, was to come.

'We're moving to Tunis,' Jacob announced one day. 'I'm fed up with those Maltese boys sniffing round my unmarried girls.'

Rachele did not expect to be abandoned by her parents. It was children who were supposed to leave home, not the other way round. For the rest of Rachele's ninety-eight years of life, she never lost the sense that her family had left her beleaguered. Soon caught up in the cycle of pregnancies and births herself, she developed an even more tight-lipped smile, concealing the gaps left by teeth lost for each of her seven children. She could barely suppress her bitterness at a fate that had made her a prisoner of the messiness of the female condition.

She felt besieged. If there was a sudden silence as she entered a shop, she was sure that people were gossiping about Banino and his lady friends. Priests continued to make her nervous. When her elder brother Victor brought his new Peruvian wife on a visit to Malta, Rachele felt insulted when Georgina started rummaging around in her cupboards in search of an eggcup.

'Oh, don't you people use eggcups?' Georgina asked out of simple curiosity.

But Rachele heard it as a reproach. Angry with the world, she was constantly impatient not only with her children, but also with the string of poor girls hired to help with the housework. She watched them closely and concluded that they were all one of two things: simple-minded or sly.

Giusa was the latter, pocketing the pennies her mistress gave her to buy fresh eggs for Rachele's anaemia. Giusa's lover, a dogsbody at the Archbishop's Palace across the road, gave her the eggs for nothing.

The stupid maids asked stupid questions. 'What is a Jew?' one of them wanted to know.

'You'd better ask your father,' Rachele replied.

'I thought Jews only existed in the Bible,' the countryman said, scratching his head. 'I'd better go and ask the priest.'

'*Sinjura*, my father says the priest told him that I cannot go on working for Jews.'

✳ ✳ ✳

Letters from the family now all far away only rekindled Rachele's view of herself as a castaway. They told her of a world in which Jews felt more at home than in Malta.

Jacob had settled his family in an apartment in Tunis and everyone wrote to say how delighted they were with their new Jewish neighbours, the Bonans and Isaachars. The Bonans, who were cousins to my mother's family, were British. The Isaachars were Greek Jews from Turkey or was it Turkish Jews from Greece? Such confusions of nationalities were commonplace around the Mediterranean. Elise, Rachele's second youngest sister, fell in love with the Isaachars' son, Guillaume. Mary, the one born just before Elise, went on an afternoon stroll down the Avenue Jules Ferry and met and fell in love with Jonas Bouhnik. They were married within three months.

From Iquitos, Raphael ordered a trousseau in Paris to be forwarded to his sister in Tunis. For the rich and newly rich, the worldwide network, which today we think is our own invention, was nothing new. After a honeymoon spent in Paris, Jonas took

Mary back to his native Sfax. There, like any other bourgeois couple in Europe, they moved into a sumptuous apartment furnished in
Art Nouveau style.

In Sfax, Mary received news that Julia had died, her womb ravaged
by cancer. Jacob had assigned the youngest daughters, Elise and
Emilia, to send telegrams to Malta, Egypt and Peru, and then
arranged for his wife's body to be placed in a zinc coffin and taken by
train to Sfax, the city of Julia's birth. In death, Julia came full circle.

Rachele wept bitterly and alone. Mary had the company of sisters
to ease her sorrow, for Jonas had persuaded Jacob to move his two
remaining unmarried daughters from Tunis to Sfax.

'There are plenty of good Jewish families here,' Jonas was able to
argue.

And so it was that, aged eighty-one, and with only a touch of
rheumatism, Jacob willingly made the third important move of his
life. A synagogue and a pool of suitors for his daughters were all he
required to feel at home in any place in the Mediterranean.

Elise, however, had to be coaxed away from Tunis because in
going to Sfax she was leaving behind her sweetheart, Guillaume
Isaachar. In 1915, Turkey was fighting alongside Germany, and the
Isaachars, originally from Turkey, were deemed to be enemy aliens.
The French authorities of Tunisia refused to grant Guillaume a
licence to marry and so there was no question of Elise staying on in
Tunis. This ban was not lifted and permission granted until 1917.

Two weeks before the wedding, the whole family returned to
Tunis where they took rooms at the Tunisia Palace Hotel. Elise was
to hold her pre-wedding ceremony, the *henna,* there. At this ceremony, women gather and paint lacy patterns on the bride's hands
and feet to ward off evil spirits. It is a custom common to both
Moslems and Jews. The *henna* is an occasion for artwork, and also an
opportunity for women to get together.

'Come on,' Jonas said as he jostled his wife, his sister and his wife's
youngest sister, Emilia, into his car. 'We're going on a pilgrimage.
Forget the *henna.*'

Jonas had decided to visit the tomb of Rabbi Fradji, a pilgrimage site on the outskirts of the inland town of Testour. Following the massacre of his family in Spain, Rabbi Fradji had set off across North Africa in search of refuge. Before he died, he said that he wanted his body to be placed on the back of a donkey and for the donkey to be left to wander. Wherever the animal came to its final destination that was where Rabbi Fradji wished to be buried. That place was Testour, which a large number of Jewish exiles from Castille and Aragon were also to make their home.

Jonas's party never reached Testour and the rabbi's tomb. Outside Medjez el Bab, Jonas, who had swapped places with the chauffeur, swerved off the road, and Mary, Emilia, Jonas's sister and the chauffeur were all thrown clear. But Jonas was impaled on the steering column and it took three farm labourers to pull him free. A passing military truck took them all back to the Tunisia Palace.

'We must take him home to Sfax,' Jacob said.

From the steps of the hotel, he had seen the would-be pilgrims returning. His son-in-law had lapsed into a coma and was not expected to survive.

'The wedding is off,' Jacob said, immediately taking command. 'The guests must all leave. Mary will keep vigil.'

Three months later, Jonas opened his eyes. 'How was the wedding?' were his first words.

When told that it had been postponed indefinitely, he ordered fresh invitations to be sent out. He had survived. He felt lucky. He felt generous. New silk dresses were to be made for his sister and the sisters-in-law. It was in these gowns, with slings made out of remnants from the same luxurious cloth, that Mary and Emilia saw Elise finally marry.

Jonas, still suffering from his injuries, was unable to leave his bed to attend the wedding. He was too ill to take care of all his businesses. So while he was convalescing he handed over the running of his affairs to his nephew.

'Only buy olives,' Jonas ordered the nephew. But the nephew

thought he knew better. Ignoring his uncle's advice but using his fortune, he decided to buy dates instead from growers round Sfax and to export them to Marseilles. Doing business across the Mediterranean is what the family did, how they formed connections with people throughout the region, and this nephew was going to make a huge success of it too.

But a dockers' strike in the southern French port blocked the unloading of all vessels and crate-loads of Moses' dates rotted in the hold. All had to be jettisoned. Jonas, the merchant with his own carriage and motor car, the master of servants, clerks, porters and drivers, the owner of warehouses in which marjoram, dates, barrels of olive oil, lengths of cloth and gum Arabic were stored, was made bankrupt.

* * *

The life her family led in southern Tunisia was very different from the one Rachele led in Malta. Her husband, Banino, was not a wealthy man though, by dabbling in the stock market, he hoped to become one. Their apartment on Strada Zecca was overcrowded. Banino seemed to be paying too much attention to other women. They had too many children. She had lost her figure and most of her teeth. She seemed to spend all her time in the kitchen. Her fingernails became infected and turned black from having her hands continually in water obsessively washing fruit and vegetables or dishes.

When Jacob died in 1919, Rachele was unable to attend his funeral. But she shared her siblings' concern about what was to be done with the youngest of them, Emilia, not yet married. From Iquitos, Raphael sent word that she was to join him in Peru.

But Emilia had other plans. At a wedding in Cap Bon, she had met a man whom she had instantly found attractive. She only held back because he was so dark-skinned that she thought he might possibly be . . . an Arab! Although it was still allowed by law and there were Jews who also had second wives, when Emilia learned that this stranger's father had a second wife, she wasn't sure if she should be in love with him.

From Peru, Raphael and Victor ordered an investigation. Raphael hurried back to North Africa to continue the enquiries. Though Victor was married to a Catholic and Raphael was to marry a Protestant from Birmingham and to father a son by a woman of Inca descent, they were men. They were not going to allow a little sister to cross the religious boundaries. So it was with relief that they learned that the stranger at the wedding was a Jew. Emilia was given permission to marry and eventually left Tunisia to settle in France.

Jacob's children were now scattered all over the Mediterranean and beyond. Only Rachele remained in Malta as the sole and fixed reference point to their place of birth. When they looked at their mother, her seven children saw a woman who felt trapped. Like her father, she had grown irascible, without the energy to muster up warmth for anyone other than the smallest and most malleable members of her brood. She loved them best when they were babies or toddlers, especially the boys.

Not that Rachele had much to do with them as babies. She brought in a local woman to breastfeed them. It was what women attempting to keep themselves a cut above others did, but I cannot imagine Rachele tolerating the block-nosed nuzzling of a pink, heart-shaped mouth. The grandmother I knew hated being touched, and kisses were rarely exchanged in her house.

Through this abhorrence of physical contact, my grandmother was beginning to take the first steps towards isolating herself. At the same time, she felt besieged within her own home for it was hard to keep up Jewish customs there even though she did her best. There being no rabbi on the island to slaughter animals in such a way as to drain them of their blood, she improvised. She rinsed and re-rinsed meat until it was almost white. To Jews blood is considered to be the life force of an animal and as such cannot be consumed. So much for the Blood Libel!

Her sons and daughters, Duggie especially, wished she had more joy in her. They froze in anticipation and hope of it when they sometimes caught her unawares humming her favourite arias. But they could not coax her to bring out the mandolin that she had played as a girl. Banino's flirtations and any perceived misbehaviour on the part of their children led her to don her grim mask more and more often. She saw such conduct as damaging to all their reputations not as ordinary people, but as Jews. This is what she came to feel and this is what made her constantly vigilant. It was her father's legacy.

'You Jews have to be better than other people, don't you?' a cleaning girl once remarked. Rachele did not beg to differ.

The difficulty of being better than others lay with Banino. On one of the family's annual summer holidays to the fishing village of Marsascala, he became friendly with a troupe of opera singers. One of these, an unmarried soprano, was expecting a baby. When Banino strolled over to the troupe's rented villa to join them in their musical *soirées*, Rachele was sure that everyone was talking about her husband. In fact, Banino had only gone over to them to show off. He had a thrillingly beautiful voice and the singers allowed him to pretend he was a professional.

I can see him setting off along Marsascala's moonlit bay. Fishing boats bob on the viscous black water. The waves hit the rocks with a rhythmic, sensuous slap. While the sleeping children breathe heavily in the suffocating heat, Rachele prowls the villa. In the tiny attic room, the maids toss and sigh, their brown limbs strong and shiny with sweat. The clock on the sideboard ticks 'dirty', 'dirty'. The ticking echoes in my grandmother's head.

Ondina, her second daughter, remembers surfacing from sleep and glimpsing her mother seated by the front door. A paraffin lamp in her hand cast a giant shadow on the plaster wall. In the next wave of wakefulness, Ondina hears the door opening and her mother's voice behind clenched lips. 'If you visit those singers again, I'll smash this lamp on your head.'

Banino, a peace-loving man, gave up his theatrical friends.

Rachele's vigilance was not just confined to keeping sexual scandal out of her family. Like every true Puritan, what she feared most was what obsessed her. In Valletta, she could not prevent Giusa from finding more lucrative, but dubious employment in a bar down by the docks. In Marsascala, she made sure that young men kept their distance from her other maids. From her vantage point at the kitchen window, Rachele would order the girls indoors if she thought they had been chatting too long with local fishermen or farm boys. They might not care about bourgeois values, but she would care on their behalf. Any overstepping of the respectability line, Rachele was sure, would reflect on her and on her religion. It was exhausting being so watchful.

Women paid a price for non-vigilance. Rachele's sister, Mary, was the best proof of this. While Mary had been absent from Sfax helping Emilia to prepare for her wedding, Jonas had begun an affair with Anna, their servant, and she had become pregnant.

'But that doesn't alter the fact that I still love you,' Jonas insisted to his wife. 'I honestly do.' As if this could console Mary for the barrenness for which Anna's swollen belly now reproached her.

'Then get that *putain* out of my house.'

'Don't be ridiculous,' Jonas replied. 'She has nowhere to go.'

'Please, Jonas. Oh, please make Anna leave.' For days, Mary whined and wept and pleaded. Rocking herself to the point of exhaustion. Waking up with the weight of her childless condition pressing down on her. Gradually, it came to her. She would have the baby.

'What do you mean, you will have the baby?'

'Yes, yes. It's simple. We'll keep Anna out of sight until the baby is due.'

Mary set out her plan. For the next few months, she would pad her stomach and wear maternity smocks. Just before the nine months were up, she and Jonas would take Anna to Rome where Daniel, the youngest of Jacob Israel's sons, was now a resident doctor at the Catolica Hospital. This Biblical drama could be entitled Conspiracies Across the Middle Sea.

'Oh, please, please, Jonas.'

But there was to be no happy ending. Anna, registered as Mary Bouhnik, was delivered of a dead son, the umbilical cord entangled round his neck. Mary locked herself into a darkened Roman hotel room and could not be coaxed out.

'*Madame,* you must eat. Please open the door,' Anna, now back from hospital, begged her grieving mistress, the woman who would have stolen her baby. 'Crying won't help.'

It was a pale and painfully thin real Madame Bouhnik who returned to Tunis. Anna, the alias and the real mother of the dead baby, was holding up her mistress as they disembarked.

'Now rest, *Madame.* I'll see to the tradesmen. Don't worry about the seamstress. I'll get the boy to fetch fruit from the market.'

Bit by bit, Anna took over all the things that Mary was too demoralised to deal with. The maid became bold and began to bully Mary with impunity. One of Mary's nieces remembers following a trail of cheap perfume down the street, knowing that at the end of it she would find Anna, playing at being the lady of the Bouhnik household. It took years for Mary to dislodge the maid, but when Anna was finally banished, Jonas still went on meeting her in secret.

*　*　*

In 1925, news reached Malta from Peru that Raphael, aged thirty-eight, had died on a trip to his rubber plantations.

'Our uncle has been eaten by piranhas, yaah!' Ondina invented this ghoulish tale to scare Rachele's 'babies', Duggie and Lilla.

The truth was almost farcical. Raphael had caught pneumonia. In order to lower his temperature, he was plunged into ice-cold bath water, which provoked a fatal heart attack.

Local newspaper photographs show a funeral procession imitating that of dead kings. In the grainy picture of Raphael's tomb, you can pick out Maltese crosses wrought into the iron railings. Rachele shuddered at these Christian symbols and buried the cuttings in the deepest drawer of the sideboard, under the impenetrable jumble of the papers revealing Banino's failed investments. She thus consigned Raphael's conversion/betrayal to oblivion.

Victor too had converted. He was now Don Victor Israel, a pillar of Peru's business community, and a man of '*inesgotable dinamismo*' (an inexhaustibly dynamic man), as an Iquitos newspaper said. The staccato of Spanish gives the description a nice ring. Rachele was proud of his achievements, but this was mixed with a sense of horror at the thought of his attending mass. Victor had reinvented himself into a man whom Jacob Israel might not have recognised.

Two of her brothers abandoned their religion. A third, Daniel, the doctor in Rome, understood that being a Jew in the newly formed Italian fascist state was going to become increasingly difficult. In 1925, most Italian Jews did not feel there was any danger. Many admired Mussolini. Some even joined the Fascist Party. Daniel's antennae for political change were, however, particularly sensitive. He showed great prescience in his decision to re-cross the Mediterranean and return to Tunis.

Although it was not a complete leap in the dark, it was a courageous move because by now Daniel had a family to support. It might be that this was the lesson he had learned from his father: when things get uncomfortable, move on.

\* \* \*

My grandmother's early years were marked by departures. In her middle years, she witnessed the beginning of a second wave of leave-takings. In 1932, Yolanda, her eldest daughter, made the short journey to Tunis to marry. In this way, the next generation embarked on the same trajectories across the Mediterranean as the previous one, and for the same reasons. Rachele could at least find comfort in the fact that her daughter had married a Jew.

But Oscar, her elder son, was now drifting towards a religious hurricane. He had fallen in love with a Catholic, a luscious young girl with high cheekbones and a cherub's mouth just like Ginger Rogers.

'A Maltese girl! How could you?' Rachele wrung her clean handkerchief. As someone who thought of herself as a lady, she always carried an immaculate white handkerchief with her.

'A Jew! How could you?' an inquisition of priests and bishops berated Oscar's eighteen-year-old girlfriend. They summoned her to the Archbishop's Palace in Valletta. Oscar, who had accompanied her, was barred from entering. He paced the pavement, then held up the trembling girl who emerged from the high-walled Palace reeling from the clerical forebodings of hell and damnation.

Worse than clerical wrath was Rachele's hysteria. She took to her bed. For a whole year she remained genuinely ill, unable to accept her son's choice of fiancée.

'If you continue to oppose this match,' Oscar finally exploded, 'I shall walk out of that front door and you'll never see me again.'

Gentle Oscar. A bit of a dandy. Who would have thought that the son who had chosen the civil service for the secure lifetime job it offered him would suddenly have found the strength to stand up to Rachele?

I remember my grandmother's way of smudging all expression off her face and of gulping down her defeats. I can clearly picture her, vanquished, creaking out of bed and giving in to Oscar's marriage. The son, who never left Malta and who was to visit his mother almost every day of her very long life, had opened up a distance between himself and his mother's influence that could not have been greater had he, like Duggie later on, emigrated to Australia.

Rachele still had control, however, over those of her children living at home and she meant to hold fast to the reins. The day Ondina, bursting with excitement, came home waving her university degree, her mother handed her a broom. 'The whole house needs sweeping,' she snapped.

For Rachele, an education was a step towards a girl becoming too free and easy. It was the bone she continuously picked with Banino. He thought daughters, more than sons, needed to arm themselves with a good education. This was his eccentricity and it maddened his wife. Next her daughters would want to marry Maltese boys! It was Jacob's refrain echoing down the generations.

Ondina took the broom and swept the floor. She swept when she came home from her work as a pharmacist. She swept to lull the pain of passion only guessed at and courage spent. For she never recovered the childhood boldness that might have allowed her to defy her mother. She never dared to cross the religious boundaries and marry the Catholic doctor who was so in love with her. She still sweeps, an old lady now lost in a cloud in the company of her imaginary children. But her mother had made her afraid of men, of stepping over the line, of flying free.

Driven out of Italy as a result of the 1938 racial laws, Banino's nephew was not welcomed by Rachele. She lectured her daughters. She nagged them. She worried that their cousin would find one of them attractive. Relative or not, he was a man, to be viewed with suspicion. Not imagining his homesickness, his longing for the warmth of a family, Rachele refused to have him in the house. But this did not stop her youngest daughter from falling in love with him.

\*   \*   \*

On 10 June 1940, Italy declared war on Britain and its colonies. Malta's harbour towns were prime targets in the air attacks that followed. So Rachele, Banino, Ondina, Margot, Doris, Duggie and Lilla moved from Strada Zecca to the house in St Julians, which had, in the early 1930s, replaced their rented summer villa in Marsascala. When this too proved vulnerable, they were evacuated to Balzan at the centre of the island.

With them went Oscar, his wife and their baby daughter. The

atmosphere in the crowded house became so tense that, in spite of the relentless air raids, Doris, Rachele's fifth child, decided to return to St Julian. Duggie followed her, but was soon to leave for India. Had it not been for the presence in Balzan of Oscar's baby, the friction between daughter- and mother-in-law would have become unbearable. But babies and toddlers brought out the best in Rachele. They softened the hardened edges and released a playfulness that often caught her grown-up children by surprise. She would take out the perennial white handkerchief and fold it into a cradle with two babies as snug as sausages in batter. If only this tender Rachele would show herself more often, they all sighed. And tried to continue life in as normal a fashion as possible under the increasingly heavy bombardments.

In Grand Harbour, the sea seethed as ships came under fire. Houses, churches, the Opera House were reduced to rubble. In a period of six weeks, half a million kilos of bombs were dropped on the island's two hundred square kilometres.

During one air raid, burglars broke into Banino's shop and stole all his stock of fine English cloth. By then the Germans had begun deploying U-boats in the Mediterranean. Few Royal Navy vessels survived the gauntlet to bring food, ammunition and fuel to the island. There was no hope of receiving new bolts of cloth. So for the rest of the blockade, which was to eclipse not only the Great Siege of 1565 but also all the other great sieges of World War II (Tobruk, Odessa, Sebastopol), Banino knew what it was like to be a prisoner of house and home.

From Tunis, Yolanda sent anxious telegrams that grew briefer and briefer as the war progressed and her husband's wages stopped coming in. 'All well' under the blue or red Cable and Wireless letterhead was understood as meaning that all Jacob's offspring in Tunisia – Daniel, Mary, Elise and Emilia, newly returned from France with her children – and Yolanda's own family, were unharmed.

By the end of 1941, Malta was still holding out, although rations were reduced to one can of beans per person and one Christmas candle. It took another eight months for the remnants of the decimated Santa Maria Convoy to hobble into Grand Harbour. When the war ended, the family looked round and was thankful that they had remained virtually intact. Two of Banino's elderly Florentine aunts had been rounded up by the SS and are presumed to have perished on their way to the gas chambers. But the rest of the Florentines were safe after their year in hiding in the Tuscan hills. Duggie was back from India and the battlefronts of Egypt and Italy. The family left the Strada Zecca apartment and settled permanently in St Julians.

✳ ✳ ✳

This was where, in 1947, my father first brought his young wife. The sisters-in-law looked Lina up and down and found her acceptable. Rachele was merely satisfied. At least this daughter-in-law was Jewish, although her skirts were far too short.

'Those are funny shoes your grandmother is wearing,' Rachele said when Zia Nina visited Malta. My mother's grandmother had found it hard to put together even the small amount that was needed to make the short journey from Tunis. But before she died she was adamant that she would see Lina again and her new baby. Who knows what sacrifices must have been made at La Goulette? As the family on the rue du Lieutenant Longello grew poorer and poorer, Zia Nina had begun selling valuable objects. Out of the glass cabinet where all the antique Hebrew books were kept, she had taken and sold the Grand Rabbi Isaac Lumbroso's great exegesis *Zera Itzhak*, the first book in Hebrew to be printed in North Africa. My mother did not know this then, and now, although she does not want to look back, she admits those books had been a real presence in her early years. They were the oldest and best proof of her family's place in the history of Tunisia's Jews.

'I'm only wearing these slippers because my feet hurt,' Zia Nina said, trying to cover up her poverty. There was no money to buy proper shoes and, always inventive as a seamstress, my mother's grandmother had made her cloth slippers herself.

Can I forgive Rachele her contempt for my maternal great-grandmother? I am not sure. But I feel sorry that her dissatisfaction turned her against herself in an odd way. After the war, she arrived at the conclusion that there was no point in ever again leaving the house in St Julians. Yolanda, Doris and Lilla were gone, but she still had two unmarried daughters, Ondina and Margot, living at home to see to the shopping. At the most, she would go out onto the high front stone parapet, overlooking the street, and call out her order of bread or fish to the baker or fishermen passing by.

What started with whispers about Banino's *inamorate* led to self-sequestration. So much secrecy surrounds my grandfather's affairs that no one can be sure that they even took place. But my grandmother closed her door against them and the rest of the world, something that would be central to the forty years of life remaining to her. Even those of us who spent summers in her house and knew the nuances of its daily rhythms tend to reduce those four decades into that one single extreme decision.

There was a strange sort of reassurance in Rachele's immovability for those of us who became scattered throughout the world. I wonder if our awe of her unshifting, if distant presence, gave Rachele a sense of her own substantiality, something which she had perhaps lacked as a daughter and then as a wife and mother. In her self-cloistering, she could not have established herself more firmly and more literally as the unshifting centre of our displaced lives, the dot on the map that connected the radiating lines to Tunisia, France, Italy, Argentina, Israel, Canada, Australia and Peru. At the end of the lines were not just her sisters and her brothers, but three of her daughters and one of her sons and her granddaughters and grandsons. In our vast family of restless wanderers, Rachele became famous for staying put so dramatically. To cousins twice-removed living in Florence, to the Swiss wife of a French nephew, to the Tunisian sister-in-law of a daughter-in-law she was and still is a sort of Miss Havisham – growing sallow in darkened, musty rooms. Although Rachele's rooms were never musty for she kept jasmines from her well-tended garden in shallow dishes in all the rooms of her house. But outsiders still prefer to think of her as the woman who for thirty, forty, fifty years (the duration varies with the teller) faded away in her house.

'If you're going to Malta, do go and see our grandmother,' was the family catchcry. Our allegiance to a fixed place was only possible because of Rachele's presence on the island. She lived so long that we foolishly got used to the idea of permanence.

Not that Rachele welcomed people from outside, but her youngest brother, Daniel, came on visits from Tunis. Her youngest sister, Emilia, swanned in from time to time from Lyons to which she had returned after the war. Emilia even sent her daughter-in-law, an Israeli prima donna, who, by singing arias at the drop of a hat, drew more attention to herself than my grandmother thought a decent woman should.

In his nineties, Victor, now a Knight of the *Orden del Sol*, was on his way to Malta for the first time in fifty years when news of an earthquake in Peru made him turn back. When Rachele's youngest daughter, Lilla, died aged only thirty-eight, her grief-stricken husband (and first cousin) sent their two little girls to Malta. They continued to go there for many summers afterwards. And were bewildered by the silence over their mother's death. It was meant to spare them pain, but it was the grown-ups who were sparing themselves. Death replaced sex as the great unmentionable.

Grief came on top of a resentment against Banino, which continued well after his death. Already years before, he had found the air so charged that he once actually started to pack his bags. Ondina, the pharmacy graduate who had as a student dissected a body, was assigned to deal with the unpleasant facts in her mother's life. This time, Rachele ordered her to plead with Banino.

'Be sensible. You can't cook and clean for yourself,' Ondina reasoned. 'It's much more comfortable at home.'

So Banino unpacked.
He died one year later.

\*   \*   \*

Because Rachele would not budge, all of us were forced to take her into account. We became Little Mohammeds journeying to her Mountain. But Duggie caused shock and horror throughout the whole family when he dared to write to his mother (from the safe distance of Australia) that his son would not be going through a *Bar Mitzvah*. We had broken away from all that religious nonsense, he wanted his family to know. We were different people. Having posted the letter, he and all of us waited for the world to fall about our ears, for our grandmother to be paralysed by shock. We listened hard and ten thousand miles away could almost hear Jacob Israel's and all the rabbinical ancestors' bones clinking in their body sacks.

Worse was to come. Brought up as a heathen under the Australian sun, I first turned up on Rachele's doorstep as an adult in 1969. I was a good granddaughter that summer, dopey with homesickness for the place and parents I had left behind in Sydney. The Old World was so different from the New. Religion, which had not figured in my childhood at all, was suddenly pressing in on me, not just here, but in France where I was living and where I first came into contact with my mother's family. Both clans were appalled by my ignorance of Judaism.

I argued passionately against religion, but having let myself already become plump among the Paris Tunisian diaspora, I grew even fatter on Rachele's courgettes fried in a batter cloud, her almond cake, her spicy meatballs served on Friday nights with couscous, the legacy of her Tunisian mother's cuisine. I took up knitting. Because, in my disorientation, I was so well behaved, Rachele allowed the boy across the road to take me out for walks along the promenade from St Julians to The Tower in Sliema. He was from what she deemed to be a good family. Usually, no man outside the family was allowed into my grandmother's house – this, too, had become legendary. An avid reader of Italian gossip magazines, she knew that the world was full of men leering down the exposed bosoms of would-be starlets.

The next summer, I turned up again with a friend. My grandmother took one look at our hippy clothes, our rucksacks, the broad-brimmed black hat on my friend's head, her generous, all too female hips, her bustling friendliness and decided that I had come under the influence of someone bad. She announced that she would only allow us to stay one night. We must find a hotel for the rest of our stay on the island. My unmarried aunts could not make their mother change her mind.

It was the aunts who gradually took over her function and became our fixed point of reference. We could still feel reassured that if we returned to Malta, we would find our umbilical cords buried somewhere there on that thin soil. This need for identification with something that does not shift continuously is hard to throw off and it is why none of us has been able to break off all ties with the island. Even those of my cousins not born in Malta seem to feel this. From France, Italy and England they send their children and grandchildren on holidays and return themselves as often as they can. We can hardly bear to imagine a future without touching base in Malta. Now that only three members of our family remain there and they are old and sick, we wonder how we shall preserve our connections with the place.

As my grandmother's mind grew misty, we spoke of the St Julians house as not just hers, but also my aunts'. We loved them all the more for having sacrificed themselves to taking care of their unyielding mother. She became their naughty child and now and then mustered a spark of humour that might have been her true essence had the course of her life been different. She once chased my husband all over the house brandishing a Hebrew Bible. On the flyleaf of this book, with its desiccated and speckled pages, Jacob had scribbled the date in pencil of one of Julia's departures to an Italian spa.

'Read me this chapter,' she insisted.

'But, *Nonna*, he doesn't read Hebrew,' I tried to rescue him.

'What is he? A Moslem?' she asked me in Italian. She had never learned to speak English and so could not communicate with this very English man. Then something must have pulled her back, made her realise that she had not been polite.

'Ginger,' she blurted out, 'Ginger,' she called, mustering the rare English word that she did know, trying to bridge the linguistic gap and to take the heat off him. My husband's hair was red.

My grandmother died in 1984. But for two years before her death, she did something that most people who cling to the image of the recluse do not know. She tried to escape from the confines of her house. To calm her whenever she became frantic and wanted to get out, her daughters would ring for a taxi. Sitting in the back of a black limousine, Rachele would travel round the block and return home at peace with herself.

I visit Malta every summer. In the late 1980s I went there with a parliamentary delegation and a team of interpreters, one of whom, an Italian colleague, lent an ear to my family's history on the island. I often feel like the Ancient Mariner, doomed to repeat my story over and over again. Putting myself in context. When I came to the climactic fact that my grandmother had for forty years not set foot outside her house, the young man turned his big blue deadpan eyes to me.

'*Finalmente*,' he said, expelling a sigh, '*una donna seria!*' (At last, a good and proper woman!) A sentiment with which neither Rachele nor Jacob would have disagreed.

*   *   *

Malta's Jewish cemetery is located far away from the city walls of Valletta, in what has become a sort of traffic-island purdah. With my aunt Ondina I have come here to see Rachele's grave. The sun beats down. The air vibrates through the fumes of cars speeding past. The minaret of the Moslem cemetery next door, well tended, thanks to Libyan funding, overlooks the Jewish enclosure. It is the Moslem cemetery's caretaker who has the keys and who opens the gate for us. The appropriateness of this does not escape me. We are a family with a long history in Arab lands.

I pick my way among the gravestones that huddle together against the encroaching weeds and struggling bushes. This is not a place people visit often and it looks neglected and forgotten. One whole corner of the cemetery is taken up by my father's family, by far the largest group among all these dead. The old inscriptions are in Hebrew, the newer ones in English.

While Ondina places flowers on her mother's grave, I stand in front of the tomb of a dead Jewish soldier. Wounded in Gallipoli, he had been brought to Malta to recuperate, but it is here that he died. The tall monument was erected by the soldier's parents resident in Jamaica. The whole of the Jewish people's wanderings are encapsulated in that marmoreal inscription. It speaks to me of people who have travelled far away – to the West Indies. With new allegiances to the British Empire, a mother and father have sent a son to fight in a distant country in a region of the world their ancestors had originally come from.

Who, once the last of Rabbi Josef's and Jacob Israel's descendants have gone, will know our story and remember our connections with the island, I wonder? That web, which once spread to all corners of the Mediterranean and beyond, will lose its heart. How then will we define ourselves?

> *There was in the Italian Jew no element of the foreigner.*
> *Established in the country already for two thousand years, he*
> *was as much a native as any component of the Italian people.*
>
> CECIL ROTH, *The History of the Jews of Italy*

## CHAPTER FIVE

# our cousins in florence

Between the two World Wars the tea-rooms of Florence each had their own specialties. Doney's was famous for its *foie gras* and caviar, Procacci's for its doll-house sandwiches. The Giacosa boasted an Anglo-Florentine *clientèle*, some of whom admired Mussolini and praised him out loud for saving Italy from the horrors of Bolshevism.

My great uncle Ugo Tayar (Banino's brother) preferred the tea-room on the dark and narrow via Monaldi. On weekday afternoons, he would leave his offices on the Piazza Strozzi and, passing Signor Carlo's posh grocery, which stocked his favourite Oxford marmalade, hurry to meet his wife, Dora.

Florence had been Ugo's city since 1913. Born in Malta, he was the seventh and youngest son of Corinna Coen and Cesare Tayar, my great-grandparents. In 1901, at the age of sixteen, he had left Malta to look for work in Egypt. In Alexandria he found employment as a clerk with Eyère and Humbert, Shippers, moving on from this post to a better job in Marseilles.

A couple of years later he moved on again to Italy where he worked his way up the hierarchy to become the manager of the Florence offices of Roditi and Sons. From its headquarters in New York, the company commanded agents in France and Italy to buy local handcrafted wares for the American market: leather goods from Florence; exquisite gloves from Naples; fine silks from Como. Ugo was not just a trusted employee; he was a pillar of Florentine commerce.

Dora always had one of the children in tow, taking their turn to be treated to afternoon tea. Seated at marble-topped tables with wrought-iron legs, Liliana, the eldest, would order hot chocolate from waitresses wearing skimpy starched aprons and frothy white caps.

On Sundays, Ugo allowed his sons and daughter to order eggs, sunny-side up. Dora always impressed on Liliana that she must speak in a hushed voice in these gathering places where English ladies clinked their spoons softly and chinked their cups. Although these women were long-established expatriates, they frowned on Latin exuberance. For her part, Dora considered these outings to be part of a young girl's education.

'Do not forget that you are, after all, half-English, through your father,' she would say.

For having been born in Malta, Shabbatai Salamone, always known as Ugo, was a subject of her Britannic Majesty.

'Tell us again how you and Mamma met,' Ugo's children – Liliana, Franco and Enzo – would beg. Although they knew the story well, it was always thrilling to hear him tell it.

It was Dora's aunt, the wife of an Italian general, who had introduced her to Ugo. The year was 1916 and Dora's Viennese-born father had been interned as an enemy alien. Dora's mother, although related to the notable Jewish families of Cairo, was also part Ashke-naz. On her father's side, she was the descendant of Jews who had fled persecution in Frankfurt at the end of the eighteenth century and established themselves in Livorno.

By the mid-nineteenth century their descendants were very much a part of Italian bourgeois society. Dora's grandparents' circle of friends included Verdi and Verga, the librettist of Mascagni's *Caval-leria Rusticana*. In her Bologna home, Dora's mother, their eldest daughter, held literary salons from which she excluded her husband. It may be that he did not meet the standard of refinement of the most assiduous frequenters of these salons. While his place as Dora's mother's cultural soul-mate was occupied by one of the salon's habitués, he sold made-to-measure shirts (which he also mended) at Schostal's on the via Rizzoli.

Dora's mother was never disappointed about not having a son. She ensured that all four of her daughters received a sound education. As a grandmother, her preference went not to Dora's boys, but to her daughter Liliana. On visits to the Tayar home on Florence's via Cer-naia, this advocate of cold water washes would arrive in her own horse-drawn carriage from which she would descend dressed in black with a feather in her hat as upright as its wearer. After retiring to her room to unpack, she would re-emerge with gifts only for Lil-iana, an unfairness branded on Enzo's memory. Franco, on the other hand, once had the dubious privilege of having to accompany his grandmother to view the corpse of her salon minion all laid out in a coffin.

Dora married my grandfather's brother in May 1917, the third year of the Great War, the second year of war for Italy. In photo-graphs taken just before their wedding, we see a man who, because of his long limbs, looks deceptively tall. Ugo's face is also long, his jaw tensely clenched. He has removed his pebble-shell glasses. Dora is short, with a square face, a high forehead, a long nose and soft dark eyes. Her hair is bobbed and the string of pearls round her neck is straight out of the convention of middle-class engagement portraits.

Their first child, Liliana, was born in March 1918, four months after 300,000 Italian soldiers laid down their arms at Caporetto. The Italian army was no longer willing to be the object of the butchery in a war in which Italy had lost over half a million men. In all the warring armies, this was a unique example of rebellion against authority, the ordinary soldier making his voice heard. The generals blamed this defeatism on the 'Reds'.

But the bloodbath was really largely the result of incompetence within the Allied Command. In March, the morale of the army was at a very low ebb. The Bolshevik revolution in Russia had freed the German army on one front. An assault was now expected on the border between Italy and Austria. In this month, however, American reinforcements poured into Italy and the offensive did not take place.

Franco was born in May 1920, at a time of great social unrest. In the elections of November 1919, the socialists had come to power. But paralysed by internal strife they were unable to maintain a balance in a country torn by strikes. Nor did they gain the necessary support for their policy of reform from the middle classes.

Enzo was born in November 1922, the month that Mussolini appeared in his fascist militia regalia, boots, spurs and all, before the Italian Parliament. 'I shall make a bivouac for my platoons of this assembly,' he bragged.

The Liberals did not seem offended by this threat and even the socialist leader, Turati, declared that Mussolini was the country's best hope against anarchy. Most middle-class Jews felt the same. In the wake of riots, strikes and a plummeting lira, the public accepted the new government with little enthusiasm but in the expectation that it would ward off chaos (which the fascists themselves had created).

\* \* \*

My father's cousins were born at a time when in Italy society was divided more between Capital and Labour and Town and Country (over 40 per cent of Italy's population were still engaged in agriculture) than between Jew and Gentile. Tuscany was never as devastatingly poor as the south of the country, but its country people still eked out a living on a difficult and steep terrain, handing over sixty per cent of their produce to often absentee landlords. On the fringes of these farming communities, there were always those who were even poorer: gypsies, hawkers, shepherds and *carbonari*, all despised for their nomadic existence. The *carbonari* produced charcoal from coke slow-burned under a blanket of moss, and by this precarious means managed to live on the edge of survival.

These poor people's existences barely impinged on the cousins' lives. As city-dwellers, the Tayars were like any other well-off Italians. And their religion did not seem to be an obstacle to assimilation. They were, anyway, not strictly observant. Liliana, Franco and Enzo might have dropped coins into the Jewish Fund's Blue Box, but the Zionist philosophy of a separate Jewish state was alien to them. Dora did not keep a kosher kitchen. The family celebrated only High Holidays, with Ugo attending services at the Moorish-style synagogue on the via Farini or at the Spanish/Portuguese congregation on the via delle Oche. They were not exceptional among their middle-class co-religionists in celebrating Carnival and in occasionally decorating a Christmas tree. Speaking to Susan Zucotti, the historian of the Holocaust in Italy, Salvatore Iona sums up the attitudes of a large number of Italian Jews in the 1920s as being a 'matter of going to temple a couple of times a year, of not eating pork at home and of not telling one's good mother that one would willingly marry a nice Catholic girl'.

If there was a sense of separateness from the rest of the community, it was only vaguely articulated. Enzo never quite knew what he was supposed to do at school when the pupils were called on to get to their feet to recite the *Pater noster*. Knowing that this was a prayer of another religion, but embarrassed by not being able to participate, he resolved the situation by half sitting, half standing while the other children chanted. One Christmas, the teacher distributed notepaper with scenes of the life of Christ embossed in gold in the margins. Each child was required to write a letter to Jesus. This time, Enzo crossed his arms and did nothing.

Sunday rather than Saturday was the family's special day. Dressed in sailor suits, with toy whistles round their necks, the children accompanied Ugo to the post office to collect his letters from the box to which all his business correspondence was addressed. Then they walked to his office, climbed the two flights of stairs above *Principe*, the elegant clothing department store, and helped their father to sort his mail. They read out where each letter came from and placed it, according to Ugo's instructions, in orderly piles on his desk.

At midday the whole family adjourned to Nandina's for lunch, meeting up with cousins, uncles and aunts.

\* \* \*

The religious barriers that would have once kept this family out of the heart of Italian society had been removed less than a century before. Yet the history of Italy's Jews is as old as that of Rome. Cecil Roth begins his *History of the Jews of Italy* with the Talmudic fable that describes how Rome came into existence. As a result of one of King Solomon's sins, an angel swooped down and planted a reed in the Mediterranean. So much mud accumulated around this reed that eventually it turned into dry land. Rome was built on it. And so in Jewish lore the fates of Jerusalem and Rome are considered to be inextricably bound to each other. The Italian peninsula is unique, after all, in having had an unbroken Jewish presence from antiquity to the present day.

This presence was marred for centuries by the church's hostility towards Jews. A concrete manifestation of this antagonism could be found in the very layout of many Italian cities. From time to time Ugo would take the children individually with him on business trips around the country. When they visited Venice or Rome, they could walk through the former ghettos and consider the fact that their ancestors would have once been confined here. Though the thought did not oppress them, it was still there as the faintest of pinpricks in their consciousness. They knew that in the past Jews had lived continually under threat of forced conversion and had not generally been allowed to own property outside the ghetto walls. Jews had not been permitted to sell retail either, except to other Jews, to practise handicrafts or to pursue the liberal professions. Opportunities were only open to them in the field of money-lending, but when, in 1682, Pope Innocent XI renewed the prohibition on usury, the Jews were also forced out of banking. Looking for economic opportunities elsewhere, former bankers became commission agents or wholesale importers and exporters (the latter traditionally Jewish niche Ugo was also to occupy two hundred and fifty years later).

At the beginning of the twentieth century, when Italy's Jews were no longer huddled in the old unsanitary, overcrowded districts, it was not as easy to remember that at one time they had not been full members of society, that they had been virtual prisoners. If anyone had attempted to leave the ghettos without the *Simman* (the yellow badge worn to distinguish Jews from Gentiles), they were subjected to a heavy penalty.

Inevitably, the Jews were driven in on themselves, creating their own institutions and relying on each other to ensure that help was given to the poor and destitute and that children were educated. The heart of the community was, of course, the synagogue. Only Livorno, later the city of Dora's grandparents and the birthplace of Ugo's mother, stood out as a haven for Jews. At the end of the sixteenth century, the Grand Duke of Tuscany, Ferdinand I had decided to turn the city – and nearby Pisa – into a free port. In his Charter of 1593, known as *La Livornina,* he had called upon Turks, Moors, Armenians and Persians to come and live in his Duchy, writing that 'none shall be able to make any inquisition, enquiry or accusal against you or your families, although living in the past outside our dominions in the guise of Christians'.

This was understood to be an open invitation to the New Christians of Spain and Portugal, the *Marranos*, to come and settle in the Tuscan trading centre. Having suffered centuries of harassment, Jews were being offered an opportunity to feel safe. It was in this wave of immigrants that most of my parents' ancestors had come to Tuscany. Many later dispersed to North Africa.

After the French Revolution, changes to the status of Jews in Italy followed in quick succession. Even when the House of Austria regained power after the fall of Napoleon, the return to social exclusion was not entire. By the 1830s, Jews were taking an active part in the liberation struggle against the Austrians, and it became clear to the country's new leaders that if they were to achieve unity, they would have to carry the Jews with them. The heroes of Italian unification, Mazzini and Garibaldi, were to be the heroes of my father's childhood and those of his Florentine cousins. Reading their history books, they were roused by tales of Garibaldi's Red Shirts (boasting touchingly that there were Jews among these liberators). In 1846, Pius IX issued instructions to remove the gates and walls of the Rome ghetto. In 1848, Italy became a republic and Jews were granted religious equality with all other Italians. By the time that Rome fell in 1870, their conditions were better than anywhere else in Europe.

Once religious barriers were removed, religious animosities quickly dissipated. Dora's family were well established in Italian society by the second half of the nineteenth century. By then, Judaism was no longer an impediment to being elected to Parliament, holding a university post, joining the armed forces (Dora's uncle was a general) or becoming a member of a club. There was nowhere else in Europe where the contribution made to cultural life by Jews was as great considering how few of them there were (only one-tenth of one per cent of Italy's total population).

Emancipation, however, also meant the disintegration of communities that had existed for centuries. With it, the great libraries of the synagogues fell into neglect and Jewish education was largely abandoned. Hebrew, widely taught in the ghetto, became a language you swotted up to get through your *Bar Mitzvah* and the major religious festivals. As Cecil Roth put it, by the end of the nineteenth century, 'the profession of Judaism was regarded as an amiable eccentricity rather than a social mistake'.

\* \* \*

What principally distinguished Ugo's family from other families living alongside them was not their religion, but that they were British. Until Mussolini's colonial ambitions in Africa collided with British interests, their nationality remained a curiosity rather than an obstacle to social integration. Like all children in Italy, Liliana, Franco and Enzo joined the *Balilla*, the fascist youth organisation, and each was assigned to one of its pseudo-military divisions. In this way, Franco became a member of the *Balilla escursionisti*, while Enzo played soldiers in the *Balilla moschettieri*. As a *Piccola italiana*, Liliana went on parades dressed in a white skirt, black shirt and a cap with a tassel. Enzo's troop re-enacted famous battles in a spotlit arena, explosions all round making their ears thrum. Everyone gave the fascist salute, which had replaced the handshake. Under Mussolini, Italian society was becoming highly militarised.

Economics rather than politics were Ugo's main preoccupation. In 1929, at the start of the Great Depression, he packed a suitcase full of samples, travelling alone throughout America trying to sell Italian goods. He could not have gone at a more disastrous time. The unexpected poverty and demoralisation of ordinary Americans convinced him that only strong political leadership could prevent such economic disasters from occurring again. Mussolini seemed to him, and to many others, to be the strong leader that Italy needed. Fascism, with its mixture of persuasion and thuggery, kept the lid on industrial unrest in the cities. In the countryside, it appeared to be able to patch up the social cracks caused by the turmoil that followed the end of the Great War.

After 'The Crash', Ugo, through hard work, was able to steer Roditi and Sons back on a successful course. When buyers came from America, he invited them to dinner. Dora would set the long walnut table with its drawers that opened on either side. Her place was always at the opposite end to her husband's, with the children to the right, the visitors to the left. Restless, first one child, then another would begin playing with the drawers. The next stage was to push the drawer into the stomach of the guest seated across the table to see if he or his good wife would splutter into her soup or wink in complicity. After coffee, everyone retired to the sitting room where, accompanied by Dora at the piano, Ugo sang, his voice with a timbre as clear as a bell.

The family spent their summer holidays with Dora's sister Lori and her family either in a rented villa or in a *pensione* in Maresca. Ugo, unable to free himself from work in the stifling city for more than a couple of days, would join them for the weekend. From the *pensione*, the children could hear his train approaching, whistling around bends, wheels screeching. Jostling each other, Liliana, Franco and Enzo would rush out of the front door and race down to the station, each trying to be the first on the platform to meet Ugo, stomachs fluttering with excitement.

But there were mornings when Liliana woke up to the sound of quarrelling in her parents' room or from the kitchen. Her stomach would turn to acid listening to her father shouting at her mother, calling her to account for money he thought she had misspent. It didn't make sense. They were not poor.

But Ugo was angst-ridden. What if one day he was no longer able to go on working? How would they all live if not on money carefully saved in the good times? These were not rhetorical questions, for the truth was that Ugo was going blind. The doctors insisted on surgery. But Ugo panicked and refused to go to hospital.

'Well, I suppose I could operate on you at home,' the doctor said.

Reluctantly Ugo agreed. Dora ordered the maid to scrub down the kitchen table. The children were shooed outside, but Liliana remembers her father's terror and the blood. To no purpose, for Ugo's sight was no better once the bandages were removed. Afterwards he counted every lira against the day when his sight would fail him completely and he would be unable to earn a living.

It was important to keep his growing blindness a secret. Ugo recruited the whole household into a game of denial: there was really nothing wrong with his vision. It made them all anxious. Sitting at home watching the clock if Ugo was five minutes late. Who knew if he hadn't been run over or had stumbled over an obstacle and injured himself? There were afternoons when he came home, his clothes in disarray, his body bruised because he had not seen a cyclist careering towards him. At least he could make out cars as shadows and manage to dodge them. Most other things were just mould-like shapes and hazy colours.

The ruse had to be maintained. This was the reason for those Sunday excursions to the post office. The children helped their father sort out the mail so that on Monday mornings, when the secretary came in, he did not have to give the game away by asking her to read things to him.

In the fights over household accounts, Dora would throw Ugo's extravagance in his face. He spent money on antiques. To which he would reply that this was a form of investment.

In other ways near-blindness made Ugo timorous. No matter how apolitical the family was he could not help feeling nervous about the encroaching erosion of world stability.

'Keep your head down. Don't draw attention to yourselves,' is what he always told his children. 'Don't do anything that will make others turn against you one day.'

Now that Great Britain was strongly urging the League of Nations to impose sanctions after Mussolini's murderous campaign in Ethiopia, the English and Italians were in opposing camps. It seemed to Ugo that the most logical thing to do was to renounce British nationality. In 1935, he applied for Italian citizenship. Banino, his brother in Malta, did not approve. He himself was so angered by Italian massacres of Ethiopians that he refused to allow his son Duggie to take up one of the fascist government's scholar-ships being offered to Italian-speakers living abroad. Ugo, on the other hand, was made a *Cavaliere* by the fascist regime for his serv-ices to Italian commerce.

By 1938, however, British nationality was no longer the main issue. Liliana was visiting one of her aunts in Cernobio when she first heard the word 'Aryan' being bandied about. It bewildered her as it did many Italians. Consternation turned to outrage when, soon after, she read a newspaper review of a concert. The article ended with this line: 'By the way, there were too many Jews in the audience.'

Although anti-Semitism had been abroad for a number of years, the campaign against the Jews seems to have crept up on our cousins in Florence. In March 1934, when Sion Segre Amar was caught trying to smuggle anti-fascist literature into Italy from Switzerland, thirty-one suspects were rounded up. These included eleven Jews (among them Carlo Levi who, in internal exile, was to write his great account of southern rural poverty, 'Christ Stopped in Eboli'). The newspapers had a field day, emphasising that the conspirators were mainly Jews, equating anti-fascism with Zionism. The Florentine branch of my father's family, like so many other Italian Jews, shrugged off the accusations.

But that was not the end of the matter. The Ponte Tresa Affair occurred at a time when Mussolini was anxious about Hitler's ambi-tions in Austria and his power among German minorities in Italy. He thought he could placate Hitler by instigating an anti-Jewish campaign. When there was no German attack on Italy after the assassination of Dollfüss in Austria, he called the campaign off. Most Jews once more breathed freely.

But by the late 1930s anti-Semitism was again being whipped up following the League of Nations' sanctions against Italy and the Ital-ian intervention in the Spanish Civil war. Newspapers such as *La Vita Italiana* and *Il Regime Fascista* were igniting more hostility against the Jews for conspiring with the Bolsheviks. My great-uncle was not a Bolshevik. The attacks seemed to bear no relation to his views and way of life. It made no sense that Jews were being accused of responsibility for soaring rents and housing shortages. It was no secret that the shortages had been caused by the fascist programme of clearing the popular quarters to make way for megalithic office buildings and luxury apartments. Food shortages, the rising crime rate, crowded schools – it was ridiculous that these were all being laid at the doorstep of the Jews.

In August 1938, the family was on holiday at the seaside when Mussolini made an announcement on the radio. Jews were no longer allowed to frequent holiday resorts. From the autumn term, they were to be banned as pupils and teachers from secondary schools. Elementary schools with more than ten Jewish children had to establish a special section for them. Jewish students already enrolled in university courses would be permitted to complete them but, from then on, no Jew could be included in any fresh intake.

Shock and disbelief followed these decrees. The family rushed to pack their bags and return to Florence. But it was a return to a life in which Liliana, Franco and Enzo and thousands of others were not going to be able to complete their education. The new law did, however, allow Jewish committees to set up their own schools with their own teachers as they had once done in the ghettos. Enzo, expelled from the Liceo Dante, was able to attend classes at a school established by his Jewish teacher from the Liceo, Fabio Ventura. Franco, however, was not going to be able to study engineering.

'Yes, he is,' Ugo said. 'We will send him to his cousins in Malta. He can go to university there.'

Franco, who had been studying German – once considered the language of science and high culture – first had to master English. Every morning Dora would bustle into her children's rooms, open the curtains and rouse them from their beds.

'Wake up, my dears,' she said in a heavily accented English. 'Today we all try to speak English.'

The racial laws banning Jews from education were the first of a whole swathe of anti-Semitic legislation. More was to follow. On 2–3 September foreign Jews without established residence were given six months to leave the country. Jews who had been naturalised after 1 January 1919, as Ugo had been, lost their nationality. On 17 November a new law prohibited marriages between Jews and non-Jews. At the same time, they were banned from owning or managing companies involved in military production and factories employing more than one hundred workers or any business worth more than a certain amount. They were no longer allowed to own land of more than a fixed value, or serve in the armed forces, or employ non-Jewish domestics. Ugo and Dora had to let Zora, their Yugoslav maid, go.

More legislative measures followed prohibiting Jews from holding jobs in banks and the civil service. In June 1939, all Jewish notaries, doctors, pharmacists, veterinarians, lawyers, accountants, engineers and architects were banned from practising their professions except among members of their own religion. And so, in the most nightmarish way, Ugo's penny-pinching was suddenly vindicated. At the periphery of his political vision, he had glimpsed the danger some time before. Now, he found himself having to wind down the Roditis' operations in Italy.

As if it were not enough to deprive people of their livelihood and education, further measures were announced preventing Jews from placing advertisements or death notices in newspapers, publishing books, holding conferences, or being listed in telephone directories. The stripping of their social identity sent many reeling.

Although the *Club Alpino*, with that disregard for central authority typical of a country with such a short history of centralised government, continued to allow Liliana and Enzo to participate in their Sunday excursions, all other activities involving mingling with non-Jews were denied them. Excluded from other choirs, they joined a choir formed by the conductor Veneziani. In their isolation, families were thrown into friendships they might not have sought in the past. This was how Liliana met Mirella Levi d'Ancona, who was to become her lifelong friend.

When Ugo closed down his offices in Florence, Enzo, who had left school to work for his father, found alternative employment in Prato. Vittorio Bemporad, a distant cousin, owned a factory that recycled rags into fabric. He said he was willing to take Enzo into his firm which, since Italy no longer had access to raw material for manufacturing cloth, was thriving – an irony given that dealing in rags had once been a traditional occupation of Jews in the ghettos.

In the spring of 1939 Franco left for Malta. War had not yet been declared so Liliana was able to visit him, travelling first to Naples on one of the *treni popolari*, then by ferry to Valletta. She spent the summer at Ugo's sister's and dazzled her cousins – Duggie (my father) and George (whose mother was Ugo's sister) – with her elegance and prettiness. Her looks, once celebrated as an example of Italian beauty, now classified as dark and alien in the country of her birth, easily passed the critical muster of the Strada Zecca girls. They liked her combination of vivacity and sweetness.

The morning after Mussolini declared war on the Allies in June 1940, Italian police began arresting foreign Jews. Some were sent to internment camps where conditions were extremely harsh. Others were placed under forced confinement in their homes or in remote villages. For most, however, life continued in much the same way. If the expulsions had been assiduously carried out, our cousins in Florence might have been forced out of Italy or gone into internal exile. But again and again, people flouted the racial laws. Even if they accepted the government's accusations that Jews were unpatriotic, they could not go along with outright cruelty to people who had been their neighbours for years. As high-ranking a fascist as Roberto Farinacci resisted dismissing his Jewish secretary. In Florence, Tullio Tamburini, who became Chief of Police, wrote letters of recommendation for the Bemporads, cousins of Dora, who were his former employers.

With the country at war, food was rationed and coupons were issued for meat and milk. To supplement the family's diet, Dora kept chickens. She went to great lengths to keep the birds healthy. A dab hand at needlework all her long life, she once knitted a fluffy coat for one chick, which had lost all its feathers and was being pecked by its fellow fowls.

Outings to tea-rooms were now curtailed, but the Sunday lunches downtown continued. At the Pensione Belletini, where they did not require coupons for soup, the family would start with *minestra* and pay an extra seven lire per person for the rest of the meal. Their aunts would regularly join them.

Ugo, no longer allowed to work, took over the shopping, accompanied by Enzo. It was an operation that required patience and tactics. Sometimes, Ruiz, the family's neighbour and a *Carabiniere* (and as such a representative of anti-Jewish authority), would add to their rations.

To Ugo, idleness was unbearable. He searched for some activity that would ward off his depression and came up with a scheme involving a hatter, Nino Donati. Using felt remnants provided by Donati and combining them with leather off-cuts, he started making gloves. Anything to keep fear and misery at bay. But the enterprise soon failed and Ugo was idle again.

Jewish men were not allowed to fight. As the war continued, it seemed to others that they were having far too easy a time of it. Partly to counteract the groundswell of envy and suspicion this situation provoked, on 6 May 1942 the government issued a decree obliging all Jewish males between the ages of sixteen and fifty-five to register for labour service. For the men, usually white-collar workers and not generally accustomed to physical work, the tasks to which they were assigned were often arduous: building roads, loading timber, heaving coal. The *Consorzio di bonifica del Sesto fiorentino*, which had been set up to drain the marshes, sent Enzo with a group of twenty-nine others, divided into two teams, to dig ditches. Under the not very vigilant eye of a fascist overseer, each man had to dig a prerequisite number of metres each day for a token wage of four lire.

Enzo would leave home by bus at 5.30 AM, taking with him a lunch packed by Dora consisting of boiled potatoes or bread made from potato scraps. These were mixed with sorghum, which made them indigestible. But Enzo made them palatable by eating them with home-preserved sardines. By winter, he was still digging ditches, and cycling to work wearing the muffs that Dora had made out of rabbit fur. In many ways it was not an unhappy time for him. He was young and fit. And work outdoors made him very healthy.

These were months of hardship but of limited dangers. At the beginning of the summer of 1943, Liliana and Enzo were able to go on a long trek from Florence to Maresca where they had once spent their summer holidays. 'Bursting out of our skins with good health,' Enzo wrote in his diary on the hike from Cimone to Garfagnano, Lago Santo and then back to Forte dei Marmi. It looked as if life would go on in this way forever; nothing was as it had been, but life had not yet become impossible. The ghettos of Lodz, Vilna and Bialystock were on the verge of extinction, but the Jews of Italy were still moving about freely. The Warsaw ghetto, where Jews were preparing a last desperate stance against annihilation, seemed far away. It was only after the war that the Florentine cousins learned of the mass destruction of another Mediterranean community, Salonika, from which 48,000 people were transported to Birkenau.

Had Mussolini stayed out of the war, he might have remained in power. But as Italian forces suffered devastating defeats in Greece and North Africa, discontent in Italy grew. Allied bombings, food shortages and rising prices also eroded support for the regime. Strikes were called in a number of northern cities. Civil disobedience spread to the countryside where the peasant farmers, once wooed by the fascists, had been badly hit by high taxes and price and distribution controls.

On 10 July 1943 American and British forces landed in Sicily. 'Tripudio generale' ('general jubilation'), Enzo's diary entry records.

On 19 July Rome came under aerial attack for the first time, but Hitler refused to send reinforcements to defend southern Italy. At this point, King Victor Emmanuel decided that the country could only be saved by getting rid of the fascists.

On 25 July, with the backing of the army as well as parts of the bureaucracy, the King nervously asked Mussolini to resign and immediately had him arrested. Marshall Badoglio was called upon to replace the Duce. Throughout the country, a series of mass anti-fascist demonstrations took place, but the new government was too fearful of German reactions to act.

Ugo, Dora, Liliana and Enzo waited anxiously while an armistice was negotiated with the Allies. It was hard to know what would happen while the government continued to reassure the Germans that Italy would remain on their side. As the King vacillated, Hitler ordered tens of thousands of troops into northern Italy. At the same time, the Allied advance was halted at Montecassino. Knowing that Franco was with the Allies, the family had hoped that the break-through would be a quick one and that they would soon be re-united. When the Germans rescued Mussolini and set him up in the puppet Republic of Salò, the Italian peninsula was split in two. The family was now even more cut off from their relatives in Allied countries; before Salò they had at least received correspondence from Franco through the Red Cross. Now they would search for clues to his whereabouts in his heavily censored letters and in the BBC broadcasts to which they listened illegally.

During the forty-five days before the King and Badoglio abandoned Rome to the Germans, the optimism of the country's Jews was restrained. Badoglio had not, after all, immediately rescinded the racial laws. Worst of all, the lists of Jews held by bureaucrats everywhere were not destroyed and were to fall into German hands. By September, as the occupation forces tightened their grip over northern Italy, it became clear to many Jews that they now risked arrest, deportation and possibly death. Hundreds of them prepared to leave their homes and go into hiding.

On 11 September official orders were issued for people to remain indoors. Defying these, Liliana and Enzo went for a walk in the evening in the centre of Florence. There were Germans everywhere. Major Carità's band, the most vicious of the fascist gangs, was also prowling the streets. When they saw someone being shot, Liliana and Enzo hurried home.

Florence's Chief Rabbi, Nathan Cassuto (who was to perish in Auschwitz), went around from house to house urging everyone to disperse. Of the via Cernaia family, it was Enzo who, as a young man, was in most immediate danger. On 12 September, the family decided that he must leave Florence. Three days later, with his friend Federico Benadì, he set off for Radda in the Chianti hills where the Benadìs owned a farm. They left on their bicycles, with only the clothes and boots they were wearing. It had to look like nothing more than a day's outing. Liliana promised that as soon as she could she would take Enzo warm clothes for the approaching winter. Dora sewed a diamond into his waistband to be bartered if the need arose. Before waving her son goodbye, she gave him her *Shaddai*, the amulet that bears the name of God.

At Radda, Federico introduced himself as Pinto; Enzo became Enrico. The farm workers were not fooled by these assumed names or by the thick beards grown as a disguise, but they were not inclined to report the presence of the two young men to the authorities. It was a region of people with strong communist sympathies, alienated from a regime that had done little to ease their lot and which had turned Italy into a battleground. Besides, to give these young men away would not have been a 'Christian' act. Any person with a sense of decency would have acted in the same way. Official Christianity, however, was proving notably deficient in protesting against the murder of Jews although, in response to the German demand for 50 kilograms of gold from the Rome Jewish community, the Pope had intervened with an offer to make up whatever amount the community was unable to scrape together.

Because the records of the Office of Demography and Race had not been destroyed, it was easy for the Germans to trace Jews. By October, they had seized 1115 of Rome's 6730 Jews and deported them to Auschwitz. Only sixteen were to survive. Neither Rome, nor Florence nor any other Italian city or town was safe. In northern Italy, 7345 Jews were captured and of these 6746 were to perish in Auschwitz. Close to Trieste, at a camp of Italian prisoners-of-war, Ukranian and SS guards murdered 620 Jews and 3000 ordinary Italian soldiers.

In Florence, SS troops surrounded the synagogue and began deportations. By now, young women were also being ordered to report for forced labour for which they would be sent up north. Ugo, forever the anxious pessimist, could not see how Liliana was going to escape this net, but she had no intention of complying with German orders. Not for the most obvious reasons to us in retrospect, the danger of being starved to death or gassed, but because she could not bear to see the family divided again. Her belief in their need to stay together is what propelled her. It was she who decreed that they must all now go into hiding.

Alone, she travelled to Poppi in the Casentino. The city with its porticos and narrow cobbled streets is perched on a hill. On the very top stands its medieval castle, like a hand with an index finger pointing to heaven, once a refuge for the poet Dante in exile. Dominating Poppi is a range of higher hills, the Pratomagno. It was a region of isolated farmhouses in which large extended families once spent all their time in backbreaking work. Their lives sometimes brutish, their social structures rigid, they did not always welcome the many wanderers who were an age-old feature of their countryside.

In Poppi, Liliana took two rooms in a *pensione* for which the proprietors asked to be paid in kind. Fortunately, the Levi d'Anconas owned a farm nearby so Liliana was able to settle her account for the next few weeks with sacks of potatoes. She did not conceal the fact that she and her parents were from Florence. Their hosts probably guessed that they were Jews. When the Germans started appearing in the Casentino, it became urgent for the three of them to move on again.

Promising Ugo and Dora she would be back within ten days, Liliana set out on foot, climbing in the direction of the Pratomagno. Her idea was to look for a farm where the occupants might be prepared to take in three adults. It would be a financial arrangement.

On her way up, she met a man named Masino.

'Keep climbing,' he advised her. 'Up there. Can you see the scattered houses? That's Larniano.'

On the hill, next to a church, stood a store. To the right, along a path flanked by chestnut trees, below the house she could see higher up and diagonally opposite the church, lived the Giorgiones, a family he knew very well. Their stone farmhouse with its terracotta tiled roof nestled halfway down another hill. Giovanni Giorgione, his wife Santina and their baby Carlino, shared the house with Santina's mother, Rosina, and her two other daughters. Marcello, their adopted brother, had been abandoned by his mother, who years before had left Larniano for America. Although she had promised to return to fetch her son, she never did, and so Rosina brought Marcello up as her own. Some might call this an act of Christian charity on a par with that of the farmworkers who later did not give Enzo and Federico away, but Rosina would have said it is what anyone would have done. The word 'Christian' in Italian is stripped of sanctimony and is a synonym for human and decent.

Liliana told Giovanni that she and her parents were refugees not from Florence but from Rome, which they had fled in the wake of the bombings. Giovanni was inclined to be sympathetic. The thought of being caught up in fighting had been so repellent to him, as well as inconvenient (given his position as chief breadwinner), that he had gone out one day and fired a bullet into his foot. As a disabled man, he could not be called up. Why should he fight the fascists' war? No, he would not turn Liliana away. His mother and sisters-in-law could move upstairs and sleep in the loft with Marcello, alongside the sacks of grain stored there.

Before returning to Poppi to collect her mother and father, Liliana had to get some warm clothes to Enzo. This meant going back to Florence. On the train from Arezzo, fellow-passengers berated the fascists, complaining of the disasters they had brought down on everyone's head, but she did not join in. One could never be sure that people weren't setting a trap. And as if to underline her position, when she left the station, she realised she was being followed. Two blocks away from the via Cernaia, she slipped into a front garden and waited for her shadower to pass.

She reached home half in a panic, half in a trance. After gathering a few items for her brother, she wandered in and out of rooms, taking in what might be a final look at everything that had been part of her life until then. In the kitchen she found a bag of flour that Dora had left untouched.

Damn it, she said to herself. I'm not going to let the SS have this.

Numbed to the danger of lingering in the apartment, she began preparing dough for bread. She cannot now explain why she did this. It was a sort of show of defiance, but there were no spectators. She froze when she heard a rapping on the front door. The only escape route was via the back of the building. Miraculously, Carabiniere Ruiz was there.

'Come quickly, *Signorina*,' he whispered. 'Climb over the balcony. The SS are rounding people up.'

She followed Ruiz to his house and waited for the SS to pass.

Before going on to Radda, she had one more place to visit – her maternal aunt Gina's villa just outside Florence. The family had stored some of their belongings there, including their British passports. Leaving the city at night, she became hopelessly lost in olive groves near a German encampment. She could hear barking voices but could see nothing through the blackness. Suddenly, the sky exploded into a solar flare, and the air vibrated. A train carrying ammunition had blown up. In the chaos, with her path lit by the blaze, Liliana found her way to the villa. The SS had beaten her to it and the passports were gone.

She reached Radda on 6 November, happy to be reunited with her brother and temporarily to ease the growing burden of the responsibility she now felt for the safety and welfare of her family. She had letters from Ugo and Dora and from the Levi d'Anconas. There was time to mend Enzo's clothes and give him a haircut.

'How do I cut round the ears?' Liliana asked. Her amateur efforts soon had both brother and sister rolling on the ground with laughter. It was a brief interlude during which they could be carefree again.

The next day, Lorenzo Bemporad arrived to warn them all that they must leave at once. The Germans had been to the offices of the Jewish community in Florence and discovered that the Radda farm belonged to Jews. Federico was to go to his parents in Carraini, but Enzo had nowhere to hide. With Liliana, he left Radda in search of another refuge.

The first difficulty was how to get across the Arno – the area around it was teeming with German patrols. Not knowing what to do, they spent the night at La Spugna, in a *pensione* so full that the guests had to share beds with strangers. It seemed as if the whole of Italy was on the move.

'Why don't you hide your brother under some hay?' one of her bedmates suggested to her. 'Then you can get across the river by cart.'

But that seemed far too risky.

At four o'clock in the morning, another woman shook her from her sleep. 'Get dressed,' she whispered in her ear. 'I've had an idea. The *carbonari* up in the hills might be happy to make some money by hiding your brother.'

By this stage of the war, the Tuscans were no strangers to men fleeing military service, partisans on the run and escaped prisoners-of-war. Whichever category Enzo fitted into, this stranger was prepared to help. She probably did not know that he was a Jew. Liliana and Enzo dressed hurriedly and, guided by the woman, they left the *pensione* before sunrise. Fear stuck in Liliana's throat, like a piece of cold gristle.

At dawn, they reached Poggiarso. As they approached, they met a *carbonaro* bending over to tie his boot-laces. He was on his way to work. The woman from the *pensione* explained Enzo's situation and an agreement was reached on what was to be paid to this poor man with his rough, half-starved children.

To be able to return to Poppi, Liliana needed a travel permit. One of the *carbonaro*'s daughters was sent to town to obtain the necessary papers. These, of course, were issued in the girl's name. Again Liliana said goodbye to her brother and boarded a packed bus to Arezzo. Seated in the back, she was too lost in her own worries and sadness to mind being pressed against swaying bodies as they trundled over gravel roads. She switched back to reality when the bus jolted to a halt.

'*Porca miseria*. Another road check,' the driver shouted, exasperated by yet another harassment on the part of the SS. Liliana couldn't breathe. She was carrying a permit with the name of the *carbonaro*'s daughter, and in her handbag she had her own ID card, which also gave her mother's maiden name, Markbreiter. The Germans were ordering everyone to get off the bus. Terror coursed from her stomach through her legs and then to her feet, weighing them down with a sensation of burning. That's it, she thought, They've caught me.

But no one was getting off the bus. Instead, they were making more noise than a piggery at feeding time.

'We're not getting off. We've had enough of these checks. Leave us alone. Let's get on with the journey.' The decibels mounted as the SS men peered into the vehicle packed with this horde of peasants.

'*Ach!*' they cursed. 'All right. Let the bus through.'

Back in Poppi, Liliana hurried to find her parents. On the way, she met some acquaintances who gazed at her in astonishment.

'Get back quickly,' they said. 'Your parents are in a terrible state. They think you've been rounded up and murdered.'

What else could they have thought? She had promised she would be back in ten days. When she failed to show up, Ugo and Dora had asked the owners of the *pensione* to phone Ruiz to enquire if he had seen her. Suspecting a trap, for he did not know these strange callers, the *Carabiniere* had replied that he had not set eyes on her for weeks.

'We're moving,' Liliana told the owners. 'Up north. It'll be safer there.'

She carried their luggage down to the train station from where she would ask Marcello to collect it, pretending that it had arrived from Rome. She was quickly learning to be cunning. It was easier to

explain their presence near Poppi as part of the wave of people fleeing the Allied advance, away from the capital.

They soon settled in with the Giorgiones in whose house conditions were cramped and basic. There was one large room with a
fireplace before which everyone gathered. In their bedroom, the
Tayars had a brick stove from which Ugo, thin, anxious and again
unwillingly idle, could never absorb enough warmth. On the other
side of the main room, Giovanni, Santina and Carlino slept in the
only other bedroom. Outside, iron stairs led to the loft. Under the
house, there was a stable and space to store wine, biscuits, apples and
the rabbits and pigeons that Santina's sisters bred and took to market. Liliana kept her bicycle there.

The farm had its rhythms and its routines, and each member of
the household his or her assigned tasks, all of them time-consuming.
Rosina baked bread in an oven outside the house. For washing,
someone had to go down to the stream with the donkey to fetch
water. The women would place all the sheets and whites in a tub
under another heavy sheet. As there was no soap, the washing was
sprinkled with wood ash and jars of hot water poured over it.

Because of his fading eyesight Ugo could do little to help around
the farm. He could not even find distraction by reading. But Dora,
the woman who had once spent her afternoons in tea-rooms and
played piano to her foreign guests, worked alongside the *contadini* in
the fields. As the Giorgiones could not stretch their supplies to feed
three extra mouths, Liliana trudged each day from place to place in
search of food. She became familiar with the hilly and rocky landscape. She soon knew where she could buy vegetables, where there
were eggs and meat for sale, in what location the biggest and juici-
est cherries grew and the spots where grapes could be found in
abundance. At the store in Larniano, she bought rice and salt. She
plucked chestnuts off the trees. In the evening, these were roasted on
an open fire, with everyone sitting so close to the hearth that their
legs became mottled with *vacche* (literally cows), which is what the
farmers called heat blotches.

As the nights drew in, neighbours would drop by to chat. Sometimes there were dances, feet raising dust as they pounded the floor. At the *veglia*, families who normally lived isolated from each other would get together to play cards, mend clothes and tell stories. On Sundays, everyone went to church. It would not have done for Liliana not to go. At Mass, she mumbled her prayers, but once caught herself doing so too loudly. She was conjugating Latin verbs and this totally bewildered the rest of the congregation. To re-establish her credentials, she offered to teach the youngest of Rosina's daughters to read from a book of poems about Jesus and Mary.

Liliana's friends, the Levi d'Anconas, had escaped to Switzerland, a feat accomplished by only a few hundred Jews, for the Swiss notoriously blew hot and cold about letting in Jewish refugees to their country. From Switzerland, the Levi d'Anconas sent two guides to escort Liliana and her parents across the border. Lodging at the Levi d'Anconas' farm, the guides sent the farm manager to Larniano to collect Liliana. When she entered the kitchen, she saw the two men sitting there, rifles resting on their laps.

'We must talk,' one of them said, taking her aside. 'Would you be prepared to come with us?'

'Yes, but first I must discuss the matter with my parents. We need to make arrangements.'

'We'll give you just two days.'

'We can't go without Enzo,' Ugo and Dora said.

'Then I'll have to go and find him.'

The next day, Liliana set off in a horse-drawn carriage for Bibbiena where she intended to get the bus back to Florence and from there begin her search for her brother. A bomb explosion, however, had made the road impassable. By now Liliana had become fatalistic. With the road blocked, she decided the family's escape to Switzerland was not meant to be. She felt lighter. It would have been a gruelling journey, with Germans everywhere searching for deserters, escaped prisoners-of-war and Jews. Progress would have been slow with the half-blind Ugo, and who was to say if the Swiss would have allowed them in? Later she felt her decision to call the escape off was justified when she learned that the farm manager, who had acted as a messenger for the guides, had been taken away and shot by the Germans.

'You were always on your toes,' she says now. 'Every day had its new and often frightening surprises.' Watching out for Germans and fascists was a constant. If a search was taking place, families all round would hang out sheets on clotheslines as a signal that all young men should head for cover. Liliana too. Dora and Ugo could be passed off as elderly relatives so they were not always obliged to 'disappear'. Once, it was her Aunt Matilda's green and brown coat that saved Liliana. The Germans got to within a few feet of her hiding place, but did not see her in her unlikely camouflage. They did, however, discover her bicycle hidden under meshing in the wine and grain loft. But it was unusable: she had taken the precaution of removing all the bolts.

It was just as terrifying when the partisans passed through, demanding that the farmers conceal their weapons. The Germans always came hard on their heels and reprisals followed any act of resistance. In Sant'Anna di Stazzema, 560 men, women and children were massacred; in Marzabotto, 1830 people were murdered by the ss. Elsewhere, whole villages were executed. The Fascist National Guard helped the Germans with these manhunts, terrorising the local people. Losses among partisans were enormous.

It was obvious that Giovanni was taking terrible risks by sheltering Liliana and her parents. Though he never said so, he was fully aware that his guests were Jews. When he had first taken them in, he might have expected that the Allies would reach Tuscany soon and their stay would not be long. The small amount of rent money was no doubt welcome but, as the fighting dragged on and the occupiers became more brutal, Giovanni exposed himself and his family to a danger no financial reward could compensate. The core of his action can only be interpreted as one of simple humanity combined with a certain dose of thumbing one's nose at oppressive authority. Time and time again, he helped restrain Ugo when, harrowed and afraid, he prepared to give himself up. Ugo felt caged in this mountain hideout, the suspense of the family's day-to-day survival corroding his already raw nerves.

For Liliana it was a lonely life, cut off as she was from friends of her own age and social background. Rucksack on back, she trudged about the countryside in the company of a farm dog, reciting poetry to herself. Sometimes she simply counted the number of steps from one place to another. Once she came across three parallel tracks in the snow: a man's footprints, a dog's paw prints and the marks of the butt of a rifle used as a walking stick. She turned back to Larniano. Another time, on her way to Bibbiena to buy books, she met someone who warned her that the Germans had got wind of her presence and were searching for a young woman, possibly Jewish, who spent her days trekking from farm to farm. She should not make the trip to Bibbiena.

As things got worse for the fascists, they came looking for both Giovanni and Marcello to take them as hostages. Every time one German was killed by the partisans, ten hostages would be put to death. The fascists were always scouring the countryside for fresh victims. Giovanni and Marcello just had time to escape and hide before the soldiers came knocking on their door. When Liliana opened it, they shone torches in her face. Beams of torchlight scanned the room where Ugo, the only man in the house, sat huddled with the women. He looked too old and frail to be of any interest.

Over the months, Enzo had been able to correspond with them, sending postcards signed under a variety of pseudonyms. From Poggiarso where the *carbonaro* had turned out to be a drunkard and wife-beater, Enzo had gone on to La Consuma where he found work as a shepherd on a farm owned by a man called Beppe. There he fell in love with Beppe's daughter, Venusta.

Later, after Enzo had moved on to a new hiding place in Montevarchi, Venusta took the risk of going to Larniano to lead Liliana to her brother's refuge.

On her return journey via Florence, Liliana met a woman whom she did not know.

'Oh, so you're still alive!' the stranger said. 'I thought you were dead. I've been to see your grave.'

Liliana was bewildered.

'Be careful. There are fascists all over the place. Watch out! Don't get caught.'

To this day, that encounter seems to Liliana as if it had been in a dream, but such was the landscape in which she moved during those months of hiding.

The Germans were now starting to requisition farm animals. To prevent these falling into their hands, Resistance fighters went from farm to farm asking the *contadini* to hand over all their cattle, sheep, goats, donkeys and horses. Then they led the animals to safety high up on the Pratomagno plateau that separates the Casentino from the Chianti region. A week later, a troop of *Brigate Nere*, the most feared of all the fascist gangs, turned up swaggering and jeering. 'So much for the partisans helping you. We've made sure all the animals are dead.'

Unsure of the truth of this boast, a group of peasants decided to go up to the plateau to see if at least some of the animals had escaped the slaughter. Liliana climbed the 1600 metres with them, taking her binoculars. She hoped that she might be able to see if the Allies had advanced as far as Chianti. What she and the group of farmers saw was more heart-breaking than anyone could have imagined: hundreds of dead farm animals, bloated and stinking, all over the fields.

They could also see, however, that the Allies had made their breakthrough. Liliana and Marcello began walking back to Larniano, but as they neared the chestnut groves a group of people came hurrying towards them.

'You mustn't spend the night here,' they told Liliana. 'Get your mother and father and take them somewhere safe.'

For the next few nights, Ugo, Dora and Liliana slept in a chestnut-picker's hut with other villagers, packed in head to foot.

'The best thing for us to do now,' Liliana said, 'is to try to get to the Allies.'

In the dark, Marcello and Dora began the climb down. Liliana followed, gently leading her father. It felt as if someone were trailing them, but each time they spun around, it was only a tree shuddering in the wind.

As they progressed down the slope, they saw two tanks lumbering towards them. From the hatch, a man's head appeared.

'Hey,' he shouted. 'What do you people think you're doing? There's a battle going on here.'

He jumped out and ran towards them. He was dark-skinned. An Indian, they guessed correctly.

'You shouldn't be in this place. Anyway, you're breaking the curfew. The two old people better get into the tanks.'

'You,' he stabbed a finger in the air near Liliana's chest, 'and that fellow had better wait here for us to come back to collect you.'

'Where are you taking us?' Liliana asked later as she and Marcello boarded the truck sent to pick them up. It was full of German prisoners. She was outraged that she should be lumped together with people who, only a few days before, might have sent her to her death.

'We're taking you to Major Piper.'

\* \* \*

In Florence, Captain Douglas (Duggie) Tayar from Major Piper's regiment was making his way to the via Cernaia to look for his relatives. Finding their apartment sealed, he decided to try the synagogue on the via Farini to see if anyone there knew of their whereabouts. But there was no one to be found among the rubble of the mined front porticos and collapsed galleries. From across the street, a sniper opened fire. Duggie ran for his life.

'What do you mean you've been into Florence? We haven't liberated it yet,' a senior officer barked at him on his return to his regiment.

Liberation took place a few days later. At the end of September 1944, Florence fell to the Allies.

When Liliana and her parents appeared before Major Piper, he was quick to make connections.

'Tayar. That's odd. We have a Captain Tayar with us. Could he be a relative of yours?'

What Liliana first thought was that this Captain Tayar must be her brother Franco. Nonetheless, a re-found Maltese cousin was a welcome second best. It was from any viewpoint a huge coincidence. And Duggie was able to trace Enzo for them. Having learnt that Montevarchi had been liberated by the Americans and that Enzo was working for a Captain Connolly, he arranged for them all to meet again.

Leaving Dora and Ugo in Montevarchi, Duggie, Liliana and Enzo set out for Florence again. It was an eerie return. The soldiers from the Palestine regiment, whom they met on their way, frightened Liliana with their Yiddish, which she mistook for German. The via Cernaia apartment, requisitioned by the fascists, had been broken into and was completely bare.

Liliana and Enzo spent their first post-war Yom Kippur in the stripped apartment. Here, they were able to take stock of the period of German occupation, grateful to have survived, but saddened by the news that Silvia and Gilda Coen, cousins of their grandmother Corinna, had been rounded up and had perished.

* * *

Approximately 85 per cent (38,400) of Italy's Jews managed to escape the Holocaust. Compared to all other European countries under occupation, this was a very high survival rate. It could be argued that Italy was not occupied for long. The situation could be compared to that of Hungary, however, where the German occupation was also brief. There, in a single period of two months, 380,000 Hungarian Jews had been deported.

The temperament of the Italians was crucial to the survival of Italy's Jews. To begin with, defiance of the state was still very much inherent to Italian culture (the Mafia still survives because of this). It was especially true in the countryside where, since unification less than a hundred years before, the central authorities had done little to bring about true agrarian reform or to correct injustices.

It also helped that, unlike the Jews of central and eastern Europe, the Jews of Italy could not be distinguished from the rest of the population by differences in custom, dress and speech. Anyway, to simple people like the Giorgiones and many others, categories such as Aryan and non-Aryan, human and sub-human, were totally meaningless. Seeing people with their lives in danger, what they did was to provide a refuge.

According to Jewish tradition, in every generation there are thirty-six righteous people (the *Lamed vav*) who, unknown to others and even to themselves, are destined to do good to their fellow men. As the Babylonian Talmud says: 'The universe exists on the merit of the righteous among the nations of the world and they are privileged to see the Divine Presence.' Without them, the world would cease to exist. In Hebrew, these people are known as the *Hasidei U'Mot Ha'Olam*. They are words which, no doubt, would have sounded exotic to Giovanni Giorgione, a *contadino*. If he were alive today, he might argue that his act of mercy was on a very small scale compared to the spectacular rescues carried out by people like Schindler, Wallenberg and the Italian Perlasca, and that he had not acted alone, for no one in Larniano chose to delve too deeply into the presence there of Liliana, Ugo and Dora.

When Ugo and Dora at last joined their children in Florence, the first thing they did was to go to the *Questura* to declare all the items missing from their home. The police were helpful, but it was up to Dora to lead Ugo from house to house to search for their furniture, paintings, cutlery and china.

It was time to re-build their lives. Ugo sent word to the Roditis in New York that he would be happy to re-open their offices with

Enzo's help. Just as his father had done in 1929, Enzo packed a case full of samples of Venetian glass, hand-painted wood, Florentine leather goods, ceramics, linens and alabaster and set sail for America in September 1946. But Roditi and Sons were struggling by now and Enzo was already planning to go into business independently with his brother.

By the time of his return to Florence, Franco had been away for almost eight years. He had joined the British Army and become a gunner in Malta. Each fresh news bulletin of the bombardment of the island or the decimation of convoys in the Mediterranean had unnerved his family in Italy. He came back a stranger to his family, reserved in an oddly Anglo-Saxon way.

Liliana went to work for Major Richardson of the American military government. Her photograph shows a very lovely woman, slim, tanned and made athletic by those solitary hikes in the Casentino. At the via Cernaia, infatuated soldiers came to call, the most besotted among them being Duggie. But Dora soon put a stop to that, recognising that the two cousins were too much alike, volatile and strong-minded. In Liliana's case, that strength had come from the months during which she had really been her family's keeper. Now she felt at a loose end, deflated.

It was a woman who had come to Liliana's office seeking information about her son missing on the Russian front who introduced her to Mrs Sherwood Anderson, the wife of the American author. Mrs Anderson had come to Italy on behalf of the YMCA to distribute funds to mothers of children fathered by American soldiers. They needed someone to help them trace these women.

'But I'm Jewish,' Liliana blurted out when told that the C in the acronym stood for Christian.

'Why should that matter?' Mrs Anderson laughed. 'If you want the job, it's yours.'

Liliana moved to the Villa Ruffo in Ronchi from where Mrs Anderson was conducting her searches. There she became friendly with the Jewish Rose de Luca and her Italo-American husband,

Philip. The couple had come to Italy on behalf of the Amalgamated Clothing Workers of America to set up a factory to mass-produce clothing that would be sold at prices affordable to ordinary workers. It was an act of solidarity with the Italian people even if a little tinged with paternalism, for the inauguration brochure of the Avenza plant speaks of helping to bring about 'the moral rehabilitation of the Italians'. Jacob S. Potofsky, the President of the ACW, travelled to Tuscany for the factory's opening ceremony.

The time spent at the villa in Ronchi was a happy one for Liliana. Rose showed her how to make jello and she taught the American woman how to make *granita di caffè*. Watched by lugubrious portraits of Ruffo ancestors, Ugo would, on his visits, entertain them all with his yarns.

When Mrs Anderson and the de Lucas finally left, Liliana went to work for her father and brothers. But she was restless, yearning for new people and new places, not content with being an adjunct to someone else's business aspirations. The war had taught her many things, but, above all, independence. Although Enzo maintains that they were all too busy rebuilding their lives to think about the recent sufferings of fellow Jews, as information on the Holocaust filtered through, it had a depressing effect on Liliana. She was moving in a world where nothing seemed to have much substance to it.

A letter from Jacob Potofsky offered her a way out. He invited her to take up a scholarship in America at the Institute of Fashion and Dress Design in New York and Mrs Sherwood Anderson agreed to act as her sponsor. None of them, however, had reckoned with the hostility of the American Consul in Florence who refused to grant a visa. Months and months of visits to his office produced no results.

'How do we know you're not just going to get married once you get to the States?' Mr Campbell asked.

'You don't. Nor do I. But if I can't have a visa, then you can stuff it.' Liliana finally exploded.

Mr Campbell, seeing that she would not be bullied, relented.

\* \* \*

In the Autumn of 1950, Liliana, aged thirty-two, set sail for the New World on the SS *Washington* of the United States Lines, captained by Harold Milde. Fellow-passengers signed her menu as a souvenir of this voyage.

'Hope you like us as much as we like you. REG.'
'If New York is too cloudy come to Oklahoma. OWEN ROBBINS.'
'May the US be what you hope for. NANCY TEAVELL.'

*I knew nothing of sequential Cairo, but sensed in some
way, I believe, a palimpsest. It was clear that Cairo – all of
Egypt, indeed – was a disorderly place in more senses than
one. It was a place of cultural confusion – I was battered
throughout my childhood with nationalities and allegiances.
British, French, Greek, Syrian, Lebanese, Turkish, Church
of England, Muslim, Coptic and Jewish.*

PENELOPE LIVELY, *Oleander, Jacaranda*

## CHAPTER SIX

# enrico and the dutch hanukkia

My father could have travelled almost
anywhere around the Mediterranean
and come across some member of his family living there. Two years before the
reunion with Liliana and her parents, he had
already found a home away from home with
the Nahums, cousins resident in Egypt.

In the middle of 1942 Duggie arrived
there from India with the Xth Baluch Regiment. Having spent time interrogating
Italian prisoners-of-war in detention camps
in Britain's largest colony, he had gone on to the military academy
in Dehra Dun to train as an interpreter from Urdu. This was all very

far removed from the fighting he had imagined. It made him feel guilty to think of his mother, father, sisters and brother suffering near-starvation and constant bombardments in Malta. So he applied to be posted to a battlefield.

'The weather here is secret,' he wrote home. His letters were daubed with black lines by the military censors and of course he could not even hint at his new location.

'Enrico took me on a visit to a Jewish orphanage,' he added, 'and Ida has a handsome young officer in tow.'

Though Duggie complained about the sand getting into every-thing, to the family in Malta this was an unnecessary additional clue to his whereabouts. The mere mention of Enrico was enough for them to know immediately that he was in Egypt.

Enrico was Enrico Nahum, whose mother, Giulia, was a grand-daughter of Rabbi Josef Tayar and hence a first cousin to Banino. Ida was Ida Pinto, the cousin who had been my father's eldest sister's great friend in the days of her 'banishment' from Strada Zecca. When Duggie was a toddler, it was Ida with Yolanda who had taken him to the opera.

*   *   *

More than forty years earlier, Enrico's father, Pinchas, had announced to Giulia that he was leaving her and their two youngest children.

'I am taking the two older boys with me to Egypt. There is more of a future for us there than here in Tripoli,' he said. 'Once we have established ourselves, I will send for you and Enrico and Fortunée.'

In moving to Cairo, Pinchas was joining the tens of thousands of other immigrants pouring into Egypt in the wake of its radical social and economic transformation. The process had begun in the 1820s under the leadership of Muhammad Ali, once a minor officer with the Albanian mercenaries who formed part of the Ottoman Empire's army. With the overthrow of Egypt's Mameluk rulers, he rose to the position of Governor and began a programme of radical reforms to make his adopted country self-sufficient and to catch up with the economic success of the West. To achieve this, he expanded agriculture, opened schools that taught science and technology and established a sound administration.

As part of his policy to turn the country into a great and respected power, Muhammad Ali and his mercantilist supporters invited people from abroad to come and settle in Egypt's cities in order to develop trade. More than half a century later, immigrants from all over the Mediterranean had made the country their home.

By the time of Pinchas Nahum's arrival in 1901, there were more than 150,000 foreigners living in Egypt, mostly congregated in two cities, Cairo and Alexandria. These settlers were attracted not only by the government's *laissez faire* policies but also by the extension of the system of Capitulations. Until the latter were abolished in the 1930s, the prospect of legal and fiscal exemptions remained a great incentive to Jewish immigrants especially.

In 1905, Pinchas was at last able to send for his wife and two youngest children. He had set himself up as a commission agent and government contractor and opened up offices and a showroom on 44 Shareh Sharif Pasha.

Like most new arrivals, Pinchas had faith that Egypt would continue to prosper. The country was ruled by the British who would, it was hoped, intervene if the Egyptians got out of hand. But the British had done everything they could to undermine Muhammad Ali's great project. It did not suit them to have a successful and vigorous power on the route to India. So they first stepped in to destroy Muhammad Ali's economic base and weaken his ability to finance his armies. When his successor fell heavily into debt and was forced to sell his shares in the Suez Canal (the building of which had cost the lives of 100,000 Egyptians), it was the British who bought up most of the stock. The 1882 rebellion against foreign influences in the country gave them a pretext for taking over the administration and setting up what became known as the Veiled Protectorate. This meant that they ruled behind a façade of Egyptian ministers who had little authority.

The conclusion most Arabs drew from this was that the West did not want the East to resemble but to obey it. This was eventually to have disastrous consequences for foreigners who, like the Nahums, believed that Britain and the other European powers would always hold sway in Egypt. At the turn of the century, one small Tripolitanian branch of my family was optimistic about its future in a new homeland.

These days, when Islamic fundamentalism has overshadowed much of what is happening in the Middle East, the confidence of the Nahums can only be the source of nostalgia. For in the past, Islam had a remarkable capacity for co-existence with other religions. No greater proof of this can be found than Istanbul at the end of the nineteenth century when Istanbul's population was not, as might be expected, made up of a majority of Moslems. On the contrary, the minorities living there outnumbered the followers of Islam. At the end of the nineteenth century, what Western city could have contemplated having more than half of its population non-Christian? Though the Cairo Pinchas had moved, his family was still predominantly Moslem, and followed the Turkish model in which Greeks, Armenians, Russians, Maltese, Syrians and all sorts of North Africans lived more or less easily alongside their Moslem neighbours.

For the Nahums, arriving from the smaller Tripolitanian capital, modern Cairo was an emporium of architectural wonders. Laid out as a replica of Haussman's Paris, its new districts mushrooming from the ancient oriental town, it displayed a mixture of styles ranging from Viennese to Italian to Art Nouveau. Along the banks of the Nile, whole areas were being opened up to development. Enrico, Pinchas's youngest son, remembered his excitement at seeing the horse-drawn trams clattering down the city's wide avenues. Near Cairo's opera house, where in 1869 'Aida' was first performed to celebrate the opening of the Suez Canal, the six-year-old Enrico and his mother visited their first department store, Les Grands Magasins

Cicurel et Oreco, whose rival was the department store which belonged to the Tunisian Jewish Chemla family. There were French *cafés* and Greek pastry shops.

Beyond these European meeting places, people of all religions and ethnic groups from East and West mingled in the market place. Moslem stallholders were prepared for all the religious festivals – Jewish, Christian and Orthodox. On the eve of Rosh Hashana, they stacked their stands with pomegranates, leeks, fresh dates and pumpkins. They knew that on Saturdays Jews ate fish. Before Passover, they stocked up with *matzot* from Marseilles and Palestine, as well as every kind of dried fruit.

'I think that Enrico would benefit from a French education,' Pinchas Nahum declared.

Back in Tripoli, his children had been educated in Italian, but in Egypt French was the *lingua franca*, spoken not only by the Turko-Egyptian élite, but also by many foreign minorities. So Enrico was sent to a French school.

At home, however, the family continued to speak Italian, but took an unusual step for middle-class non-Moslems in ensuring that Enrico also learned to read and write Arabic. Most Europeans only spoke kitchen Arabic. It was English, the medium of Egypt's business and official communications, which Enrico stumbled over. Since his father had marked out a career for him in commerce, he changed his mind about the French school and transferred Enrico to an English one. At the synagogue, Enrico's linguistic education was completed with lessons in Hebrew.

If Enrico's mother, Giulia, felt disoriented by the move to Cairo, it was soon remedied by the arrival from Malta of her sister, Emma. Emma, as her Maltese cousins never fail to point out, was plain. Lanky and with a wire-drawn neck, she had failed to find a husband among the island's minuscule pool of suitors. In Cairo, a widower with a small daughter was found for her. In 1910, she presented Isaac Pinto with a second daughter, Ida. When Isaac died only three years later, Emma crossed the Mediterranean back to Malta.

At the age of fifteen, Enrico Nahum's formal education came to an end. He was now apprenticed to the import-export firm of family friends. For the first six months, he worked without pay from seven in the morning until midnight. For the rest of his Dickensian indenture, he received one Napoleon (approximately $1) a week. This regime was meant to toughen him for the time when he would join his father in business.

His informal education continued especially after the outbreak of World War I. For most Egyptians, the Allied soldiers pouring into their country on leave from Gallipoli and Palestine were an alien horde. In the first volume of his Cairo trilogy, Naguib Mahfouz describes how Australian troops terrorised the local population with their drunken sprees and rowdiness. They crowded into camps with other troops around the cities like invaders from another planet. But among them Jewish soldiers were always welcomed into the Nahum household. Every Australian child of my generation has grown up with Gallipoli stamped on his consciousness and so I wonder how many young men who helped Enrico make progress with his English were later to die on the shores of Turkey.

The Nahums were a religiously observant family but, by World War I, they, like many Egyptian Jews, were fairly secular. As most of them felt at ease in Egyptian society, they considered Zionism as no more than a remote political ideology, an offshoot of German imperialism. Just two years after Enrico's birth in 1899, Theodore Herzl, drawing upon the long tradition of messianic hope in the restoration of the Jews to a homeland in Palestine, had convened the First Zionist Congress. Pinchas was already resident in Cairo when, in 1903, the Khedive declared himself willing to grant an area in the Sinai peninsula for Jewish settlement. This startling offer was, however, soon withdrawn.

Most middle-class Egyptian Jews thought of Egypt as their home. Many of them still benefited from the system of Capitulations, which remained in existence even after the dismantling of the Ottoman Empire at the end of World War I. Why should they not feel comfortable when they were exempt from conscription nor could their property be confiscated?

With Tripoli in Italian hands since 1912, it was not clear what the nationality of Pinchas and his children was, but they also thrived in Egypt's general climate of tolerance. Nationality was not an issue that bothered them at this stage. If they were worried about the rise of Egyptian nationalism as promoted by the pro-independence *Wafd*, they were lulled into a sense of security by the party's temporary eclipse in the wake of the assassination of the British Commander-in-Chief. The conservative Turkish élite picked up the reins of power again and most Jews breathed a sigh of relief.

Politics did not at this stage greatly impinge on the young Enrico's consciousness, although it seems to me that they were always there hard at his heels. With Europe constantly undermining the East, the sense of security most of Egypt's foreigners felt was, with hindsight, very fragile. But Enrico was too busy building a career and enjoying himself to ponder such matters. He honed his compact body by working out on the parallel bars at Cairo's German Gymnastics Club and loved to go running. Only tennis bored him a little.

When he discovered opera, he was bowled over. He learned arias from them, undeterred by even the soupiest Wagnerian melodies. In the evening, he rushed to the Opera House through crowded streets and lanes, slaloming round men in *jellabahs* and trying not to bump into veiled matrons. Ignoring the clamouring of street vendors, he dodged through avenues congested with slow pedestrians, donkey carts, trolleys and cars. The air was pungent with the smell of incense mingled with the dung of shabby animals. Flies hovered above in stagnant clouds. At the theatre, Enrico left all these oriental scenes behind and merged into a European world of classical music or plays written in iambic pentameter.

From March until May, the *khamsim*, the putative Ninth Plague of Egypt, whipped leaves around the municipal gardens. In spite of Giulia's efforts to keep a spotless house for her family, everything would be covered in a thick film of dust. Still, it was a comfortable home. She attended to all of Enrico's domestic needs. Meals were ready when he returned from the shop. His clothes were laid out, washed and pressed for the next day's work. After the death of Pinchas, Enrico's father, the symbiosis between Enrico and his mother grew stronger.

Enrico's business interests were varied. He was agent to a number of European pharmaceutical firms, selling proprietary medicinal products. These days, when Jews are not welcome in most of the Middle East, it seems unimaginable that Enrico travelled freely in Palestine, Lebanon, Syria and Iraq as the representative of publishers Hodder and Stoughton. He was also 'Our Man in Cairo' for Hazell, Watson, Viney Ltd. His photograph can be found in the company history published to celebrate their centenary; in it, he appears alongside their other agents scattered throughout the British Empire. He is wearing frameless round glasses, his hairline is receding and an imposing nose seems to tug his thin lips upwards in a tense grimace. In 1932, those tight lips give him the air of a man about to be frozen into a mother-dominated middle age. In need of a break from work and family, he has decided to take a cruise.

\* \* \*

In the summer of the same year, Sadie Berman, a schoolteacher, crossed the Atlantic from Boston, Massachusetts. In Europe, she boarded a ship for a journey that would take her round the historic sites of the Cradle of Civilisation. Her reward to herself. The daughter of Latvian immigrants, she had already been working for a number of years, first in order to pay her way through college, then to get through teacher training school. She was a tiny, delicate woman, the kind who makes men feel protective. Her liveliness attracted several gentlemen passengers. When she removed her beret, worn tantalisingly *à la midinette*, her dark hair came tumbling down. As a young girl she had grown it so long that it reached down to the back of her knees.

Sadie was not drawn to any of the men who buzzed around her. She had noticed one man, a little older, who held himself back. He was not handsome, but she liked his wiriness, his slim wrists, the way he affected nonchalance by crossing his legs as he sat sipping his coffee. Like a sophisticate, he drank it black and bitter. She learned that his name was Enrico Nahum and that he was taking time off from a business in Cairo.

When people fall in love, there is sometimes a sense of instant recognition. At other times, it is the unknown that draws them most powerfully. To a young American, Enrico was exotic, the embodiment of the East. As an educated 'gal', Sadie might not have read the novels of Elinor Glyn, but she must have at least seen pictures of Valentino in his full eastern regalia. Enrico had the advantage over a fictional Sheikh in that he possessed a European polish, a commonplace among the merchant classes of the Levant.

He was not looking for a wife, but he found Sadie's vivacity irresistible. She was a modern, working woman, very different from the women he knew in Cairo. Even when well educated, most of them led lives bound by convention and tradition.

It was pure serendipity that Sadie was also Jewish, though she made it clear that her family, like so many immigrants in the New World, had abandoned strict religious observance. She and Enrico strolled round the decks of the ship, discussing not love, but the nature of Judaism.

I imagine an exciting mix of intellectual and sexual tension between them. I know he spoke to her gently of the beauty of Judaism's rituals because he spoke gently of them to me, with a touching simplicity and a shrug of the shoulders when I lost concentration.

'I have no wish to impose my views. I only hope that you will come to see things for yourself,' is what he said to me decades later and so I hear him uttering the same words to Sadie.

Sadie and he agreed to meet again in Europe the following summer. In his letters to Boston, Enrico continued to debate religion.

Giulia was dismayed. She could not understand why her son had set his heart on a complete stranger, a woman travelling unchaperoned. On her next trip abroad, Sadie had got the message and brought her mother along with her. Giulia could see that Jennie Wagenheim Berman was a perfectly respectable, plump Jewish matron.

The following autumn, Jennie accompanied her daughter to Cairo as the sole representative of the Berman clan at Sadie's and Enrico's wedding.

The shipboard romance had survived. It was the bit that came afterwards that was to prove more difficult, the clash between East and West as embodied in this newly married couple. Daphne du Maurier, who lived in Cairo as a young bride at the same time as Sadie, gives us an idea of how repelled a Western woman might have felt. She wrote of her disgust of the natives defecating in the streets and added that most people had a limp or a sore. She was overwhelmed by the stench outdoors. Sadie's judgements were less harsh, but she was also depressed by the heat, dust, flies and battered animals. She could not get used to the clamouring beggars.

Having once had a career, she hated having nothing to do because she was not expected to keep busy by taking up paid employment. Nor was housework an option as Giulia was in charge of the servants and cooking. Giulia did the shopping too, arguing that as Sadie spoke no Arabic, she would not be able to haggle with traders for the best bargains. With Enrico out at work all day, the suburban household in Garden City was stifling.

So Sadie threw herself into the only life open to a middle-class wife, that of the socialite. It was an existence she could not have dreamed of in America and a world away from her parents' and grandparents' origins in the *shtetls* of the Baltic. Visits to the dressmaker filled in time. As did taking tea at Groppi's or on the terrace at Shepheard's Hotel. On Gezira Island, she relaxed at the sporting club, which had its own polo fields, golf course, and tennis courts, cricket pitch and gardens. To blasé Europeans, this way of life might have seemed provincial, but Sadie was, at least initially, dazzled by it.

On Friday nights, as usual at the Nahums', it was open house after synagogue and she enjoyed playing the generous hostess.

It is also part of a society lady's role to be benevolent. But Sadie took her charity work at the *Goutte de Lait* seriously. This was one of the many institutions established by the Jewish community to help its many paupers. There were also hospitals and clinics for Jews as well as soup kitchens for the sick, all subsidised by donations and property taxes. They existed alongside associations providing interest-free loans for the penniless, funds to ensure that girls from poor families received a dowry and charities assisting Jewish travellers. These were all part of a long Mediterranean tradition of Jewish welfare institutions.

The *Goutte de Lait* had been founded by Isaac Benaroio. Seeing so many malnourished children in the community, he undertook to provide them with a breakfast of *café au lait* and a huge chunk of bread. By 1919 the charity was clothing and feeding 450 children. A year later it was providing them with vocational training. Enrico was the association's treasurer.

In 1934 Sadie returned to Boston, snubbing the standard of hygiene and medical care offered by Cairo's hospitals. She wanted her first child to be born somewhere 'civilised'. The birth of Ruth Phyllis was followed eighteen months later by that of Jeanne for which Sadie made the same sea-crossing to the east coast of America. If her mother-in-law thought her a bit above herself, Enrico was simply pleased to be a father.

For Sadie, each return to Cairo was hard, a confirmation of the distance between her past and present lives and of the huge cultural gap between East and West. When Jeanne fell ill, the women of the household busied themselves preparing cupping glasses. As Sadie watched helplessly, they dowsed cotton in alcohol, stuffed the glasses with it and set it alight. The glasses were then applied to the small child's back. It seemed to Sadie to be some ancient primitive ritual and she did not hesitate to say so. When one of the cupping glasses slipped and badly scalded Jeanne's back, Sadie refused to continue with the treatment. Her tolerance was beginning to crack.

But she continued with the social whirl. An Egyptian *ayah* was hired to take care of the girls. There were parties and outings in the Ezbekiah Gardens alongside other children with their nannies and the kites scavenging for crumbs. Summer was the season of the exodus to Port Saïd, Alexandria or Palestine.

In 1934, Giulia's sister, Emma, came back to Egypt. With her, she brought her daughter, Ida, now twenty-four years old. The problem of finding a suitor in Malta had arisen in yet another generation. Again one more generation crossed the Mediterranean in search of a spouse. Giulia mumbled that it was a pity Enrico had not waited for Ida to grow up. She would have preferred him to have married 'one of his own' and not a foreigner like Sadie.

These were troubled times in Egypt. Italy invaded Ethiopia in 1935 and Italian expansionism was becoming a growing menace. Egypt had ceased to be a British Protectorate in 1922, but in 1936, Nahas Pasha's *Wafd* government signed the Anglo-Egyptian Treaty under which Britain undertook to defend Egypt and the route to India. For a while, the country's minorities felt reassured.

In the same year, however, the Convention of Montreux abolished the Capitulations. Increasing anti-Zionist propaganda, linked inevitably to anti-Jewish sentiments, was also becoming a feature of the Egyptian political arena. In 1938, the Moslem Brotherhood called for a boycott of Jewish businesses and shops. To counteract these actions, local Jewish leaders drew upon their extensive contacts with Egyptian politicians. Still, Enrico, like every other non-Moslem who owned a business, felt uneasy. There was nowhere he could turn to because those Jews who had lost the protection of foreign embassies when the Capitulations were rescinded were not, as had been promised, granted Egyptian passports. Their status remained unclear.

Meanwhile, war in Europe seemed more and more likely. Enrico was worried for his family. In August 1939 Ali Maher was made Prime Minister Lieutenant of the Realm, and General Wavell arrived to help build up the defences of the Delta and Western Desert.

'I'm not sure it's going to be safe in Egypt for much longer,' Enrico told Sadie. 'Perhaps you should take the children to America. Go and see the World Fair. Stay until the storm passes.'

While Sadie and their daughters were in New York, Germany invaded Poland. In September, Britain declared war on Germany. Egypt thus broke off all ties with Britain's enemy and placed its airfields and railways at the disposal of British forces. By April 1940, Denmark and Norway were occupied. The Low Countries were overrun in May. On 10 June 1940 Mussolini declared war on the Allies. By July it looked as if Egypt was going to suffer the same fate as Ethiopia.

Enrico sent word to Sadie to stay where she was. She, in turn, pleaded with him to join her and the children in Boston. But he could not, would not leave his ageing mother behind. Nor was he able to transfer money easily to the US and he had no idea what he could do to make a living if he went to America.

As the situation worsened and money transfers from Enrico ceased completely, Sadie had no choice but to go back to work. If she had stayed in Egypt she probably would have provided tea and cakes for Allied soldiers on leave. It was what Enrico's cousin Ida was doing. And having a wonderful time playing hostess to Allied soldiers. A photograph of Ida taken at the time shows a young woman looking a little like the captain of a girls' hockey team. She is tall. Her face is long and her top teeth slightly overlap her bottom lip. In another photograph, she is sitting on a snooty camel and in yet another she is dressed in the costume of a Tripolitanian Jewish woman, her feet bare and with giant hoops in her ear lobes.

While in Boston, Sadie donned a hard hat and went to work at the Boston Naval Yards. She became responsible again, a breadwinner.

'We're only here for the duration,' her daughters chanted.

But the months turned into years and the memory of their father grew blurred. In a short time, both Phyllis and Jeanne forgot their French and Arabic and became monolingual young Americans.

Sadie did her best to keep up their religious education. She sent them for lessons at a Reform synagogue and to Jewish summer camps. But it was all rather half-hearted. By 1941 their return to Egypt was only a remote possibility.

For France had fallen and the French Navy in the Mediterranean and the French Army in Syria could no longer be relied upon to protect the Delta. By 13 April 1942 Tobruk was besieged. By mid-May, Sollum, on the westernmost fringe of Egypt, was taken by Axis forces. In the middle of June, Alexandria was bombed. 140,000 Allied soldiers now poured into and around Cairo.

Among them was young Captain Douglas A. Tayar (Duggie). As a guest at the Nahums' he made Aunt Giulia laugh with his singing. And she amused him by reciting the birth dates of all the members of the British Royal Family. Ida introduced him to pretty young women. It was at this time that Enrico took him to the Jewish orphanage about which he wrote home.

'The girls were a bit rude and began asking me a lot of questions in Hebrew, which were translated by the teacher. I felt important and finished the day with an awful headache.'

Enrico also took him to a Friday night service. When they arrived he grabbed hold of the synagogue caretaker's arm. The man was shabbily dressed.

'Wouldn't you say he needs a coat more than you do?' Enrico asked Duggie.

This was typical of Enrico. It seemed logical to him. If Duggie had other good clothes to wear, he could surely part with his over-coat. So Duggie divested himself of this heavy possession and only regretted it when he found himself on the other side of the Mediter-ranean, shivering through a Tuscan winter. There was something about Enrico that made people want to please him. Perhaps it was the lack of the self-righteous in his goodness.

I suppose, Duggie thought, since his wife and daughters are in America, he has transferred his gift for affection to the needy. He knew little about the absent wife and the two little girls whose pho-tos Enrico kept between the pages of his prayer book. There they were, all three with big dark eyes, staring shyly at the camera. In 1942, they had been in Boston for two years already.

In June of the same year, Tobruk fell and the Eighth Army, of which Duggie's regiment was a part, retreated. By 29 June, Rommel's troops were only sixty miles from Alexandria. In early July, British HQ began burning documents. Women and children were put on trains leaving for Palestine or South Africa. But others saw no point in leaving and, as El Alamein held, those who had left started returning to Cairo. On 12 November, the Eighth Army, under Field Marshall Montgomery, recaptured Tobruk.

*    *    *

The war had a huge impact on Egyptian economics and politics. Large numbers of agricultural workers poured into Cairo and Alexandria, exacerbating the problems of urban growth. The gap between rich and poor was especially blatant in the capital where the rich ostentatiously displayed their wealth. The presence of Allied soldiers also created social tensions. Anti-British feeling ran high. In 1944 the Balfour Day commemorations deteriorated into riots. In Cairo's Muski district, stores owned by Jews were plundered and a number of Jewish homes looted. Jews, after all, were considered to be pro-British and supporters of the corrupt British-backed Nahas regime.

When calm was restored, Chief Rabbi Haim Nahum Effendi re-affirmed the Jewish community's allegiance to the Egyptian state. He also reiterated his wish that the Allies would find a homeland for the Jews in a place other than the narrow confines of Palestine. In spite of growing Egyptian nationalism, the community still seemed to think it would be able to continue living as it had done for decades. Enrico and Ida went to their clubs, attended services at the synagogue and were guests at parties. For a short while, it was possible to ignore the fact that in an Islamic state, the status of non-Moslem minorities would inevitably change.

Throughout their six years of enforced separation, Sadie pleaded with Enrico to leave Egypt and settle in the United States. There seemed to be no watertight explanation of why he would not. She felt resentful that he gave so little consideration to her wishes. Keeping that feeling churning inside her, at the end of 1945 she prepared to return to the Middle East.

As she arranged for new passports, booked passages and shopped for items she knew she would not find in Cairo, Phyllis and Jeanne were spinning with excitement. Throughout their years in Boston, they had been telling their friends about their father who lived in the Land of the Pharaohs. They spoke of the nannies they had once had, the servants.

'You're such liars!' their school friends taunted. Everyone could see that Sadie was poor. The only childminder she could afford was her own mother.

In November 1945 Sadie and her daughters set sail on the SS *Santa Paula*. In the officers' quarters, they had a cabin all to themselves, with nine bunks. It seemed the fairytale had already resumed even before they set foot ashore at Port Saïd ten days later. Enrico was on the dockside to meet them. The small girls held back.

'Don't be silly,' Sadie laughed. 'It's your father. Give him a hug.'

Everyone was nervous and shy. Realising that this might happen, Enrico had arranged for them to spend a few days in Port Saïd. This would enable them to adjust to being a family again. He was, anyway, not in a hurry to return to the apartment where Giulia had died just a few months before.

It was to be their last period of happiness as a united family.

After the Garden City house where they had lived before the war, the Maadi apartment into which Enrico had moved seemed terribly small. Sadie hated it.

'We can't afford anything bigger now, my dear,' Enrico said.

In the wake of the Egyptianisation of the economy, it was becoming harder and harder for non-Egyptians to carry out business. Enrico was finding it increasingly difficult to receive imports and he was living on the proceeds of stock bought before the war. His expenses were greater too: the fees for the Cairo School for American Children; the Sporting Club dues for all four family members; the running costs of a larger household. Sadie was not going to be able to live in the old style.

But a return to the old way of married life was not necessarily what she wanted. Like so many women separated from husbands during the fighting, she had learned to be a decision-maker. For six years she had not had to defer to anyone. So she did not ask Enrico's permission when she went looking for a job. It was the most sensible thing to do in their relatively reduced circumstances.

'I've found work as a relief librarian at the girls' school,' she announced at home.

Enrico's affronted silence was worse than a slap. She could not understand it. It seemed so unlike the gentle man she thought she had known. So unreasonable.

'We'd like to speak to Madame Nahum,' tradesmen would croon as she opened the door to them.

'You are speaking to Madame Nahum.' Sadie, her daughters tell me, never shouted, but she certainly must have felt like doing so now. For here were hawkers and stallholders telling her that she couldn't possibly be Madame Nahum.

'She's a tall lady,' they responded with humility. 'Very elegant.'

'What do you mean?'

The truth was that, during Sadie's absence, Ida and her mother had moved into the Maadi flat. It was all presumably above board though no one has been able to tell me. Enrico and Ida were first cousins and this was a practical arrangement allowing Ida to look after Enrico's mother also. But tradesmen had got used to thinking of Ida as the mistress of the household.

Bitter recriminations followed. Bouts of accusations and door-slamming. Then long silences. Phyllis and Jeanne were distressed. They watched in dismay as their father moved out of the main bedroom into the spare room no bigger than a cupboard.

Enrico felt harassed not only by the strife at home, but also by the growing crisis in the Middle East. His business and his marriage were disintegrating before his eyes. So was the political situation.

In the United Nations, the Palestine Question was under debate. The Egyptian Ambassador intervened with warnings that a wave of anti-Jewish feeling would ensue throughout the Arab world should Palestine be partitioned. On Balfour Day 1946 and 1947 the Egyptian government offered police protection to all Jewish institutions. In December 1947 it felt obliged to deny publicly rumours that Jews had caused the recent cholera epidemic. To the descendants of the people expelled from Spain and Portugal, this sort of accusation had a familiar and chilling ring; it was the discourse of European anti-Semitism now transferred to Eastern soil. When the UN voted in favour of partition, demonstrators attacked shops owned by Europeans, Jews and Copts.

In 1948 the tension between Enrico and Sadie came to a head. They decided to divorce. Enrico insisted that this be carried out following all the due processes of Jewish law. Sadie found this outrageous. In the presence of witnesses, Enrico handed her the *get,* the bill of divorce. Its archaic wording appalled her: 'The power of divorce is vested in the husband in the event of his having found something unseemly in the behaviour of his wife . . .' Sadie felt utterly humiliated.

Pulling Phyllis and Jeanne out of school, she left for Boston. She never saw or spoke to Enrico again and forbade her daughters from communicating with him.

* * *

With a failed marriage to a woman from the West behind him, Enrico now looked no further than his cousin Ida. Now man and wife, they clung on to a way of life that was becoming more and more precarious. They could not, however, imagine another country where they would feel as much at ease as they did in Egypt. Anyway, if Ida, as a British subject, could leave, Enrico had no passport allowing him to settle in another country.

In Maadi, he and Ida continued in a semblance of their old routines. At dawn, Ida would rise and open all the windows to let the cool air in. Before the sun rose, she closed the shutters, creating a cocoon of coolness indoors. She then dressed and waved Enrico goodbye as he left for his showrooms which were virtually empty now. Still, it was important to maintain an air of busy-ness. In the afternoons, Ida went to Maadi Sports' Club where she met friends, took tea, played tennis. Between April and May, she went swimming.

By the early 1950s, the backdrop to their lives was the Egyptian struggle against the British presence on the Suez Canal. When, in 1952, forty Egyptian policemen were killed in street riots, Ida and Enrico sat holed up in their apartment as demonstrators burned down large parts of modern Cairo. The attacks did not target Jews specifically, but were aimed at all those benefiting directly from British rule, which included the Jews. It was becoming clear that Egyptians were no longer prepared to support the old social and political order. The attacks were a prelude to the takeover the following July of the Egyptian State by the Free Officers led by Colonel Nasser.

We in the West have a pale idea of how heroic a figure Gamal Abdel Nasser was not only to Egyptians, but also to millions of people throughout the Arab world. His immense popularity would be unimaginable even by the standards of today's pop stars. Whenever he broadcast one of his three- or four-hour-long speeches, crowds huddled round transistors hanging on to his every word. Songs written in his honour blared out all day on radio and on street loudspeakers.

If Nasser's modernisation policies had succeeded, he might have been able to avert many Moslems from thinking of the state as the emanation of one religion. The rise of Moslem fundamentalism was to a large extent a reaction to his military failures and to his inability to put an end to Egypt's chronic underdevelopment. Nasser was no friend of the religious establishment. They tried several times to have him assassinated. He led Egypt not in the name of Islam, but in the name of the nation-state.

In this respect he was Egypt's Jews' best hope. In fact, he took great pains to reassure all religious minorities living in Egypt that their way of life would continue as before. Enrico and Ida could stop feeling anxious. After all, Nasser and the Free Officers had invited Chief Rabbi Nahum to attend national celebrations as the rabbi had done in the days of the monarchy while General Muhammad Najib paid official visits to synagogues and Jewish schools.

But most Jews did not feel reassured. Many now began preparing for departure. If they were fortunate enough to have family and friends abroad or to possess foreign passports, they got out fairly easily. In each district, almost overnight, neighbours packed their belongings and left for Italy, France, Canada and Australia. When I was a child in Sydney, many of my mother's friends and French-speaking colleagues were such exiles from Egypt. That they had come to Australia with whole families intact made them exotic to me. There were grandmothers and aunts within easy reach, something that I did not have.

Those who did not have the means to leave Egypt continued to hang on. For Enrico, the problem was less a financial one than the fact that he had no nationality. Israel would have willingly granted him a passport, but there was no direct route of emigration between Egypt and the new Jewish State. So he and Ida swallowed their uneasiness when police came round to the showrooms looking for a certain Dino Judah Nahum.

'There's no one of that name at this address,' Enrico said truthfully. His elder brother Dino had been dead for years, but his name was still on Enrico's shopfront from the distant days when Dino had run the business with their father Pinchas. The police wanted to interrogate Dino as the registered owner of the shop.

'We believe that these premises belong to a Jew,' they explained, but did not delve too hard.

Enrico was relieved. He had heard of people being arrested for simply applying to leave the country. Soon, however, it seemed that he and Ida would never be able to get out. In 1953 a member of a Zionist Youth Movement was put on trial accused of having tried to undermine the rapprochement between the Egyptian government and the United States. This case further damaged relations between the local authorities and the Jewish community.

In October 1956 a decisive blow to the shreds of inter-communal harmony was struck when Israeli, French and British forces attacked the Suez Canal. To Egyptians, this secretly co-ordinated campaign represented ultimate proof of the link between Zionism and Imperialism. Mass arrests followed. British and French nationals were expelled with a number of stateless Jews. Another 40,000 Jews left of their own volition.

Ida, who had grown up in Malta and was a British subject, was placed under house arrest.

'It's not your fault,' her kindly Egyptian neighbours tried to console her. 'We don't blame you personally.' No one could think of her as the enemy. So they sent their children upstairs every day to keep her company while she was under detention.

By 1961 Enrico's business had collapsed completely. The government embarked on a series of nationalisations, depriving most non-Egyptians of their livelihoods. Only about eight thousand Jews now remained in the country. Their existence became more and more precarious.

To fill in long days spent without employment, Enrico undertook the running of the centuries-old Jewish cemetery at Bassatine. Once the special branch line to the graveyard had ceased operation, it was a long, sad, hot hike to reassure his own and the community's ghosts. As the circle tightened around him and Ida, he whiled away the creeping hours by restoring Bibles. Pasting and patching, humming quietly to himself, he thus nursed his anxieties.

It was the Arab-Israeli War of 1967 that finally galvanised him into action. The authorities began rounding up Jews, sending them to prison camps in Abou Zabaal, Tourah, the Barrages and the Citadel. The United Nations and the Red Cross tried in vain to obtain the release of detainees. The Arab League, led by Syria and Iraq, was exerting pressure on Nasser to rid Egypt of its remaining Jews. Nasser responded by further random arrests.

Before each arrest, the police ransacked property. Afterwards, they took over the apartments whose occupants had been evicted. In the Muski district, two policemen sodomised a girl. A seventy-three-year-old doctor, locked in a cell, had his trousers removed and his cellmates could hear him groaning and weeping all night. Such lurid stories fuelled even more frightening rumours. Ida and Enrico could no longer doubt that departure was the only solution.

Foreign embassies hurriedly issued passports to almost everybody applying for them. The Spanish Embassy, accepting claims of connections with the Iberian peninsula dating back to before the Inquisition, did the same for any applicant asserting Sephardic descent. Enrico now began a round of the embassies. He would not be able to leave unless one of them provided him with the necessary papers.

In the end, it was the most unlikely European country that granted him a passport. For more than a hundred and fifty years, the Nahums had had in their possession a Dutch *hanukkia* made of brass and embossed with a tulip and tilted coffee pot, the emblem of one of the Dutch ports. It was, so the family story goes, a gift presented to a venerable Nahum ancestor who had taken Dutch merchants across the desert from North Africa all the way to India.

Enrico trudged to the Netherlands Embassy, carrying the candleholder in a soft cloth. He waited patiently for an official to emerge from an office. Slowly, he unfolded the cloth and recounted the story of his ancestor's caravanserai.

'You need go no further. When do you wish to travel?'

On the basis of this most tenuous link with the Low Countries, the official issued Enrico with a Dutch passport.

At the end of 1967 he and Ida left for Amsterdam.

Aged sixty-eight and fifty-seven respectively, they did not find it easy to adjust to life in the Netherlands. They first found themselves living in an Ashkenaz community whose customs differed from their own. Ida went to work sewing clothes for the dead. The rules were strict. She was forbidden to tie a knot in the thread and everything had to be stitched by hand. I can imagine her peering through her pebble-shell glasses, but sitting always with her back very straight for I never saw her slouching. She would not have complained, but she was happier when she found the same kind of work within the Sephardic community. They allowed her to use a sewing machine.

Enrico began making plans to settle in Israel and finally, in 1971, he and Ida returned to the shores of the Mediterranean. Physically, it is a short distance from Cairo to Tel Aviv. The drab suburb they moved to, however, was a world away from their pre-war life in Egypt. To get to Bat Yam, you drive through Jaffa. Not the restored, bijou old city, but the Palestinian one, with its low concrete houses, shabby façades and jobless men hanging about in cave-like *cafés*. The suburban apartment blocks are grey, with metal shutters like armoured tanks. This is where Ida and Enrico lived for the rest of their lives.

✳ ✳ ✳

In the late 1950s Enrico had resumed relations with his two daughters. Unknown to Sadie, Jeanne had visited him and Ida in Cairo on her way home from Turkey. It was another fourteen years, however, before Phyllis was to meet Enrico again. By then Sadie was in a nursing home, ill, hardly aware of what was happening around her, but still clutching to her fury against her former husband. The nurses were bemused.

'Who is it who has made your mother so angry with the world?' the resident psychiatrist asked Phyllis.

Having lived with her mother's rage for decades, Phyllis felt that it would serve no purpose to tell Sadie that she had invited Enrico and Ida to her son's *Bar Mitzvah* in Boston.

'I'd like to see your mother again,' Enrico told his elder daughter.

'That would not be a good idea,' Phyllis replied with great sadness. 'But I can take you to the home so that you can at least see how nice it is.'

So she drove her father to the other side of town and sat with him in the car in front of the home. He did not catch a glimpse of Sadie as he had hoped he might.

She died shortly afterwards and so their differences, which were basically the differences between East and West, were never laid properly to rest.

*Tunisian independence forced a difficult and painful choice*
*upon the Jews of Tunisia. They could no longer be*
*satisfied with a history created by others in the hope that it*
*would not be too unfavourable to them. They had to*
*choose, for themselves and for their children, the country in*
*which they wished to live, the nation with which they*
*intended to share their destiny.*

PAUL SEBAG *Histoire des Juifs de Tunisie*

CHAPTER SEVEN

*ninette*

When on 5 June 1967 Egypt, backed by a coalition of Arab states, attacked Israel, the Nahums could no longer delude themselves that there was still a place for them in an Islamic society.

For another member of my father's family, Ninette Israel, resident in Sfax in southern Tunisia, living in North Africa had also become a problem. The events in the Middle East saw hundreds of demonstrators pouring into districts where Jews lived. Policemen stood by as men smashed shop windows and tried to burn down Tunis's Great Synagogue. The Scrolls of the Law were lost in the flames. There were, however, no serious casualties and President Bourguiba went on air to condemn the violence and reassure the Jewish population.

These attacks came after several years of petty humiliations. Walking down the street on the day Tunisia declared its independence in 1956, the husband of one of my mother's cousins had his hat knocked off by a passer-by elated to be able to give at least one European his comeuppance. Each time Pierrot bent down to pick up the hat and put it back on his head, the man knocked it off. He did this again and again. Later, when his employer, having mismanaged his business, did a midnight flit, Pierrot was arrested in his place. But it was a Moslem fellow-prisoner who kept up Pierrot's morale during the three months spent in gaol by playing endless card games with him. Pierrot, who felt completely naked when only bare-headed, kept his hat perched firmly on his head throughout his imprisonment.

After the Six Day war, the mass departures from Tunisia were speeded up. When the Jews left, they left behind them more than two thousand years of presence in this part of North Africa. Seeing Zionism as the only solution to precarious tenure in any place other than a Jewish state, some of them left for Israel. Others emigrated to France. After seventy-five years of French rule in North Africa, they at least did not have to learn a new language there. Anyway, they were partly acculturated through the French education system by which, it was once said, you could set your clocks. At any given time of the day, French school inspectors knew precisely what textbook each child in Paris, Algiers and Tunis was hunched over.

There were people, however, who decided against leaving. Some were frozen by inertia. A small contingent stayed on as an act of faith in the new regime. Yet some remained because they had no choice.

This was the case with Ninette. Self-employed, and with no pension rights, departure would have meant becoming financially dependent on relatives abroad. Her British passport, the legacy of her Maltese-born father, gave her no right of abode in the UK or anywhere else in Europe. She became one of the countless people cast adrift by the twentieth-century's historical upheavals.

\* \* \*

In November 1995 I set out on the last leg of my Mediterranean journey to visit Ninette. On my first evening in Sfax, I found myself seated at her dining table in the company of an old man. In the dim light cast by one naked bulb, his whispered conversation lent a conspiratorial air to our tiny gathering.

'They've gone. Both – the father and the son,' he said.

I could hardly make out the words, but gathered that two unnamed acquaintances had left for *ha'aretz* or The Land. For Jews there is no need to specify that what is meant is Israel.

The stranger sighed and hugged himself. For warmth or perhaps comfort. Bending creakily, he fished out a parcel from his fraying basket. Like Ninette, he was in his eighties but, unlike her, he was fit enough to be able to go out. He had undertaken to collect and deliver her order of kosher meat each time the rabbi from Tunis came on his monthly visit to Sfax to supervise the ritual slaughter of animals. This time the soggy parcel came with the news that two more men had left the community. It was no longer possible to form a *minian*. I had heard this kind of story before and pricked up my ears.

While Ninette shuffled on swollen feet to the kitchen to fetch the old man some fruit, he turned to me.

'I'm a jeweller. No, not retired. Can't afford it. I used to own a shop in the *souks*. These days I work from home. But it's hard to get hold of materials.' He sighed again, allowing his spine to sink down further.

I sympathised. This encouraged him. He suggested that if I had a ring or a brooch to repair, he could do the job for me for a reasonable price. My left hand shot up to my ear before I remembered that I had just recently had one of the earrings I was wearing re-soldered. It made me feel uneasy, gave me the same sense of guilt I feel when I glance away from homeless people begging in the street. I know I have a comfortable home to return to.

'Co-habitation,' the jeweller, said in a murmur, 'is so . . . difficult.'

I assumed he meant Jews and Arabs living as neighbours. I waited to hear some stunning revelation about the position of Sfax's tiny Jewish community within the wider Moslem one. But as the man

kept glancing over his shoulder, I slowly realised that he was referring to someone sitting on the other side of the glass door, which
divided the sitting room into two separate lounge areas. A dust-
encrusted curtain, hanging by two rings, partly concealed a figure
sitting on a chair in the darkness. We were being watched and over-
heard. But neither Ninette nor her visitor asked the person in the
shadows to come out and be introduced.

It was twenty years since I had last seen Ninette. With relatives
from all over the world, we had been invited to Lausanne for the
engagement party of a young cousin, a boisterous family affair and,
as far as my English boyfriend was concerned, totally confusing. All
those Israels and Benmussas. He knew none of his own cousins,
uncles or aunts, and the sheer number of mine amazed him.
Although I tried to explain my relationship to each of the guests, he
soon gave up trying to follow me.

Ninette, one of my father's numerous first cousins, was sixty-five
then, a plump and vigorous woman. She had been placed in charge
of Aunt Emilia, my grandmother's youngest sister, shepherding her
about with patience and good humour. Whenever Emilia snatched
one of the Swiss chocolate bars intended as a present for the guests,
and stuffed it into her Queen-Mother handbag, Ninette discreetly
recovered the stolen gift. With a delicate smile, she returned it to its
proper place next to the guest's nameplate.

In 1995 Ninette was older than her Aunt Emilia had been at the
time of this party. But whereas the family network had even twenty
years ago been strong enough to ensure that an unmarried niece
could be summoned from across the Mediterranean to take care of
an ageing aunt, now that Ninette was an old woman herself there
was no one to take care of her. Not even the woman sitting behind
the dusty curtain. For by the next day, I had ascertained that it was
a woman. She was younger than Ninette, able-bodied, and with hair
hennaed to the colour of blood oranges. Her make-up was smudged
so that she looked like an exhausted clown following an afternoon
spent entertaining spoilt children.

Throughout my week-long stay in Sfax, no one introduced this woman to me, but I understood that she was Ninette's lodger. I also noticed that they spoke to each other as little as possible.

'Come,' Ninette snapped at me as she stuck her head out of her room. She did not want me to speak to that woman. I was her guest exclusively.

She had been expecting my visit for months, planning menus of local specialities. Some of the cakes and biscuits had been prepared so long in advance that they tasted mouldy. But I made an effort to eat what was set before me, knowing how important my being there was to Ninette. Apart from the jeweller, as far as I could see, there was no one left to come calling on her.

While the autumn sun warmed the air outside, we sat in her darkened apartment, talking about her life. Looking round what had once been my great-aunt Mary's salon, I was dismayed by the decay and dilapidation. A few pieces of dark and lugubrious furniture still remained from what had been Jonas Bouhnik's lavish wedding presents to his wife. They were dotted with woodworm holes. Damp patches had appeared on walls, where the paper had peeled off. On the ceiling, the frescoes of hunting scenes and blowsy flowers were almost completely cemented over. Only one Tiffany-style lampshade was left.

In contrast to the derelict interior of the apartment, the façade was receiving a fresh coat of brilliant white. Painters suspended in harnesses were daubing the Art Nouveau stucco vine leaves, morning glories and cherubs of this building designed at the turn of the century by the Sicilian architect Mone. The stained-glass window panels and the tiles of the staircase, with their intricate leaf motif in olive green, cream and mauve, spoke of a once-confident European presence in Tunisia. Before box-like constructions had been put up, blocking the water view, you could see the harbour from the balcony. Now, you could only smell its iodine whiff in the sticky air.

Through the open balcony window, a painter appeared. Like an extra in some surreal drama, he did not excuse himself, but marched across the room and left the apartment through another window at the side of the building. I wondered if it was lack of respect for an old woman or contempt for a Jew. Ninette seemed impervious to his presence each time he popped into the room.

In a week's time, President Ali would be passing through Sfax. The city council had decided that the president should not be offended by the sight of rundown buildings as he passed by in his speeding motorcade and so all the façades along the main avenue were being whitewashed.

'You should have seen this place once.' Ninette's eyes shone. 'Nothing but the best. Do you think I can sell this bedside table and the lamp for a good price?' she asked as I examined and admired them.

Throughout the week, she put this question to me several times about the few valuable items, still unsold, which she had inherited from Mary.

'They don't give me much for these things,' she said, speaking of her Arab neighbours.

It was not a reproach. She liked these people and knew that, for them, musty European furniture had no value. One man's antiques are often another man's junk. The neighbours only bought the things to help her out and were always willing to do her other favours such as sending the children on errands or allowing her to use their telephone.

On the ground floor, *Sidi* Trabelsi, the owner of the souvenir shop and the Hertz Car Rental outlet, received her mail. Until she and *Sidi* Trabelsi had come to this arrangement, the postman used to throw Ninette's mail away. The word 'Israel' being anathema to some Tunisians, we in the family learned to leave her surname off all correspondence, addressing envelopes only to Mlle Ninette, c/- Hertz Car Rentals.

\* \* \*

When Ninette was a young woman she would take her sewing machine out onto the balcony. At sunset, as the walls of the Arab city turned a pinkish gold and sparrows seethed in flocks in the palms lining the city's main avenue, she would drag out her chair and finish off a hem or a few buttonholes. As the muezzin's call lassooed through the cooling air, all the day's tensions would fall away.

Later, when everyone was asleep, Ninette returned to the balcony to smoke her one cigarette of the day. At her feet, her pet terrier snuggled and snuffled. From the sitting room came the voice of Caruso singing *E lucean le stelle* or the sound of Fritz Kreisler playing the *Méditation* from Massenet's 'Thaïs'. These were favourite records. In 1995, she had them still, with their original brown covers. Sometimes, above the fluctuating whistling static, she could pick up crooning on Radio Monte Carlo from across the Mediterranean.

Stories of true romance were her other great entertainment. She was pretty as a young woman, with high cheekbones, her features small and fine. As was the fashion in the 1930s, she used to pluck her eyebrows into pencil-thin lines. With her hair brushed off her face, you could see that her expression was one of frankness, though she does look tense in her passport photo. She would not have dreamt, however, of pouting for a portrait.

If only some handsome, feminist-minded man had come to woo her on her balcony, she said to me. 'Not the widower, of course,' she chuckled. In old age, she had no regrets on that count. 'Or the one who was a doctor and who Aunt Mary thought would do me nicely. Or that terribly short man. Imagine! He was so small I could have easily eaten a bowl of soup off the top of his head.'

There was an element of the bully about all these potential suitors. Living with Jonas Bouhnik, she had learned that men can be petulant and bossy. If that was what marriage was about, she preferred being single.

It was when her mother had died in 1917 that Ninette first realised that in the end we are all alone. At the time, she was just seven years old. 'It left a void which I have carried around with me all my life,' she confessed.

She remembered her father, Samuel, taking her to see her mother at the sanatorium in Nabeul, the old Phoenician city. Her mother had caught a cold, which soon developed into galloping consumption, a disease that had already killed four close members of her family.

'You mustn't kiss your mother,' everyone warned Ninette. This puzzled her. 'Don't touch her either.' That seemed very cruel. Especially as her mother was grieving for the death of a baby girl born a year before. Ninette would have liked to hug her mother, comfort her and be comforted.

'She won't survive the loss of the baby. You'd better take her home to die,' the doctors told Samuel. And when she died, he and his two remaining children, Ninette and Giacomino, vacated the contaminated apartment.

But there were plenty of family members around to reassure Ninette that her world had not been turned completely upside down. Her grandfather, Jacob Israel, was still alive. Ninette remembers him as the Terror of the Temple on Sfax's rue de la Synagogue.

That Ninette knew him radically changes my perspective of historical time. Jacob was born in 1834 and must surely have known people born in the eighteenth century, before the era of Jewish emancipation in Europe. When I touch Ninette's hand, I touch my connection with a past that seems far less remote because of her. Many of Jacob's descendants no longer claim any religious beliefs; the speed of the weakening of our ties to Judaism is brought home to me with force.

With the exception of Victor, Ninette met all of Jacob's children. She remembers Rebecca arriving from Cairo with her three offspring. She recalls Raphael, fabulously wealthy from his Peruvian rubber plantations, coming to Sfax to see his three youngest sisters. Every two years, he would set sail from South America, travelling to Paris and Tunis. In 1920, he arrived with his bride, the lovely

Gertie from Birmingham. All her nieces and nephews in Tunisia and in Malta have kept a vision of her English beauty, but none knows what became of her after she tired of the heat of the Amazon and separated from Raphael. The suites in luxury hotels, the coachmen in coaches bearing Raphael's invented coat-of-arms were not enough to make Gertie want to stay married. Ninette took note.

She never met the other Rubber Baron uncle, although he did come to Sfax once when she was a child and stayed at the Hôtel des Oliviers. Before his departure the following morning, he went to the cemetery to say *kaddish* over his mother's grave. This was a proper thing for a Jewish son to do even if, in South America, he was no longer a Jew.

Through her maternal grandmother, Zula Fellous, Ninette is connected to other Mediterranean Jewish communities, those of Algeria and the island of Djerba. So she is my link not only in time, but also in a space that reaches to other parts of the Mediterranean. Zula, who lived with and took care of Ninette and Giacomino after their mother's death, led a life not unlike that of Moslem women. She was the one who taught Maltese-born Aunt Mary how to cook local dishes. At Yom Kippur, they baked eggs in pastry baskets. At Passover, there were two boiled eggs not one. The bitter herbs were dipped in wine and not in salt water. At Shavuout, they ate *bollo*, a sort of pound cake made with oil rather than butter and the children were given pastries shaped into cushions, birds, blankets, watches, scissors and reading glasses. Celebrating birthdays was an affectation some Tunisians had assumed, but girls usually received presents at Hanukka, while boys got their gifts on the Feast of Jethro. This festival commemorated the conversion to Judaism of Moses's father-in-law, an Egyptian nobleman. On this day, people ate roasted pigeons.

Ninette is of the opinion that when she was a child there was a greater religious divide between Moslems and Jews than there is now. But there are so few Jews left in Tunisia that it is impossible to make comparisons. What is certain is that Jews once shared many customs with Arabs. Women hennaed their hair and lined their eyes with kohl. They covered their faces when they went out in the street. Often Jews even worshipped at the same shrines as Moslems and shared a number of their superstitions.

Paul Sebag, the historian of Tunisia's Jews, thinks that they had been present in Sfax as early as the tenth century. He offers some evidence of trade with Egypt in olive oil, lac and purple dye. Ships from Alexandria and Syria frequently moored in Sfax's harbour which, because of its sheltered position, was spared the attacks of marauding Corsairs. The town itself, with its mosque and ramparts built in the ninth century, has seen many rulers: the Normans of Sicily from 1148–1159; the Catalans from 1287–1335; the Hafsids in the sixteenth century; and from 1588 until the French Protectorate, the Ottomans under whose stewardship the city grew rich from commerce and investments in land.

When the Jews were expelled from Spain in 1492, the Moslem states took many of them in willingly. Jewish refugees settled in the towns and cities of the eastern Barbary coast, mostly in Morocco and Algeria. Some got as far as Tunisia. But the first permanent Jewish colony in Sfax was only established in the nineteenth century. The authorities, keen to make use of Jewish commercial expertise and of their links with other Mediterranean ports, invited four families from Djerba to settle on the outskirts of the walled Arab town. Banned from living within its precincts, they built their houses on leased land outside.

Other families soon joined them, among them the Zanzuris, whose descendant Julia was to become Jacob Israel's fourteen-year-old bride. By the end of the nineteenth century, there were approximately three thousand Jews living in Sfax. Some were poor and worked as porters and domestics. There was also a small class of traders and craftsmen. The 'aristocracy' was made up of the original settler families. They remained deeply observant, with a strong sense of responsibility for the institutions and associations of their community.

\*　\*　\*

Ninette had little schooling. Her first lessons were taken at a convent where the nuns forced her to kneel and recite prayers. When Emilia, her youngest aunt, who was taking piano lessons at the convent, heard of this she was outraged and reported the matter to Samuel.

'You must reprimand the nuns most severely,' he told his sister. Since his wife's death, he had been drinking more heavily and preferred to delegate responsibility to anyone willing to take it. The paralysis of one half of his face, the result of a childhood accident, made Samuel look fierce, but he was really a weak man.

'They still keep forcing me to say prayers,' little Ninette complained.

'Then we must withdraw her from that school and send her to the Italian one,' Emilia decided.

Within a year, however, Ninette had changed again to the Alliance Israélite's co-educational school. Although most of the pupils there were boys, it seemed the best solution. But when the number of girls dwindled to just three, Samuel announced that Ninette could no longer attend the Alliance's school.

'No, no. I'm not changing again,' Ninette protested. 'I've changed schools enough.'

'*Testa dura*' (mule-headed) they called her at home and tried to make her obey. In the face of her stubbornness, Samuel caved in. He imposed one condition, however, which was that she was not to sit anywhere near a boy.

'I'd like to learn shorthand and typing,' she said confidently. And when her formal education ended at the age of thirteen, she had visions of going to work in a bank. But Samuel would hear of no such thing. He acted as if he had not frittered away all his inheritance, as if his daughter was the daughter of a man who could afford to have her sitting idly at home until marriage. He was living in a cloud of alcohol fumes.

Once he briefly emerged from it and informed the family that he wished to marry again.

'That is out of the question.' All three of his sisters living in Sfax swooped down on him like a squall of banshees. 'You cannot re-marry. What will become of your mother-in-law? After all the help she's given you with the children!'

Mary, the only sister married at the time, took Samuel aside and added, 'If it's a woman you need, there are places you can go to for that!'

This is what Ninette told me, laughing in her chin. I was rather surprised by her pleasure in recounting Aunt Mary's advice to her father. In my own father's family, elderly unmarried women do not usually mention sex.

Not permitted to work in a bank, Ninette taught herself to sew and started working from home. Tailors in town soon got to know her and would bring her clothes for finishing. Gradually, she began making dresses and suits for well-to-do women.

Motherless, she was always the darling of her childless Aunt Mary. Together they went to the cinema every Sunday. And each afternoon they took exercise by walking the two kilometres to the villa of the Guez family whose father was the head of the Jewish community. From there, Mary's husband would pick them up in his car.

Ninette loved these outings as much as she had loved childhood excursions to the beach with her grandmother and younger brother. Those had been happy times, with Samuel at his least confused and most affectionate. At three o'clock, he would join them for a picnic by the sea. At sunset, they drove home bleary-eyed from sun, salt water and fresh air. Along the shore, they passed the Greek sponge divers, stretching their twisted hands out for a few centimes. Ninette always felt sorry for these men crippled by the bends, the great haz-ard of their profession.

As Ninette grew older, she and Aunt Mary drew even closer. In a way, this ready-made companionship prevented Ninette from seek-ing friends outside the family circle, as did working at home. And she kept away from the synagogue not out of a lack of religious con-viction but because she hated the gossip in the women's gallery.

I wondered if her lodger had once been one of those chattering women.

'Oh, I wouldn't think so,' Ninette replied. 'Her family weren't our class of people. We wouldn't have known them.'

Was it shyness or diffidence that made Ninette turn down invitations to dances at the Hôtel des Oliviers? Perhaps having missed out on having a mother, she was unable to let go of the role of Mary's surrogate daughter. They were inseparable. On summer evenings, they strolled together on the promenade leading to the train station. There, in the cloying night air, an orchestra entertained the crowds from a pagoda at the centre of the square. It was an easy, uncomplicated existence.

In 1929 Uncle Daniel took Ninette and her brother on holiday to Tripoli, driving the 150 miles or so to the capital of Libya, an Italian colony since 1912. These days when there is no direct route from the West to one of the greatest pariahs of all modern states, we tend to forget that travel to Tripoli was once relatively easy. Still, the Libyan capital was a scary place. Everywhere Daniel and his party went, people gave the fascist salute. Ninette remembers the streets in the city centre as being particularly devoid of Arabs. That would have been unthinkable in Sfax and seemed sinister here.

By 1936 the family was watching events in Spain closely. The political situation in Tunisia was also worrying. In 1937, seven thousand people marched through the streets of Sfax, rioting and attacking shops in a wave of anti-European and anti-Jewish feeling.

This was nothing new. In 1917, at the height of World War I, similar demonstrations had taken place in Tunis, Sousse, Bizerte and Sfax. A regiment about to leave for the front attacked a Jewish crowd. The French colonists were often openly hostile to Jews. Like people in mainland France, they harked back to the Dreyfus Affair. Many still objected to having Jews in the armed forces. After the Great War, however, the French authorities introduced new regulations giving more people access to French citizenship. All those with at least one parent born in Tunisia were now entitled to a French passport.

Ninette's father decided not to give up his nor his children's British nationality. Years later, when Ninette wanted to leave Tunisia, Samuel's decision was to have disastrous consequences.

At the beginning of World War II, Jews were allowed to join in the defence of Tunisia, but this open attitude did not outlast the Armistice of 25 June 1940. The French authorities introduced discriminatory measures not unlike the racial laws of fascist Italy. An administrator was appointed to every Jewish-owned company; Jews were banned from the civil service, the editorship of newspapers and the management of cinemas; a *numerus clausus* was introduced for all professions. In 1941 a decree set the number of Jewish doctors allowed to practise at five per cent. People were alarmed, fearing that this measure would drastically reduce the number of medical practitioners available to care for Jewish patients. Similar quotas also came into force for lawyers, and a new regulation banned Jews from working in banks, commodity exchanges and real estate agencies.

However, until the Germans invaded Tunisia the war remained relatively remote to Ninette. Aunt Emilia had managed to get out of France with her three children. But she had had to leave her husband behind in Switzerland. Unable to register fully what the new laws of the Vichy regime meant, he had returned to Lyons to try to plead with the authorities against the confiscation of his textile factory. He only managed to get out of the country again by the skin of his teeth, but incredulous and inconsolable, he died soon afterwards of a heart attack.

The Axis Forces occupied Tunisia in November 1942 and soon began arresting the leaders of the Jewish community. By 9 December about one thousand men had been rounded up and sent on forced labour assignments in camps located throughout the country. Giacomino, Ninette's brother, was not one of them. He had gone into hiding.

'It was in someone's garage,' she told me, 'but where exactly, we didn't know.'

Aunt Mary's apartment was requisitioned. She, Jonas, Ninette and

Zula (Samuel had died of cirrhosis in 1940) were evacuated to a half-bombed villa on the outskirts of Sfax. Jonas suffered a stroke and became even more irascible, shouting not only at Mary but also at Ninette. Ninette responded by dawdling each time that he issued a command. I wonder where this steeliness came from in a society in which men still had tremendous power over women. The death of her mother notwithstanding, I suppose Ninette's confidence is that of someone who was a much-loved child.

On 10 April 1943 Sfax was liberated. Ninette stood on the side of the road and glimpsed General Montgomery entering the city. It was time to return to Mary's apartment. But just as they were coming into the building, they saw a group of Italians dragging Mary's bathtub down the stairs.

'*Questo è mio!*' Aunt Mary barked, startling the Italians by demanding her property back in their own language. She did not let them skulk away, but ordered them to take the tub back upstairs immediately.

Many things were missing from the apartment. Some furniture and fittings had found their way into Arab homes. Jonas's offices had been broken into and vandalised. The silver he had hidden in a coal box, however, was still there.

Giacomino came out of hiding. British passport in hand, he volunteered for the Eighth Army and spent the rest of the war as an Allied soldier.

But family life did not return to what it had been before. Mary's apartment was now requisitioned by the British. Ninette, her grandmother and her uncle and aunt returned to the half-demolished villa that had been assigned to them under the German occupation. On 31 December 1943 they only just missed being burnt alive when a firebomb fell on the town.

Zula died just three months later. With all the terrible events in the world, it was sometimes hard to believe that people could actually die of old age. Especially once news started filtering through of the mass deportations in Europe and the death camps. Ninette learned that a cousin in Marseilles had been transported to Germany and had died there. Fifty years later, leafing through a family album, Ninette pointed out this cousin to me. The woman's name stuck in a sob in Ninette's throat. She turned to the next page. When I asked who this woman was, she sighed, 'Celle qui a été déportée' (the one who was deported). This was all she could bring herself to say. The central fact of one woman's life had become for Ninette the thing that had led to the woman's death. In this way, the Holocaust touched on the lives of some of my family who had been lucky enough not to suffer more than six months of German occupation.

Ninette loved Mary and would have gone on living with her forever. But she had grown tired of Jonas's bad temper. When the war was over, she decided she could take no more. Aunt Emilia, now back in Lyons, was offering her a new home in return for companionship. In 1947, closing her ears to Mary's tearful appeals, Ninette sailed for France.

She did not feel disoriented. She had so many relatives around, not one of whom regarded her as the poor relation. Emilia took her shopping to Lyons' most expensive shops. In the afternoon they sat in elegant cafés, and in the evening they went to the cinema or the theatre.

When she was returning from a performance of Molière's The Miser, Ninette received news of Jonas's death. She had been living in France by then for two years and had no thoughts of returning to Sfax. Aunt Mary, however, began sending letters begging her to come home.

'You must return. Think of all the years we spent together. I gave you a home.'

The arguments were powerful, but Emilia would not let her go.

'She has three children,' Mary wrote. 'I am all alone.'

When even this failed to have the desired impact, Mary sent Uncle Daniel to Lyons as her emissary. He pleaded with Ninette. Aunt Emilia felt betrayed.

'Well, if I do go back, it will only be a temporary arrangement,' Ninette said to please everyone.

But whenever she spoke of returning to Lyons, Mary would burst into tears.

Having come back to Sfax, Ninette was not happy. Giacomino had moved into Mary's apartment with his new wife whom Ninette deeply disliked.

'If she and Giacomino don't find a place of their own,' she announced, 'I'm going back to France.'

Ninette was no mild-mannered, subservient companion to Aunt Mary. Her companionship was not negotiable. And she felt vindicated when her sister-in-law proved incapable of looking after her children. On a visit to Giacomino's apartment, Ninette found her nephew covered in dirt and sores and whisked him off to Mary's apartment. The boy was ill and unable to speak for weeks. No matter how much his mother missed him, Ninette and Aunt Mary were going to keep him.

'After all, the woman cannot even take care of herself,' they said, trying to justify this kidnapping, and smothered the boy with all the energy of women who would have liked children of their own.

When people regret the disappearance of large extended families (and this book is in some measure the product of my nostalgia for the multiple ramifications of my own), they sometimes forget that close-knit clans can have a paralysing effect on individual members who do not meet its standards. Ninette and Mary maintained that what they had done was for their nephew's good, but the dark side of their action was that another woman had lost her son.

By the time Mary died of cancer in 1957, the nephew was well entrenched in her household. He was never again to live with his parents. Or share a home with the two sisters born after him who also spent much of their free time in the apartment Ninette inherited from Mary.

\* \* \*

I visited Ninette there for the first time in 1971. Her nieces were with her, as they were every day, taking their meals, watched by the goddesses on the ceiling. They did their homework in the light of the Tiffany lamps not yet sold. They also ran errands for their aunt. Whenever she ran out of thread or needles, she sent them to the Arab city to buy more. There, shops spewed wares into a huddle of narrow lanes. Pungent bleach, sloshed over the cobbles, masked the foetid smells.

The girls' brother had already left, joining the growing Jewish exodus that had begun in the wake of Tunisian independence. At the end of World War II, there had been approximately four thousand Jews living in Sfax, a population second only to Tunis's with its forty-one thousand. Their departure was not an inevitability; a small number of the country's Jews had played an active part in the struggle for independence from France and in 1956 the new government had passed legislation banning religious discrimination. It called upon the Jewish élites to join forces with them to build the post-colonial state. In the first cabinet, the Reconstruction and Town Planning portfolio was held by Albert Bessis, a Jew.

But this did not prevent a large number of Jews from feeling uneasy. Even before they themselves left, there were families who sent their children abroad to complete their studies or find work. Ninette's nephew, her surrogate son, travelled to France leaving behind in the master bedroom, which had been his since he was a small and coddled boy, walls peppered with drawing pins. These had once held up posters of his favourite football and pop stars. In my 1995 visit, a few torn poster corners were still attached to the pins.

The smaller the community became, the more vulnerable it felt and the more fearful of potential explosions of violence. Tensions increased with the Arab world's growing hostility towards the State of Israel. The Algerian war exacerbated the malaise. When, in 1961, the Tunisian government ordered French forces stationed in Bizerte to leave the country, it was rumoured that Jews had backed the French. In the battle that ensued, there were thousands of casualties.

During the Six Day war, tensions came to a head. Ninette found herself being turned away by Arab shop owners. I first wrote this sentence without much thought about what that meant. Re-writing it, I feel now her humiliation and anxiety. Ninette was too ladylike to make a fuss, too vulnerable as a woman on her own.

This is when her father's decision to remain a British subject came to haunt her. With French nationality, she could have perhaps settled in France. Samuel had been British because he was born in what was then a British colony. But Malta had been independent since 1964. Ninette was in the same position as most Hong Kong residents were to be more than thirty years later. As in their case, her British passport did not give her right of abode in the United Kingdom.

In June 1967, while crowds of demonstrators thronged the streets, Ninette and the children remained holed up in her apartment for two days. Not understanding what the commotion was all about, the younger niece rushed out onto the balcony. Caught up in the excitement, she shouted encouragement to the people below. Her brother had to grab her and pull her back in. But he did it so roughly that, furious, Ninette broke a stick on his back. Jacob Israel, her grandfather, might have been proud of her.

In the mid-1970s the nieces also left for France. Ninette was now left alone in the apartment on the Avenue Bourguiba. If she felt lonely she did not say so. Even if she could have gone to Paris, she could not afford an apartment in one of those bleak and flimsy tower blocks that had started mushrooming all round French cities. Thousands of people, displaced by the death throes of French colonialism, had had to be accommodated. France is still living with the aftermath of decolonisation. People are still seeking new definitions of what it means to call oneself French. In recent years this has given rise to Le Pen's National Front and an assault on multiculturalism.

\* \* \*

As long as her eyesight remained intact, Ninette could go on working. She probably did not expect to grow old and be unable to look after herself. Gradually, however, her sight started to fail. Rheumatism had already begun to make it difficult to sew. She decided to take in a lodger. It should have been a happy arrangement. The lodger was a widow and her family had also left for France.

'She's always hovering about,' Ninette complained to me. 'Always trying to listen in. She's so vulgar.'

We often lump old people together, their personalities blanked out because of their age. This is what humiliates the old, more than their disobedient bodies. We stick them in retirement homes and expect them to get on with each other. There was no reason for Ninette to like her lodger other than that they were both elderly. Judaism might have been a bond, but it did not turn out that way.

Ninette could not let go of her contempt for someone she considered to be her social inferior. With only a handful of Jews still left in Sfax, it seemed ridiculous to cling to such notions of class. But I half admired Ninette for not allowing her sense of who she was to be erased. She refused to be placed in the same old-abandoned-lady category as the other woman. And the lodger gave Ninette tit for tat by never offering to do a little shopping for her.

However, a few days into my visit both landlady and lodger approached me in an unexpected show of unity.

'Are you afraid of lizards?' they asked. 'If you aren't, please go into that room and see if you can find their nest.'

The room they were referring to had once been Aunt Mary's bedroom. It now served as a storeroom and had been, they told me, invaded by lizards. Both women were terrified. So I went in and searched under the cupboard. I lifted suitcases and boxes. I poked gingerly under furniture and into cracks in the plaster. There were no signs of any saurian inhabitants.

The more I looked, the more nervous I became, remembering that lizards are only one remove from snakes. I hadn't been in this room before. Its decay was even more advanced than the rest of the apartment's. In the end, I was unable to dissipate the women's fears. A black cloak of depression enveloped me. It seemed that the invisible animals, hidden in dark corners, had turned the apartment into an even more precarious place of refuge for Ninette.

On my last morning in Sfax, I returned to the apartment to say goodbye. I had spent most of the previous night glued to CNN in my hotel room. With the first news flash that the Israeli Prime Minister had been shot, I realised that I would not be able to sleep until more definitive news came in. Had Rabin's life been saved or not?

By early morning I could no longer stand being cooped up in my room. I went down to the lobby although I did not hope to find another soul there to share my sorrow for by then I knew Rabin was dead. Behind the reception desk a television was flickering this message and crowded round it were not only the receptionists but also the valets, waiters and doormen, all huddled over the counter. By morning we knew that it was not an Arab who had killed Rabin but an Israeli whose family were of North African origin. There was no jubilation in that lobby, only stunned silence as profound, I imagine, as in most public places in Israel.

Standing outside Ninette's door, waiting for her to shuffle down the hall to open up to me, I was bursting with the news.

'Oh no, how terrible!' she gasped. But without skipping a beat she asked, 'Was it an Arab?'

'No,' I told her. 'It was a Jew. A religious fanatic.'

'Thank goodness,' she exhaled. 'I'm so glad it wasn't an Arab.'

The implications of an Arab assassin had been immediately clear to her. In a flash, she had seen the delicate truce between her and her neighbours unravelling in the wake of Israeli reprisals against Palestinians and Palestinian counter-reprisals. It would have been terrible if the family next door had stopped speaking to her because of some act of violence in another country. The two thousand or so Jews still living in Tunisia had, after all, found a *modus vivendi* with their neighbours. It was solid enough not to have collapsed even when, in 1985, the Israeli Air Force bombed the PLO headquarters in Tunis. But no one could predict if the delicate balance would remain the same.

*  *  *

When I left Sfax I thought I would probably never see Ninette again. Terribly worried about her living conditions, I phoned several cousins to discuss what should be done. Ninette's nephew flew down within a few days to see the situation for himself. He was horrified. Cousins in Paris offered to take her in. But she delayed taking a decision for another two years. Finally, the insults of physical decline could not be ignored and as one of her nieces was now offering her a small flat in the twentieth *arrondissement,* Ninette gave in to family appeals.

It is not a totally happy ending, however. In that Parisian wasteland of towerblocks, that fringe of the city that most tourists do not see, she leads an isolated existence. Everyone is too caught up in their busy lives to visit her regularly. Her arthritis and near-blindness have made her a prisoner in an overheated room looking out on an industrial estate. And she has no insurance to cover her growing medical expenses. Although a social worker has visited her, the question of her increasing need for physical care has not been resolved.

Her tourist visa is only valid for a year at a time. On the last occasion when she went to renew it, she was told she was no longer British. Although she has only visited Malta once in her life, she is now deemed to be Maltese.

This only adds to her sense that she has been cast adrift. Now, none of us is a hundred per cent sure that she would not have been better off in Sfax with her kind Arab doctor and her warm Arab neighbours. Whenever their mother baked a cake, a slice was reserved for Ninette. Who among her French neighbours even knows of her existence?

*Our country lay beyond the sand, beyond the black silk of
the night sea, away to the south, away to the east.
Distant, yet so tantalisingly close. Our troubled land.
Palestine. Israel. The boy whispered the new word to
himself, weighing it carefully on his tongue, rolling it from
one side of his mouth to the other, until happy with its
presence. He looked across at me.
'And in Israel the fruit is on the trees?'
'The fruit is on the trees.
You can take the fruit straight from the branch.'*

CARYL PHILLIPS, *The Nature of Blood*

## CHAPTER EIGHT

# the promised land

'But the place is full of Jews!' my grand-father blurted out when Duggie announced his plans to settle in Israel.

Banino shook his head as if a mosquito had flown into his ear canal. 'Anyway, joking aside . . .'

Duggie usually shared his father's quirky sense of humour. When presenting him with his shiny new idea, however, he had not expected a negative response.

To Banino, the plan was totally crazy. Why would anyone want to be going to a country that looked as if it were not going to survive? The day after Ben Gurion had read out the Scroll of Independence on 14 May 1948, the Arab armies had invaded Israel. The Old City of Jerusalem was lost to King Abdullah's

Arab Legion. Although, within three months, the Israelis had regained military supremacy and, by the following spring, armistice agreements were signed with four out of five Arab states, Israel remained in a formal state of war with all five: Egypt, Lebanon, Transjordan, Syria and Iraq.

'He has a home in Malta,' Duggie's sisters puzzled over the matter. 'Israel is, after all, for people who have nowhere to go!'

'Why do you want to settle in Israel?' said the Israeli Embassy official from Rome processing our immigration application. He sounded as if the family in St Julians had hired him to play in their Greek chorus. 'You already have a country and a nationality.'

This divided attitude to Israel will not be unfamiliar to many people born Jews. On the one hand, we want the state to exist; on the other, we prefer to leave it to other people to live in it. In 1949 the Holocaust was a fresh memory. Israel might have seemed the greatest guarantee against such a thing ever happening again. But for my grandfather, the notion of a Promised Land was only theoretical, the vow of 'Next Year in Jerusalem' merely something you galloped through once a year at Passover.

Lina, however, was urging Duggie to leave Malta. It was not so much out of a sense that, after Hitler and Mussolini, Jews would be safer and happier in a country of their own. She felt dissatisfied with the confining nature of Maltese society. When she had married and moved to the island, she had hoped to leave small-town claustrophobia behind. Instead, she found her mother-in-law critical. The Maltese language, so similar to Arabic, was not completely impenetrable, but it was hard to find a way into Malta's Catholic society. If La Goulette had one asset, it was the relative conviviality that once existed there between its different religious and national communities. Oppressive as the house on the rue du Lieutenant Longello had been, she felt lonely in Attard, where Duggie and she now lived. Every afternoon she pushed me in my high pram round and round the Sant Anton gardens, laid out three hundred years before by the Knights of the Order of St John.

These were a cool haven of greenness on the arid rock, but she still felt she was moving round and round in ever-diminishing circles.

After seven years' absence in the army, Duggie was also eager to get away. His job as a Customs Officer was dull. He dreamed of living off the land. The idea of a place where hard work and its rewards would be shared equally was also enticing. If my parents were going to Israel, it was not to live in a town or a city, but in a kibbutz, applying the ideals of socialism. Theirs was a vision of a new society in which people could live a 'clean' life. With all their material needs catered for, they would be free from the usual things that oppress us, more particularly that exhausting striving for economic and social ascendancy over one's neighbour. Their aspirations were a far cry from the small-scale mercantile traditions of both their ancestors.

Duggie set about preparing for departure in a methodical way. He fished out his army *Teach Yourself Hebrew* and bought a book entitled *The Collective Settlements of Israel*. No one laughed when he pored over another book on dairy farming in African climates. For all anyone knew, Israel might have an African climate.

\* \* \*

In the autumn of 1949, Duggie, Lina and I set sail on the SS *Grimani*. At our first port of call in Syracuse, from the deck of the ship, Duggie illegally photographed the swarms of army jeeps sent from the Italian mainland to round up members of Salvatore Giuliano's gang. Murderous bandit to some, freedom fighter to others, Giuliano's dream was to make Sicily a part of the United States of America. This view was as lunatic as the idea of the Jews returning to Jerusalem after two thousand years of exile.

Ours was a leisurely journey to the Promised Land, not the desperate voyage of the survivors of Europe's devastation. From Naples we visited Rome and then travelled to Florence to see my father's youngest sister, Lilla, now married to her first cousin, Franco. We

made another detour to see the ice and the snow on the Rhône Glacier. My mother held me up to the camera, the two of us laughing
cheek to cheek. At twenty-three, my mother was not a great beauty,
but there was a certain lusciousness to her clear pale skin and her thick
crop of shiny curls. Her greatcoat hid the small bulge on her stomach.

'Your wife is pregnant!' exclaimed the recruiter from Degania can-
vassing members for his kibbutz. Duggie and Lina were anxious to
get away from their temporary accommodation in a city of tents
housing thousands of new immigrants. 'We can't take you. Not with
her in that condition.'

'We're building a new children's house in our kibbutz.' The
recruiter from Kvutzah Schiller, a small settlement three miles south
of Rehovot, was much friendlier. 'Perhaps you can help us with that.
Then your new baby will be able to live in it.'

But it did not quite get rid of the bitter taste of Degania's rejec-
tion. When, on the way to Kvutzah Schiller, Duggie and Lina passed
through Rehovot, they were even more disappointed by what they
saw. On that day, the Weizmann Institute of Science was being
inaugurated. Outside the building, Lina caught sight of women
dressed in furs being helped out of limousines. This was not her idea
of freedom from materialism.

'Why have we come here?' she wondered out loud. 'It's the same
as any other country.'

The weather further dampened her enthusiasm. She and Duggie
settled into their new lives at the start of Israel's harshest winter in
forty years. Only a few miles from the Mediterranean, they woke up
to a white hush and marvelled at the cacti and orange trees sagging
under snow.

My father sauntered to the dairy. One of Banino's eccentricities
was that he thought a university education for his daughters was
more important than for his sons. He argued that men always had
the option of undertaking hard physical labour. Now Duggie found
himself labouring hard by choice, lifting bales of hay, hoisting milk
churns, wading through mud to round up lumbering cows.

In the kibbutz, work was held up as the supreme value, a purify-ing and sanctifying force. Lina was assigned to sainthood in the communal kitchens. One of the oddities of her childhood under her great-grandfather's roof had been that she had done no housework. Now she underwent an initiation into the drudgery of early risings and preparing food for large numbers of people. At night, she and Duggie took their turn on guard duty, once a year.

My brother was born in March 1950. Since these days he is so quintessentially 'Aussie', we like to pull his leg about his being the family's first *sabra* (native-born Israeli). His name, Michael, is a Hebrew one. Name changing is often part of the migrant's slough-ing off of his past and by then we had all taken on Hebrew names. Lina simply reverted to Leah, the first name on her birth certificate. I became known as P'nina, my second given name. David, my father's new name, was in the same fighting league as General Douglas Haig, after whom Banino had registered him in 1918. As for our surname, Tayar, it could not have been more appropriate. In Modern Hebrew, it means 'tourist'.

Nine months after Mickey's birth, Kibbutz Givat Brenner, a short walk away from Kvutzah Schiller, accepted us as members.

Only three to four per cent of Israel's population live or have ever lived in kibbutzim. But the image many outsiders still have of Israelis is gleaned from depictions of bronzed, sinewy kibbutzniks labouring to make the desert bloom. These pioneers stood in sharp contrast to the pale-skinned, black-gowned Jews of the ghetto.

There was something appropriate in our joining a kibbutz founded by an Italian Jew, Enzo Sereni. He had chosen the site for his new settlement in 1926. Located on a ridge facing the Mediterranean on one side and the Judean hills on the other, its fifty acres, covered mostly in gravel, were not very promising ground. But the Jewish National Fund agreed to set this land aside for workers from Rehovot, ignoring the opposition of the World Zionist Organisation.

When, after two years, this organisation had not moved its stance, thirty-five people took the situation into their own hands. They climbed the ridge, pitched their tents and set about buying another two hundred and fifty acres from an Arab farmer living nearby. They ignored the organisation's orders to dismantle the settlement. By the autumn of 1928, Sereni had given up regular employment and taken over as the new kibbutz's secretary and representative. The orange groves began to bear fruit. The communal kitchens were erected. Sereni set about looking for fresh recruits among German immigrants arriving in Palestine.

It might seem strange that a Sephardic Jew should have practised this sort of exclusivity. But Sereni believed that Germans, Russians and Ukranians, with their grounding in socialism, had more to contribute than oriental Jews. He maintained that eastern and central Europeans were more ideologically prepared for the regimentation of kibbutz life.

In 1929, however, his kibbutz and ideals were already under threat. The Moslem Council, which owned the Wailing Wall in Jerusalem, had refused to allow Jewish congregants to install prayer benches near the Wall and to blow the *shofar*. When a Jewish group demonstrated against the ban, Arab fears were aroused. In a planned assault, Arabs attacked the Jewish quarter of the city. In Hebron and Safed, towns where Jews had lived peacefully with their Arab neighbours for centuries, the attacks were more ferocious. Lives were lost. The Haganah, the covert Jewish self-defence organisation, ordered the evacuation of Sereni's settlement.

The reverberations of the riots were felt beyond Palestine's borders. Italy demanded that Great Britain give up the Mandate and entrust it to a Catholic country. The Jews of Palestine, feeling they could not rely on British protection, began organising their own defences. Once peace was restored, Sereni's settlers returned to their hilltop site and put up their first stone structure, planning to retreat there in the event of another attack. Feeling reassured by this, they finally gave their kibbutz a name, Givat Brenner (Brenner Hill), after the writer Chaim Brenner. At the naming ceremony, all rose to drink a toast and sing the 'Internationale'.

Displacement of the Arab population was not part of Sereni's discourse. In his opinion both Jewish and Moslem labourers would eventually achieve an agrarian democracy together. The Jewish worker had no future, Sereni felt, if efforts could not be made to improve the living conditions of the Arabs. But it was a sad reflection on his policy of recruiting members from Europe that an Iraqi Jew, speaking to him in 1942, should have confessed that 'among the Arabs we felt like Jews, here we feel like Arabs'.

By the time of my family's admission to Givat Brenner, it was the biggest kibbutz in the country, supplying fruit and vegetables to the outside market. Sereni's aim had always been to establish a large settlement, believing that the public confessions and the dredging of souls, which are part of the ritual of kibbutz life, would be less oppressive in a community of some size.

In 1951, the year we joined his old kibbutz, he had been dead for seven years. Haunted by the suffering of Italy's Jews, he trained as a parachutist and was dropped behind enemy lines in an attempt to rescue as many people as possible. But he was captured almost immediately. After being transported to Dachau, he was tortured and murdered.

\* \* \*

Having left Malta with high hopes of an 'open' life, Lina and Duggie found themselves trapped in a society even more confining than those of their childhoods. Everyone in Givat Brenner knew everyone else's business. There were no personal secrets, not even about your own body. As showers were a communal affair, word soon got round if a woman was particularly hairy in the wrong places or if a man was especially well endowed.

You had to be tough not to succumb to group pressure. When the husband of one member was revealed as a womaniser, the whole kibbutz called for his expulsion.

'Look,' his wife argued, 'this is something between him and me. If I can accept his behaviour, no one else has the right to interfere.'

Voicing one's dislikes at the *sicha*, the general meeting, or in study groups, could get people's backs up. Because my father was (and still is) a purist in all his beliefs, there was little room for tact, even when this might have kept the peace.

'Here he goes again!' the *haverim*, or fellow kibbutz members, said when Duggie got up to grumble about that Ashkenazi penchant for putting sugar on vegetables and in fish. He thought the latter detestable enough in its unsweetened condition. Coming from a hot climate, he could never adjust to the central and eastern European fillers of yoghurt and cheese. As everyone ate whatever the communal kitchens were able to concoct out of strictly limited rations, there was no leeway for individual dietary preferences.

Everyone was always hungry. Whenever any social gathering took place, the subject invariably turned to food. They were, on the whole, a bunch of young people, but they mulled over past menus with the nostalgia of war heroes in their dotage. Each *haver* had his own account of a memorable meal, real or imaginary. There were few areas where the divide between Ashkenazim and Sephardim was as marked as in their food.

Except for the Holocaust, of course. In Israel in the 1950s most survivors were reluctant to dredge up the horrors of the past. To spare their children, they spoke little of their sufferings. But the mass exterminations weighed heavily not only on them, but also on those who felt guilty that they had been spared. Some, like my parents' friend, Giorgio Morpurgo, concealed their pain with humour. Giorgio had made an epic journey to the Promised Land. On his way, he had stopped in Rome where, in front of Saint Peter's, he remembered his mother's words.

'Don't give yourself away as Jew. Just watch what other people do and behave like them.'

Giorgio looked at the pilgrims removing their shoes. They were preparing to cross the piazza on their knees. He too took off his

shoes. He was embarrassed when he discovered that his socks had
rotted on his feet during his journey.

'As I shuffled on my knees,' Giorgio laughed when telling the
story, 'I noticed the growing gap between myself and the other pilgrims. I remembered then that I hadn't washed my feet in weeks.'

\* \* \*

In spite of having spent crucial years in Givat Brenner, from the age
of one to the age of seven, I have no memories of life in the kibbutz
that I can with certainty call my own. Most of what I know is based
on my father's stories. These are always geared to demonstrating the
failure of the kibbutz ideal and the crushing of his faith in this new
society.

'I have something to show you,' Duggie said to Lina. 'You mustn't
breathe a word to anyone.'

Lina hesitated. If she didn't get to the babies' house soon, Mickey
would be screeching the place down. He was ravenous.

'Come on,' Duggie said. 'Forget the baby. It's only a short walk.'

Lina followed him to an enclosure behind a hut. In the middle,
she saw a small tree, dark-green pears hanging from its branches.

'What are they?'

'Avocados. It's an experiment. They're growing them for fancy
restaurants. In Switzerland.'

This was economic realism. Although the *haverim*'s stomachs
rumbled, no one could forget that they lived within a wider world
and its market economy.

Duggie would have preferred not to know that the product of
kibbutz labour was going to feed the rich Swiss.

'I've got to get back. Mickey will be screaming his head off. It ter-
rifies the other babies.'

Sometimes I think that my brother was screaming for the personal
attentions of a mother rather than for food. As he grew into a toddler,

he was always injuring himself. In every photograph he looks a little sad, a chubby child with a perennial plaster on his forehead or a bandage around his head. Once, he fell on a barbed wire fence. A barb pierced his left eye. Duggie scooped him up and ran to the infirmary where they managed to save it.

'What is it? What is it?' Duggie asked when Mickey woke up howling. He had been allowed to spend the night in our parents' hut.

'The moon. The moon,' Mickey pointed to the crescent in the sky. 'Someone's gone and broken it.' He had never before noticed that the moon waxed and waned.

The result of the early days of the kibbutzim, when few adult workers could be spared to look after children, childcare was organised in a rational way. Babies and children were grouped into houses where carers watched over them during the day and where they slept together at night. Only afternoons and holidays were reserved for visits to parents. This system is now widely discredited for it failed the generation it was initially intended to free from the restricting influence of the biological family, viewed once as inimical to society. The kibbutz itself was supposed to be the family. When a child woke up afraid at night, however, and there was only a nursery nurse to comfort him or her, the security the system was meant to provide proved hollow.

My parents tell me that I was a sickly child, prone to raging sore throats and ear infections. When a professional photographer visited Givat Brenner and asked to take a photograph of a child crying, they sent him to take a picture of me. Often in pain and unhappy, I would withdraw into a world of my own, willing my limbs into a state of paralysis. No one, except my mother and father, could coax me into relaxing my arms and legs.

'We'll keep her with us until she's calmer,' Duggie decided, breaking the communal rule again.

I wonder if it was in those kibbutz years that he developed the fierce scowl that he carries behind his thick glasses. It certainly makes people nervous. My father has the physique of a fighter and something of a lioness about to attack. So his tenderness with children comes as a surprise. He decided that he could not trust any house-mother with his own cubs when a visiting friend asked him one day:

'What's the matter with P'nina?'

'What do you mean?'

'Well, they stick her in a corner in the playroom. The house-mother says she's backward. But I don't think she is.'

This was the first that Lina and Duggie had heard of this, but it had been going on for months. Duggie had to be restrained from doing violence to the housemother. He felt no pity when people pointed out that she had a retarded child of her own. That was meant to excuse her habit of picking on one child in each group passing through her care and classifying them as mentally handicapped.

'What is this a drawing of?' my father asked me. 'Why is the little girl walking on tiptoes?'

'Well, it's 'cause she's walking on eggs. She's trying not to break them,' I am told that I replied.

I was probably too young then to be able now to remember that reply. But it bothers me that I have no memories even of my later years in Givat Brenner. It's almost as if in leaving the kibbutz, I lost part of my history. I have to rely on my father's stories, repeated so often that they have come to take the place of forgotten events themselves. One such story is The Radio that Laid an Egg.

In their one-room hut, Lina and Duggie kept a shortwave radio, a present from Nonna Rachele in Malta. With no premonition that one day we would be living on the other side of the world, Duggie tuned in regularly to Radio Australia. Its call sign was the crazy cackle of a kookaburra. Each day, like a magician, he plucked a freshly laid egg from behind the radio. He had invented this game to account for the eggs that he took from the chickens pottering about in the muddy yard by the dairy. He did not want Mickey or me to blabber to everyone where the eggs truly came from.

Once my father is in story-telling mode, this story always leads to The Chicken Story. The underlying theme of the failure of ideology in our kibbutz is always there as is hunger.

One night, on guard duty with Lina by the chicken coop, he was struck by a bolt of inspiration.

'Isn't it true that, in the social order of the kibbutz, everything belongs to everybody?' he said to Lina.

She was not sure what he was leading up to. The Cartesian emphasis of her French education makes her inclined to reject new ideas on reflex when their logic is not instantly evident. Duggie, on the other hand, had been schooled in British pragmatism. Sometimes the differences between my parents are echoes of the clashes of the two different empires in which they grew up.

'Look! If everything belongs to everyone, then we all own the hens.'

'You're not trying to tell me that you're about to steal one? Because if you don't consult the *haverim*, it would be stealing.'

'But no one consults us about food parcels from America.'

It was a resentment that had been simmering for a long time. Although everything was supposed to be shared equally, some members of the kibbutz were better fed than others. They received food parcels from relatives in the United States and rarely shared their booty.

It was easy enough to catch the chicken, but much harder to kill it. Although Duggie kept twisting and pulling its neck, the bird refused to die. The neck just grew longer and longer.

Suddenly, there was Shlomo trudging towards them.

'Quick, let me wrap the hen up in my jacket,' Duggie whispered to Lina. 'Good evening, Shlomo. Anything to report?'

'No, it's been pretty quiet.'

'Here too.'

Shlomo was patting his chest for a cigarette. He looked as if he intended to stay and chat.

'How about taking a look at the dairy?' Duggie had to try to make him move on.

Just then the chicken came squawking out of the bundled-up jacket. It plopped to the ground and tottered about.

'Hello! What's this?' Shlomo peered at this surprise apparition.

'I believe it's a chicken,' Duggie said as if he were a scientist reading out some weighty conclusion. 'We'd better put it back into the coop. I wonder how it managed to get out.'

A cloud briefly formed a moustache across the face of the moon. In the dark, it was easier for Duggie to appear nonchalant and to conceal the sliver of laughter in his eyes.

The following morning, on his way to the milking shed, he was intrigued by a group of people huddled round the coop.

'What's happened?' he asked.

'It's the hens. We've had to call in the vet.'

'What for?'

'We're not quite sure.' One of the group spoke up on everyone's behalf. 'But see that hen over there, stumbling about? The one with the long neck? The vet thinks it's a vitamin deficiency. Like rickets.'

This was not the end of my father's attempts to supplement the two-ounce ration of meat assigned to each kibbutznik. Whenever he tells the tale of the vitamin-deficient chicken, he goes on to tell the story of the Slaughter of the Peacocks. It's a routine that he has off pat. In lieu of my own memory of the events, that routine has become itself a comforting childhood memory of a ritualistic sequence in my father's storytelling. I have never groaned in exasperation at its repetitiousness. My father never re-tells a story in exactly the same way.

The lawns sloping down from the *Beit Tarbut* (Culture House) had for some reason become the display grounds of peacocks whose only function seemed to be to keep everyone awake with their metallic caws. On nights when a full moon sailed over the orange groves, there was something disconcerting about those outspread luminescent feathers with their kohl-rimmed eyes. Something even more unnerving in the aggressive way these decorative birds strutted about in garden patches, uprooting plants.

'Shoo! Get away!' Duggie threw a stone at a peacock. The bird had wandered into his sweetpea and strawberry plots. With total insouciance, it strolled into a neighbour's garden. The man had been watching.

'Did you know,' he mused, 'that peacocks are edible?'

Which planted the seed of an idea in Duggie. It soon led to an open season on peacocks in Givat Brenner, a season of madness in which everyone's hunger was satiated. Duggie, having learnt from the chicken incident that the trick to a clean kill was to snap the neck, got Lina to pluck the feathers. They stuffed them tightly into a rubbish bin. In the dead of night, as the rest of the kibbutz snuggled and snored, my mother and father sat down to The Feast of the Roast Peacock.

It was Mickey who discovered the feathers in the bin when he came home on his afternoon visit. He showed them to his best friend, Lillith Ravà. She showed them to me.

'Look what I've got,' I boasted to my best friend, Yacov, holding up a silky plume.

By the end of the year, most families in Givat Brenner had tasted peacock. Not one bird was left to bestow its idle beauty on the lawns kept neat through the kibbutzniks' hard toil.

\* \* \*

Hunger was not the only matter that gradually eroded my parents' enthusiasm for kibbutz life. They began to feel trapped by the cheek-by-jowl existence and the hothouse political climate. The kibbutz movement was deeply marked by the central and eastern European political circles from which its founders, Marxists to varying degrees, had originated. It was divided between those who were doctrinaire Marxists and those who took a more Social Democrat line. A tendency to dispute and argument lay at its very core.

In 1951, a year after our arrival in Israel, the movement was torn violently apart over the issue of whether or not the Soviet Union

should still be held up as the leader of the international class struggle. Ideology and politics split the kibbutzim right down the middle.
People were called upon to take sides.

Duggie argued against this tendency to schism. He is naturally
inclined to make hasty judgements. This often leads him to adopt a
simplistic and ferocious approach to issues. When confronted with
extremism, however, he is also capable of mustering genuine mod-
eration. This is something I have learned about my father over the
years. As a child in Australia, I was often confused by these sudden
shifts in stance. Especially when he swung from support for the State
of Israel to anger at its policies. As an adult, it is this version of him
that I hold to. It should not be forgotten that those Jews who had
thrown off religion often replaced it with hard ideology. Having
been brought up in a family with only a loose connection to religion, my father felt no need to fill the religious vacuum with any
ideology.

The *haverim* never knew what to make of Duggie. When he
argued against taking sides, they thought him right wing. It seemed
to them that he had also infected his wife with his views for, at a
general meeting, she refused to stand up for the 'Internationale'.

'I will stand up for the *Hatikva*,' she proclaimed, 'but not for any
other anthem.' As my mother usually tries to be conciliatory, no one
believed that she was expressing her own opinion.

Suddenly, they all remembered that Duggie had been an officer in
the British Army.

Someone recalled the BBC World Service Broadcast on which the
announcer had thanked a listener in Givat Brenner for informing
them about the best wave-lengths for reception in Israel. It could
only have been Duggie. In small and insecure communities, conspiracy theories easily flourish.

'Anyway, he should not be allowed to keep private property,' some
of the *haverim* pointed out. There was always this wrangling over
what was allowed and not allowed.

To be allowed to travel, for instance, kibbutz members had to seek permission. Without the agreement of all the *haverim*, Daniel Sereni had not been permitted to travel to Italy on his honeymoon, although his family was paying for it. Later on, Daniel and his wife Ofra were to attend a gathering at Ma'agan near the Sea of Galilee. It was being held to commemorate all the parachutists from Palestine who had died during World War II. The couple set off on an open-top truck crowded with other kibbutz members who were taking advantage of the free ride to get to Tel Aviv. During the ceremony they must all have heard the buzz of the Piper Cub plane hired to drop a commemoration scroll over the crowd. One man shouted 'Duck!' and tugged at his wife. But she and the fifteen other passengers did not react fast enough. Everyone, except the shouting man, had their heads severed.

'How can the sun be shining?' Duggie wondered on the day of the mass funeral. 'Who would have thought it would ever shine again?' Everyone in Givat Brenner had lost a friend, but these deaths truly ate away at Duggie's ebbing morale.

He loved his work in the dairy. On his gloomiest days, he went about saying that he preferred cows to humans. But the strain of hard physical labour was taking its toll. Then a kick from a bull broke his back.

'We don't think you'll ever walk again,' the doctors said. 'We'll see if traction helps.'

So they kept him on a rack for months and months. When he started begging for more morphine, they withdrew it completely. The only way to kill the pain was to drink methylated spirits. The nurses handed this out for the purpose of cleaning itching skin under the plaster cast, but Duggie found that with a bit of freshly squeezed orange juice it was a pleasant analgesic.

The doctors eventually realised that traction was the wrong approach to his broken back. They did not, however, apologise for the pain caused by their error.

'Perhaps you should go back to Malta,' they suggested, thinking Duggie would never be able to walk again.

'Not until I'm able to get around without help,' Duggie barked. Why should the kibbutz chew him up and spit him out, a shell to be sent back to his family?

Unable to stand, he crawled. Crouched on all fours, he dug in the garden. On hands and knees, he planted more strawberries and sweet peas and watched them flower. By sheer force of will, he learned to raise himself. Stooped low, he hobbled about. Slowly, he began to half uncrook his back. He would not leave Givat Brenner until he could walk straight again.

He spent his convalescence in the company of Lina. She too had been seriously ill and nearly died from amoebic dysentery complicated by double pneumonia and pleurisy.

'Stop moaning,' the Ashkenaz nurse snapped as Lina fought for breath. There were no oxygen tents in the kibbutz infirmary. 'You Sephardim! You have no idea what it is like to really suffer.'

There it was. Out in the open. The deepest division of all. That terrible moral pressure of the survivors. When you cannot breathe, however, it is hard to respond. Lina heard the nurse's words as she struggled for air. Another voice in her head was also reproaching her.

'You can't die now. You're only twenty-five. What will become of the children?'

The doctors were leaning over her bed. It was what one of them said that pulled her back to life:

'Her husband, that mad Englishman, will kill us when we tell him she's dead. Let's wait a while before we make the call.'

'What do they mean?' Lina felt as if she were wading through mud to get to the other side of a river. Had she really died?

\*   \*   \*

While recuperating together my parents had time to reflect. It seemed to them now that their dream had finally evaporated. There was little use in staying on in a place where people held their 'Mediterranean-ness' in contempt, no point in trying to adhere to ideals when the majority were failing to do so. The hugger-mugger of kibbutz life also left them deeply depressed.

'Oh, yeah? You'll never leave,' Malka sniggered. She worked in the dairy with Duggie. 'Because you'll never walk again. Where else in the world would they take in a cripple?'

For her spite, Duggie placed a live baby rat in her gumboot. He had come across it in a bale of hay.

'Malka,' he remained calm as she hopped about, 'if you just relax your foot and stop yelling, I'm sure your boot will come off.'

'You did it! You did it! You Goy! You filthy Goy!' The greatest insult she could muster was to call my father a Christian. After all, everyone was convinced that our departure had something to do with conversion to Catholicism. Rather than attempting to deny these rumours, Duggie enjoyed fuelling them. I think contrariness is something he learned as a child in a minority community clinging with difficulty to its sense of separateness.

'Have you seen the Madonnas tacked to the walls of their hut?' People were appalled.

Duggie had cut out reproductions of Raphael's Madonnas from a book and decorated the room with these gorgeous Renaissance pin-ups. They hung side by side with photographs of big-bosomed Princess Elizabeth, her pale-lashed husband and their two Aryan-looking children, Charles and Anne.

'Who are they?' visitors asked.

'Our Royal Family.' Duggie, never a royalist, would muster his most reverential tone.

'What can you expect,' everyone said, 'from a Britisher?' This was the other insulting label they stuck on my Maltese father.

Moshe Dayan was more sympathetic. As he was Duggie's senior officer, his permission was needed for a discharge from the military service all males up to the age of fifty-five were and are still expected to carry out annually.

'I'm so sorry that things have not worked out for you and your wife. Sorry to see you leave. But if ever you decide to come back to us, you will be more than welcome.'

\*  \*  \*

We sailed back to Malta via Italy. No further proof of our conversion was necessary. Travelling steerage, women separated from the men, Lina and I were assigned to one cabin, Duggie and Mickey to another. This they shared with two Jesuit priests.

'Wouldn't it be wonderful if someone from the kibbutz could witness this?' It would have been Duggie's last victory over Givat Brenner. Viewing our departure as a betrayal, not one person had come to see us off.

On board, Duggie was in his element. Throughout the journey he debated religion with the clerics. All the themes I learned as a child were there: how religion is a divisive force; how people turn to it because they cannot accept that they are dispensable; how Popes, Mullahs and Rabbis all cash in on our conceit and fears. The seagulls hung above the belching funnel, swooping down from time to time to scavenge. The ship ploughed its way across the Mediterranean.

'Look at this,' Duggie waved a newspaper obituary for the author Colette whose writings had been condemned by the Catholic Church. 'They're refusing her a Christian burial. Don't you think it's shameful?' he asked one of the priests.

'Well, not really,' the Jesuit said. 'Not at all, in fact. It's like this. The church is a club. If you don't pay your dues, you cannot expect to enjoy the facilities.'

Duggie was not flattened by this casuistry. After all, he had grown up in one of the most rigidly Catholic societies in the world. He knew how Jesuits were taught to sound rational.

'God, if He exists,' my father simply had to have the last word, 'would be more generous.'

In Naples, my father's cousin George came to meet us and photographed us walking down the gangway. My brother and I look dazed as we are shepherded by our mother in the same greatcoat she had been wearing five years before on the Rhône Glacier. Duggie, aged just thirty-seven, is so bent that he looks like a man of seventy.

'Let's celebrate,' George said as he steered us all to a pastry shop.

From his pocket, Duggie drew out a piece of paper and handed it to the girl on the other side of the counter. In return she gave him a box of chocolate cakes, miniature tarts with strawberry pyramids on top and paper-thin wafers oozing with jam.

'I want some of that paper too,' I am reported to have said as I tugged at my father's jacket. In the kibbutz, I had never seen money. I was convinced my father was performing another of his tricks, like the egg behind the radio.

We were back in the materialistic world that my parents had sought to escape. On reaching Grand Harbour, we discovered that we were not wanted in that world either. The police refused us permission to disembark. To them, our story seemed implausible. Who had ever heard of people from Israel wanting to settle in Malta? His brother Oscar had to race round all over the island in search of witnesses to testify that Duggie had been born there.

It seems to me that in my family we are always having to explain where we come from. The more we have moved around, the harder it has become to find a simple identifying label. Even hyphenated identification tags such as Italo-Maltese, Maltese-Australian, or Judeo-Maltese are over-simplifications.

'Now that you are back in Malta, why don't you stay?' family and friends asked my parents. 'Why do you want to leave again?'

But Lina and Duggie saw their return as a defeat. Broken-backed and broken-spirited, my father did not have enough money to pay for a roof over our heads. He accepted a front room at his parents' house in St Julians. Lina impressed her unmarried sisters-in-law by her ability never to get in anyone's way. It was almost as if by tiptoeing around the house and keeping everything about her neat and tidy, she would succeed in obliterating our failed experiment. Hadn't Duggie's family advised us not to go to Israel? No one appreciated the depth of her yearning to be free – of small places, small minds, the kind of society she had been born into and still hadn't managed to escape.

We were all disoriented. Mickey felt most deeply the loss of his friends. To distract him and me, our aunt Ondina, the one whom the family still assigned to the difficult tasks, took us on long walks. She would tell us stories in a mixture of languages, English, Italian and Maltese.

'We're not moving again. We're not. We're not,' my five-year-old brother grumbled. He was remembering the time he had come home with his first English sentence, scintillant in its completeness. 'The sea is full of fish and ships.' Everyone had burst out laughing.

'Fish and ships. Fish and chips.' He couldn't see the difference. Why did they keep repeating that it was so funny? They tousled his fair hair and laughed again. That only strengthened his wish never again to change place and language.

Our father went to work for George, and we moved to St Elija Street. But Duggie and Lina had already decided that they would not be staying long. They sent off emigration applications to Canada, the US, New Zealand and Australia. There was even talk of my father going to England to work as a miner. That shows his determination to get away from the island for how was he going to do backbreaking work when his back was already broken?

In this year of waiting, I lost my own memories of the kibbutz. My parents were not eager to keep reminders of Israel alive. They were in a hurry to move on, to try out another new life, another identity. So they sent Mickey and me to a special school where an ancient lady crammer taught us English in record time, in prospect of our leaving for Canada, America or Australia. On the front balcony of our grandfather's house, we sat at Banino's feet and listened to stories in English which, week by week, became more and more comprehensible. By our first post-kibbutz Passover, my brother and

I were not so much puzzled by Banino's idiosyncratic pronunciation of the Hebrew prayers as by a language we by then could hardly remember.

At Carnival, Aunt Ondina made Mickey and me Dutch costumes. No one thought that this was a Christian festival in which Jews should not participate. But our Uncle Oscar's Catholic children taunted us.

'You're going to burn in hell. You haven't been baptised.'

We didn't have a clue what they were talking about. Neither Mickey nor I had ever heard the word 'religion' let alone understood what baptism was. No one had explained to us why we were different from the Maltese people who went through a fascinating ritual of crossing themselves as they boarded a bus, went over a threshold or plunged into the sea. Sometimes, I was tempted to copy that reflex hand waving across the heart just so as not to appear different. I watched curiously as girls in their best floral frocks, men in cotton shirts starched to paper-cut sharpness, and widows in black clung to the shade of the high whitewashed walls lining the street as they shuffled to church in the morning.

'Get away from the balcony,' Nonna Rachele, our father's mother, would scold. 'Don't stare. That's nothing to do with us.'

From North America, my parents received offers of farm work. New Zealand turned us down because we did not have a capital of £500 required for all new immigrants. Australia, keen to populate its vast expanses, was paying all but £10 of the fare for anyone willing to go and settle there.

'Don't go so far,' George pleaded with my father. 'Stay here and work for me.'

Duggie, however, was adamant. 'I'm not a businessman. I'm not interested in making lots of money. Besides which, I don't have your kind of luck.'

One day, on his way to his cousin's warehouse, Duggie was caught in a storm, one of those that wash the island's thin topsoil into the sea and are a reminder that summer does not last forever. He arrived shivering.

'Here, take that shirt off,' George fussed. 'Have one of mine. I always keep a spare in the office.'

'You know what?' Duggie said to Lina when he got home. 'I don't think I'll give the shirt back. I have a feeling that if we keep it, some of George's good fortune will rub off on us.'

So George's white shirt, as precious as the shrivelled finger of a saint, was put away in the two suitcases which is all we had to take away with us to the New World.

*   *   *

By the time we arrived in Australia, a year after leaving Israel, my brother and I no longer spoke Hebrew. In part, the decision to abandon the language had to do with its not being the first language of either of our parents. To continue speaking it at home would have been totally artificial. Away from Israel and a Hebrew-speaking environment, it would have become a strange language, caught in a 1950s time warp. Inevitably, we would have had to enrich our vocabulary in the way most immigrants do by adding or adapting words from the language of our new country. At home, we still often laugh at those wonderful inventions of the Italian immigrants who live in our suburb, *'giumpa'* for jumper and once, amazingly, *'tina di rubiscia'* for rubbish bin.

The other part of our parents' decision to discard Hebrew was based on their strong desire to leave the scalding experience of Israel behind. However, in Australia we were not free from being labelled by the people among whom we found ourselves. It was the usual confusion. To some, we were Maltese. To others, Italian. In the 1950s, immigrants from southern Europe had not yet radically changed the nature of Australia's closed, Anglo-Saxon society. Maltese and Italians, southern Europeans in general, were still despised for working 'too bloody hard', eating strange food and being Catholics.

My mother was the only one spared the snubs. Everyone assumed that, because her first language was French, she was also French. That carried a certain air of sophistication. We were very poor in our first years in Sydney, but my mother taught herself to sew with a second-hand Singer sewing machine, using strips torn from our tough kibbutz bedsheets to practise straight seams. Sartorial elegance on a shoestring was one further proof of her Frenchness.

We became a family not without a past, but with a mislabelled past. At least, in other people's eyes. It might have been less confusing if we had been able to incorporate Jewishness into our self-definition. But we had abandoned religion because my father saw it only as a source of divisiveness.

I don't know if I would have forgotten my first seven years anyway, but I wonder if, in losing my first language, I also lost the very thing that would have anchored me to my childhood, giving me a sense of belonging to something. All I had was my father's stories, the humour of which did not hide his grim disillusionment. Over the years, he developed a conviction, verging on superstition, that if ever he were to set foot on Israeli soil again, it would be the death of him. He would have pushed his survivor's luck one step too far.

So that when, in 1989, I announced I was going to Israel to study Hebrew, he was very nervous for me. A bomb could blow up on any Jerusalem street or on a Tel Aviv bus. Equally worrying was that I might suddenly turn religious. The only ideology our father had ever tried to instill in my brother and me had been that religion, like nationalism, set people against each other.

*   *   *

On a January day of low skies, the inter-city bus dropped me off on the main Jerusalem-Rehovot highway, in front of a sign pointing to Givat Brenner. The air was charged with humidity because here you are close to the sea. On the other side of the road stood the orange and lemon groves, a dirt track running along the left side of their perimeter and disappearing beyond the horizon. In a film, there might have been someone to meet me. Or a flashback, memories rushing towards me. I picked up my suitcase and started to trudge towards my early-childhood home. The only sounds were the scrunching of my shoes on the gravel and the rhythmic tip-tapping of water sprinklers.

I heard the coughing of an engine before I spotted the motorbike on top of the slope. As it approached, I realised its helmeted rider, dressed in trousers and a sweater, was not a man but an elderly woman. It was Mimma Ravà. I had had some difficulty in tracing anyone who still knew my family, but once I had identified myself as P'nina, the daughter of David and Leah, in a phone call from Jerusalem, the Ravàs remembered me. That had given me a feeling of great warmth.

'Hop on,' Mimma said.

Her husband, Dino, was not far behind, puffing towards us on his bicycle. After four decades in Israel, he was still more the softly spoken *Dottor l'Ingegnere* than the Israeli pioneer, his voice more womanly than his wife's. His stylishness would have been more familiar on the streets of his native Milan than in blowsy Tel Aviv.

The first thing we did was to tour Givat Brenner. Its greenness in winter and its air of prosperity were not what I had gleaned from my parents' stories. At the heart of the settlement, a new *Beit Tarbut* was being built to replace the box-like, cement structure of the old Culture House. The children's houses and infirmary huddled close by. When I was a child, the adults lived in single-room huts. Now, they had small, well-designed apartments set in landscaped gardens.

Some distance away from this area, we walked round the *refet*, the dairy, where my father used to work. Like all families, we had our own few special words at home. We never called the kibbutz dairy by anything other than the Hebrew word. Long after I had forgotten Hebrew, *refet* remained a rare remnant of the language.

At lunchtime the Ravàs and I joined the queue in the communal dining room. Though Givat Brenner is the largest kibbutz in the country and there are many volunteers from outside working in it, people still picked me out as a stranger. Of my generation, it would have been expecting too much for anyone to remember me. But I was surprised by the brusqueness of a woman Mimma introduced me to. Apparently, we used to live in the same children's house.

'How do you do?' This woman was polite, but cool. She looked over her shoulder while shaking my hand and did not even wait the few seconds necessary to feign politeness before walking away. In spite of the Ravàs' friendliness, I knew I hadn't come home.

After two days I went back to Jerusalem to my class in an *ulpan* (school for new immigrants), which was made up predominantly of Jews from the former Soviet Union. They knew only marginally less than I did about Judaism. As they were a majority, part of each lesson was devoted to explanations of the Jewish religion and its rituals. Our teacher was a woman of unlimited energy, but she must have sometimes felt exhausted by our ignorance.

Unbelievably, the Russians suffered as much as I did from the Jerusalem winter. We had to get to class early in order to claim possession of the chairs closest to the one-bar radiator. It was an alien environment for the Russians, but when you consider that they had no grounding in Old Testament Hebrew, they set about learning their new language with remarkable speed. The Americans in our class annoyed them and me by their slowness in putting even the simplest sentences together, hampered above all by their total ignorance of grammar though not of the Bible. All of us irritated the girl from Paris who was good at both language and religion and had the frightening fervour of a West Bank settler. There are enormous problems in building a nation out of such a heterogeneous group.

Choosing always to sit at the back of the class, two Palestinian boys never appeared to be dismayed by the patriotic songs the teacher made us learn, which stuck at the back of even my throat. During the morning break, these boys ate their homemade snack quietly in the corridor. The Russians hung about coughing and wheezing from respiratory ailments and pungent cigarettes. Those of us who had money to spare rushed out for a coffee, a Danish pastry and a bitch at the oriental slowness of Israeli workmen, the officiousness of bank clerks and the Byzantine ways of the bureaucracy.

Having lived in Israel as a child, my feelings about the country are perhaps more complicated than those of other people. When non-Jews criticise Israel (the state), I cannot help detecting a hint of that age-old hostility to Judaism (a religion). Although my stomach literally heaves at the extremism of West Bank settlers interviewed frequently on the BBC World Service, I wonder why Jewish fanatics get more of an airing than other extremists. My over-sensitivity on this issue is not uncommon among Jews.

\* \* \*

After two months in Israel, I looked forward to the end of my course and to my return to England. At 4 AM, the police at Ben Gurion Airport asked me to step aside with my luggage. While a policewoman eviscerated my suitcase, emptying it of its dirty washing, leaking toiletries, exercise books, dictionaries and novels in Hebrew, they steered me to a partitioned area where they interrogated me. They examined my British passport from four different angles, then disappeared. They returned accompanied by a senior officer.

'It says here that you were born in Malta,' he said, shoving the relevant passport page under my nose.

He was confused. In 1990 Malta was the notorious place where, it was claimed, a bomb had been placed on a Pan Am flight. The plane had blown up over Locherbie.

'What is your business in Israel?'

'Learning Hebrew,' I replied.

'So you're intending to make *aliyah*.'

He did not like my snappy, 'Certainly not!' *Aliyah* is a term that has always rankled with me for its true meaning is 'ascent'. People do not emigrate to Israel, they ascend.

My answer did not fit in with the officer's list of stock responses. He had never heard of anyone coming to Israel to learn the language without intending to settle. He was starting to make me feel I was guilty of something.

'I didn't know there were Jews in Malta,' he said.

By then, my suitcase had been whisked away to be X-rayed. It came back with a clean bill of health.

'There are Jews everywhere,' I replied with a laugh in my voice.

His scowl told me that he thought I was verging on being a bit of a smart aleck, but he let me pass.

'*Plus ça change . . .*' my father said when I recounted this incident. He reminded me of the time when, thirty-seven years before, the police had hauled him in. They wanted to question him about a letter from Malta that they had intercepted. In it, Banino spoke of cashing in some of Duggie's shares. As my father had not seen the letter himself, he was unable to answer their questions.

'It's your own fault that they stopped you,' one of my father's sisters said when I told her about the airport police interrogation. 'You needn't have gone to Israel.'

This aunt is always vigilant about criticisms of the Jewish state in Malta's local press. She tends to see an anti-Semite between every line of newsprint.

'You aren't a refugee,' she said, using the same argument she had used almost four decades before when Duggie said he was leaving for Israel. 'Your father should never have gone either. He had a country. He shouldn't have taken the place of those who didn't.'

It was the same sort of schizophrenic response as Banino's all those years before.

*Since someone will forever be surprising*
*A hunger in himself to be more serious*
*And gravitating with it to this ground*
*Which, once he heard, was proper to grow wise in,*
*If only that so many dead lie round.*

PHILIP LARKIN, *Churchgoing*

EPILOGUE

## at the villa serena

Once, when my mother, her sister and her two brothers were small children, they huddled round their dead grandfather's *table d'esprits*.

'How many times shall I cross the sea?' Lina quizzed the three-legged table.

In response, it started jumping up and down in a frenzy, not unlike the broom of the Sorcerer's Apprentice. No one could keep count.

In 1947, when Lina married Duggie, her first sea crossing was only a short one to the island of Malta. Within another decade, she was to travel further than any of her ancestors had ever done, ten thousand miles away to Australia.

Even if she had not married and left Tunisia when she did, she would have lost her homeland only a few years later. The seeds of severance had been sown before the birth of her great-grandfather, Rabbi Jacob Arous. In Europe, one culture, one state was an ideology underwritten by early nineteenth-century Romanticism. As I write this, only a few months from the end of the second millennium, thousands of Kosovan refugees are escaping for their lives, the victims of this ideology. By the middle of the twentieth century, it had also been implanted in North Africa and the Middle East. All that was required for a once colonised people to assert their separate identities from the coloniser and to grasp independence was a congruency of the political and the cultural. Gradually, in Arab states, non-Moslems were to be excluded from national self-definitions. Most Jews saw no place for themselves in the new Tunisia.

My mother's surviving brother, left in charge of the family after her departure, now began making plans to leave. He had already buried his grandmother and mother. The problem was what was he to do about Simone. Certified as insane, his sister could not emigrate to France with him. There was no hope that Australia, where Lina now lived, would take her in either.

One afternoon, at *La Jetée*, the pier at La Goulette, my uncle had a chance encounter with an official from the Italian Embassy. It was this stranger who suggested a solution to him. As the Lumbrosos were Italian, my aunt was entitled, he said, to a place in an institution in Italy. And as our ancestors had come from the Tuscan town of Livorno, the appropriate institution would be the mental asylum in Volterra, also located in Tuscany. The Italian Embassy would undertake to pay the costs of the journey for both my aunt and my uncle as her escort. Their generosity even extended to an alarming offer to pay for police protection along the way. But that would have given Dani's lie away for he had told Simone that they were going to visit a cousin in Rome. He did not want her to panic.

\* \* \*

The Tuscan countryside in winter is monochrome. Trellises of vines with naked crucified arms hang along the contours of steep terraces.

Villas with peeling stucco façades squat on hilltops and in hollows. The smoke from their chimneys is barely less grey than the sky that compresses the horizon. Even after midday, the gristly sunlight does not always break through the mist.

When you travel to Volterra from Florence, you have to change buses in Poggibonsi. To arrive early at your destination, you leave Florence in the dark. By the time the light cracks open the sky and the bus has jiggled you up and down hills and round slippery bends, you experience the same sort of queasiness as with jetlag. To warm up, you spend the connection time in a bar, stomping sensation back into your feet as you post yourself before the counter and order a centimetre of the rocket fuel known as an *espresso*. Stomach rumbling, you point to a pastry, which is handed to you in a tiny square of greaseproof paper. Like a sleepy child, you try not to let the sugar sprinkle onto the front of your coat. You ask the barman for a key to the toilet. As if it were as precious as the key to a safe, he reluctantly hands it over to you, making you feel apologetic about having to use the dingy facilities before continuing on your way.

I made this journey several times in the 1970s to visit my aunt in Volterra so I know this landscape well and have an inkling of how Simone must have felt when she arrived there. It was one of the coldest winters of the century when she first came from Tunis to this town perched high on a hill. Volterra is most famous for its Etruscan tombs and its prison. In the 1950s and 1960s it was also famous for its mental asylum. Years later Simone confided to my father what she had felt when she arrived. Slipping and sliding on the black ice, its treachery unknown to people used to a Tunisian winter, she realised she was going to be abandoned here. I will always remember her words. 'Every breath singed my lungs.'

It was on a sunny winter's day in 1976 when I first walked through the asylum gates. The air crackled with cold. My stomach was churning from too many cappuccinos. When making the arrangements on the phone to visit my aunt, I had confused the staff member I had spoken to. Lumbroso was a ward, named after the nineteenth-century psychologist, Cesare Lumbroso. Instead of being put through to my aunt, I was put through to a nurse in that ward.

I had also mistakenly persisted in saying my aunt's name in the French way, the final 'e' silent. In the asylum they pronounced the final 'e' in the Italian way, which turns it into a man's name rather than a woman's. Though Simone was well known and much liked in this institution where she had lived by then for almost twenty years, I was irritated on her behalf by the blurring of gender. It was enough that years of electroshocks and medication had un-sexed her. Finally, one of the staff realised who I was asking for.

When I arrived at the hospital, I was shown into a common room. 'Simone's at the hairdresser's. She'll be along shortly,' I was told. 'Take a seat.' In Italian they say *si accomodi*, which also means make yourself at home.

I did my best. Seated all round the perimeter of the room with its glass walls were my aunt's fellow inmates. Some were dozing. Some watched me with the unnerving dulled curiosity of caged creatures. Others stared blankly. I smiled back. A woman paced up and down in front of me. It was like watching a sequence of film rewound and played over and over again. Where she continuously scratched her head, there was a bald patch.

A few minutes later, a woman whom I recognised from photos as my aunt waddled in. She was wearing a neat overcoat and looked like any plump matron about to set out on a day in town – she had been given permission to go out with me. I noticed she was trembling and took it at first to be excitement at seeing me for the first time since I was a baby. She hugged me. I hugged her back, trying to inject all the warmth I felt for her and for her blighted life. She patted her hair lacquered into place only a few minutes before by the asylum hairdresser.

'I want you to meet someone,' she said, taking me by the hand and pulling me over to a man seated at a table and staring into space.

'This is my niece,' she said in English. During the war she had learned to speak the language well and had not forgotten it. 'She's from your part of the world,' and, turning to me, 'He's from New Zealand.'

Then, switching to French so that he would not understand, she explained that, two decades before, he had gone to Florence to study art. When he suffered a breakdown, the authorities wanted to send him back to the other side of the world, but discovered he had no relatives alive there. They sent him to Volterra instead.

In all those years since his committal, he had not learned to speak Italian. Simone was almost the only person with whom he could communicate.

'What are you doing here?' I asked him and immediately felt foolish. What I meant was, 'Oh, but you're so far away from home.'

The man looked up at me with eyes as sad as a bloodhound's.

'I'm mad, of course,' he said.

His exile was really much more dramatic than my aunt's. She at least had ended up in a place where she knew the language. When she was not in deep depression, she was able to help with the hospital's accounts. The heavy medication, the cause, I realised later, of her tremor, did not prevent her from going into town whenever she felt able to do so.

As she and I puffed up the hill, people in doorways called out *Ciao* and asked how she was and who I was. She knew them all. Each time we moved on, we had to re-think the way we held onto each other's arms, whose arm was to go on top and be supported, whose arm underneath to do the supporting.

We spent a strange day wandering from one place to another. Simone took me to the museum with its endless collection of sarcophagi, the principal relics of the Etruscan civilisation of which Volterra was once the capital. The next port of call was a coffee bar followed by an elegant restaurant for lunch, and afterwards to more coffee bars and pastry shops. By late afternoon, the sun had faded into winter mist. If Simone had had a home of her own, we would not have spent our day in this way. We would have had somewhere

warm to retreat to and I would not have felt as if we were the epitome of The Wandering Jew.

Simone spent twenty years in Volterra. When the Italian government closed down all the mental asylums, she had nowhere to go.
But another stroke of luck led her to the luxurious Villa Serena in
Livorno where the nuns agreed to take her in and look after her.
There she at long last found some equanimity. And there she made
the one true friend of her sad life in the woman who shared her
room.

When her friend died, my aunt decided that she too had had
enough of living. One cannot begrudge her the sanest act of her life,
which was to decide to end it. As her great-grandfather had done
when he knew he was dying, she turned her face to the wall, refusing all nourishment. She died six weeks later, in March 1993.

Had it not been for a vigilant nun, Simone might have been
buried twice. But on the eve of what was to be her first funeral, one
of the Sisters at the Villa Serena remembered that my aunt had been
born a Jew. A phone call failed to find Dani, the sole relative the
nursing home had recorded in Paris. If my aunt's files contained any
information about a sister living in Sydney, no phone number was
available at which my mother could be reached.

So the nuns decided to contact the leader of Livorno's once large
Jewish community, the one our ancestors had left more than three
centuries before in order to settle in North Africa. The leader of the
community was surprised to be asked how one went about burying
a Jew. Why hadn't he been told that a Jewish woman had been resident in a Catholic nursing home? Had he known of Simone's
existence, he maintained belatedly, he would have made sure that
someone would have visited her regularly. On Jewish High Holidays
they would have taken my aunt to the synagogue and someone
would have been assigned to invite her into his or her home for the
festivities.

In the nick of time my aunt did not end up having to be disin-
terred from a Christian grave. Dani, finally back from holiday, stood

at his sister's final resting place. As he had done for all the women of the rue du Lieutenant Longello, he went through the Talmudic rituals which are meant to ensure the dignity of the dead and to ease the sorrow of the mourners. By his side stood only strangers from the Livorno Jewish community. They alone heard my uncle recite the blessing:

'May the Lord comfort you among the mourners of Zion and Jerusalem.'

# select bibliography

\* \* \*

ATTAL, Robert and SITBON, Claude (eds), *Regards sur les Juifs de Tunisie*, Albin Michel, Paris, 1979

ATTARD, Joseph, *Britain and Malta, The Story of an Era*, Publishers Enterprise Group, Malta, 1988

AZRIA, Alice-Dolly, *La communauté juive sfaxienne* in *Programme de la Journée du Judaïsme Tunisien*, 4 May 1986

BLOUET, Brian, *The Story of Malta,* Progress Press Co. Ltd, Malta, 1989

BONDY, Ruth, *The Emissary, A Life of Enzo Sereni*, Robson Books, London, 1978

CAFFAZ, Ugo (ed.), *Discriminazione e persecuzione degli Ebrei nell'Italia fascista*, Giuntina, Florence, 1988

CASSAR, Carmel (ed.), *Everyday Life in Malta in the Nineteenth and Twentieth Centuries* in *The British Colonial Experience, 1800–1964*, Victor Mallia Milanes, Minerva Publications, Malta, 1988

COOPER, Artemis, *Cairo in the War, 1939–1945,* Penguin Books, London, 1995

DI FELICE, Renzo, *Ebrei in un paese arabo*, Il Mulino, Bologna, 1978

FORSTER, Margaret, *Daphne du Maurier*, Arrow, London, 1993

FRANKEL, William, *Israel Observed,* Thames and Hudson, USA, 1981

GILBERT, Martin, *The Holocaust,* Fontana/Collins, London, 1986

GINSBORG, Paul, *A History of Contemporary Italy, Society & Politics 1943–1988,* Penguin Books, London, 1990

GELLNER, Ernest, *Nationalism*, The Orion Publishing Group, London, 1997

GERBER, Jane S., *The Jews of Spain, A History of the Sephardic Experience,* The Free Press, New York, 1994

GUBBAY, Lucien and LEVY, Abraham, *The Sephardim,* Carnell Ltd, London, 1993

HALIMI, Gisèle, *Le lait de l'oranger*, Gallimard, France, 1988

HASSOUN, Jacques, *Histoire des Juifs du Nil, Série Culture et Société*, Minerve, Paris, 1990

HOURANI, Khoury and Wilson, *The Modern Middle East*, I.B. Taurus & Co. Ltd, London, 1993

KRAMER, Gudrun, *The Jews of Modern Egypt 1941–1952*, I.B. Taurus & Co. Ltd, London, 1989

LANDAU, Jacob M., *Jews in Nineteenth Century Egypt*, University of London Press Ltd, London, 1969

LIVELY, Penelope, *Oleander, Jacaranda, A Childhood Perceived*, Viking, London, 1994

MCCARTHY, Justin, *The Ottoman Turks*, Longman, London & New York, 1997

MASMOUDI, Mohammed, *Sfax, Collection Villes du Monde*, Sud-Editions, Tunis, 1990

PILGER, John, *A Secret Country*, Vintage, London, 1989

PROCACCI, Giovanni, *History of the Italian People*, Pelican Books, London, 1970

ROTH, Cecil, *The History of the Jews of Italy*, The Jewish Publication Society of America, Philadelphia, 1946

'The Jews of Malta', Paper read before the Jewish Historical Society of England, 28 March 1928

SEBAG, Paul, *Histoire des Juifs de Tunisie*, Harmattan, Paris, 1991

SMITH, Denis Mack, *Mussolini*, Weidenfeld, London, 1993

WETTINGER, Godfrey, *The Jews of Malta in the Late Middle Ages*, Midsea Books Ltd, Malta, 1985

WHEATCROFT, Andrew, *The Ottomans*, Viking, London, 1993

ZUCOTTI, Susan, *The Italians and the Holocaust*, Basic Books Inc. Publishers, New York, 1987

## Also available in Picador

Stravinsky's Lunch
**Drusilla Modjeska**

*Why are people allowed — and women encouraged — to stake their lives, careers, economic position, and hopes of happiness on love?*

STELLA BOWEN

*All form has an inarticulate grace and beauty: painting to me is expressing this form in colour — colour vibrant with light — but containing this other, silent quality which is unconscious, and belongs to all things created.*

GRACE COSSINGTON SMITH

Stella Bowen and Grace Cossington Smith were born a year apart, in the antipodean autumns of 1893 and 1892 respectively. Beyond this fact their lives were very different. One was a good cook; the other was not. One left Australia on the eve of the First World War and lived the rest of her life in Europe; the other lived for decades in the same house on the outskirts of Sydney. For one Paris and famous names; for the other the quiet life of a provincial suburb. One went off to find a life of art; the art of the other grew out of the life she lived. The bohemian and the spinster. They are like mirror images of each other, two sides of a coin.

*Stravinsky's Lunch* is both a continuation of Drusilla Modjeska's previous work and an exciting new departure. In telling the stories of these two extraordinary women, it asks how an artist finds a balance btween her art, love and daily life.

(and so forth)
**Robert Dessaix**

In this selection of his short fiction, essays and journalism from the last decade, Robert Dessaix offers insights into the many selves at play behind the mask of well-known broadcaster and author of *Night Letters*. Traveller, thinker, linguist and self-confessed dilettante, Dessaix muses in these pieces on an astonishing array of subjects from Orientalism to Aboriginal spirituality, from the art of translation to the nature of creativity, from covetousness to gay fiction, from Albanian tourism to adoption and the suburban family.

Underlying these finely nuanced conversations with the reader is a passion for language and for finding ways to write with simplicity about intricate yet vital things – intimacy, mortality, time, love.

*(and so forth)* amplifies the themes in Robert Dessaix's bestselling novel *Night Letters* and autobiography *A Mother's Disgrace*, and reveals the workings of a brilliant, if unorthodox, mind.

The White
**Adrian Caesar**

*Mawson decided to turn north … when he was suddenly plummeted downwards with the fearful rush of nightmare. As the rope and harness attaching him to the sledge unravelled, so did his hope. But then he was arrested by a mighty jerk which felt as if it might remove his weakened arms. The rope pulled up, and he was suspended, slowly revolving fourteen feet into a giant grave of ice. He felt the sledge tugged by his weight towards the lid of the crevasse. So this is the end, he thought.*

It is 1912, the heroic age of Antartic exploration. Scott's journey has ended. Mawson's is just beginning. Adrian Caesar's stunning stroke of imaginative re-creation transports us to the last days of those perilous expeditions in the heart of the white continent.

Sweeping through deaths and disasters with the pace and inevitability of a thriller, *The White* inexorably lays bare the forces that drove these two adventurers, the values that inspired them, and the remorseless obsession that dominated them.

The Twelfth of Never
**Louis Nowra**

*'As you grow older you will hear many stories about how I killed a man,
but you are not to listen to anyone's version except mine. I will tell you the
truth on your twenty-first birthday.'*

Louis Nowra, an acclaimed playwright, novelist and screenwriter,
never understood why, as a child, his birthday was not celebrated.
Only later was he to discover that exactly five years before his birth,
his mother killed her father, a Gallipoli war veteran.

In this funny, razor's-edge memoir, Louis Nowra looks back at a
fractured family: a beautiful and demanding mother, whose standards
could and would never be met by her children or her husbands; a
father in love with long-distance; a mad grandmother; a hideous head
accident; and a childhood filled with strangeness and obsessions: with
a one-armed Dutch girl, flying saucers and aliens, an Italian movie
starlet, and the stylish, black American political leader, Adam Clayton-
Powell.

*The Twelfth of Never* is a moving and wonderfully original evocation
of an unconventional boyhood, of growing up believing that aliens
might just walk among us, and of the realisation that to be normal is
harder than you think.

Too Many Men
**Lily Brett**

*It means 'too many men', a young man passing by said to Ruth. She is saying to you, you have too many men in your life. Ruth laughed. Too many men. She didn't have any men in her life.*

Ruth Rothwax is in control. She keeps her mind sound with her successful New York-based letter-writing business; she keeps her body sound by running and lifting weights. There's no one she has to report to since her three marriages ended. A good life, all in all ... But there's something missing.

Ruth has a burning need to travel with her father Edek to Poland. She needs him to help her make sense of the past – to make sense of the murder of her family. She needs him to help her understand who she is.

So why are people staring at her as if they've seen a ghost?

*Too Many Men* is Lily Brett's most powerful and imaginative novel to date, a dazzling exploration of the places between past and present, tragedy and comedy, sanity and lunacy. It is the novel that confirms Lily Brett's unique status as one of Australia's wittiest and most loved writers.